HOLLYWOOD
GOES TO
WAR

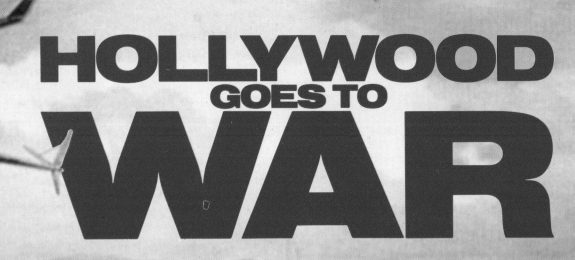

HOLLYWOOD
GOES TO
WAR

Edward F Dolan Jr

GALLERY BOOKS
An imprint of W.H. Smith Publishers Inc.
112 Madison Avenue
New York, New York 10016

A Bison Book

Published by Gallery Books
A Division of W H Smith Publishers Inc.
112 Madison Avenue
New York, New York 10016

Produced by
Bison Books Corp.
17 Sherwood Place
Greenwich, CT 06830

ISBN 0-8317-4511-8

Printed in Hong Kong

1 2 3 4 5 6 7 8 9 10

Page 1: German planes attack in *The Blue Max* (1966).

Page 2-3: Helicopters move in in *Apocalypse Now* (1979).

Page 4-5: The British advance in *Waterloo* (1970).

CONTENTS

THE OPENING GUNS 6
The Earliest Years

WORLD WAR I 14
Up from the Trenches

WORLD WAR II 36
On Land, on Sea and In the Air

THE BATTLES STILL RAGE 66
World War II Films of the Post-War Era

HOT & COLD WARS 100
From Korea to Vietnam

LIVES IN UNIFORM 132
Military Biography

OTHER WARS, OTHER BATTLES 152
Empire Building and Revolutions

MEDALS WON 176
The Most Decorated

FILMOGRAPHY 180

INDEX 190

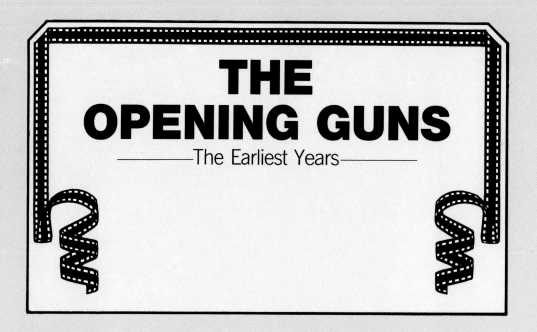

THE OPENING GUNS
The Earliest Years

The Spanish-American War was the first conflict to erupt after the early-1890s birth of the motion picture in Thomas Edison's laboratories at Menlo Park, New Jersey. But, declared in April 1898, it was a war that came too early in the film industry's life, passed too quickly (the actual fighting lasted hardly four months) and was, in some parts of the world, of too little interest for producers to take note of it as possible subject matter.

In the Europe of 1898, France's Lumière brothers – Louis and Auguste – were delighting audiences with their endless stream of experimental and imaginative short film stories (numbering by that year more than 1000), among them such ambitious offerings as *Faust* and *The Life and Passion of Jesus Christ*. Their fellow countryman, Georges Méliès, was playing with trick photography and bettering his former vaudeville magic by having performers abruptly disappear from the screen (done simply by stopping the camera, removing the player, and then advancing the film once more). He was already preparing for his 20-scene *Cinderella* (1899) and was just four years away from his pioneering tour de force in cinematic fantasy – *A Trip to the Moon/ Le Voyage dans la Lune*. Germany, France, Great Britain and Russia were struggling to get their industries started; France and Italy would soon be turning out the best of the world's first feature-length pictures, spectacles such as *Jeanne d'Arc* (France, 1900) and *Othello* (Italy, 1907). In all, concentrating as they were on getting acquainted with a challenging and magical medium, European producers had neither the time nor the inclination to think about the thematic potential in a far distant and somewhat minor war over Spain's colonial behavior.

As for the United States, its picture offerings in 1898 looked like child's play when compared to the Méliès and Lumière projects. The entrepreneurs in the vanguard of the new industry – all the visionary show people and ex-salesmen who could already hear the death rattle of much live entertainment – were just now getting rid of Edison's hand-cranked Kinetoscope (beyond which the inventor had thought filmed entertainment would never go) and were experimenting with material for the first projectors and screens. The film that told a story had yet to put in an appearance and would not do so until 1903, when the most inventive director of the day, Edwin S Porter, turned out *The Life of an American Fireman* and the nation's first genuinely successful motion picture – critically and economically – *The Great Train Robbery*.

Filmed snippets of rushing trains, assorted natural phenomena, racy kisses and bits of slapstick tomfoolery were the US order of business. Work-

D.W. GRIFFITH'S IMMORTAL MASTERPIECE

THE BIRTH OF A NATION WITH SOUND

Above: Henry B Walthall defends his Southern troops in *The Birth of a Nation* (1915).
Right: The tanks arrive in *Patton* (1970).
Opposite: Alvin York (Gary Cooper) receives his Congressional Medal of Honor from General Pershing in *Sergeant York* (1941).
Below: Helicopters on their napalm raid in *Apocalypse Now* (1979).

ing usually on a financial shoestring, the producers were content with them. And why not? The little things were not only paying for themselves but were also financing future works. Every week, there were longer lines of customers at the nickelodeons springing up across the country. They were customers happy to watch and be thrilled by any film simply because it *moved*. So why bother with outfitting a let's-pretend army and having it fight a let's-pretend version of a war that was over almost as soon as it had gotten started?

The single known exception among the early US producers was a transplanted Englishman, J Stuart Blackton, a former journalist and cartoonist. Hoping to have his Vitagraph Company cash in on the hostilities, Blackton in 1898 quickly turned out a few minutes worth of battle titled *Tearing Down the Spanish Flag*, in which he himself played the heroic soldier who finally replaced the hated banner with the Stars and Stripes. He claimed – and the most gullible of the day's almost universally gullible audiences believed – that the footage had been shot during actual fighting down in Cuba. In truth, the whole thing, which holds the distinction of being America's first propaganda film, had been staged at Blackton's open-air studio atop the Morse Building at 140 Nassau Street, New York.

In later years, the Spanish-American War was to remain just ignored. Only a scant number of films ever used it as a theme or background, chief among them *The Rough Rider*, with Sidney Blackmer in one of his more-than-a-dozen stage and screen portrayals of Theodore Roosevelt; the Barbara Stanwyck-John Boles spy piece, *A Message to Garcia* (1936); and Robert Montgomery's *Yellow Jack* (1939), an adaptation of the Broadway play detailing the efforts of the Walter Reed medical team to isolate the mosquito responsible for yellow fever, a disease that took several hundred American lives during the Cuban occupation. Actually, the war is probably best remembered theatrically, in the play *Arsenic and Old Lace* and its filmed version (1944) – namely, in the person of the contentedly insane Brewster brother who, thinking he's Teddy Roosevelt, continually echoes Roosevelt's much publicized but historically doubted shout, 'Charge,' at the base of San Juan Hill.

The early thematic blindness to war persisted through the opening years of the twentieth century. With few exceptions – among them Italy's *El Cid* (1910) and Russia's *The Defense of Sebastopol* (1911) and *1812* (1912) – war and its battles were shunned as film topics until the outbreak of World War I in 1914. European producers, as filmmakers everywhere would do in future wars, then quickly began turning out propaganda fare for domestic and foreign consumption, fare in which, predictably, the homeland's soldiers and civilians were noble and selfless

heroes pitted against a brutal and sneaky enemy. Germany, foreshadowing the Hollywood of the wartime 1940s, also flooded its home market with a string of diverting pieces meant to give everyone a few moments of respite from the terrible realities of the times.

US producers ignored the news of the European crowds lining up to see the propaganda stuff. Likewise, they failed to sense the box office potential in the massive war debate that was taking shape on their own doorstep. The nation, just as it would do 25 years later in Hitler's 1930s, was dividing itself into two camps over the question of its continued neutrality. On the one side were those who argued for preparedness against the day when America, as surely it would, found itself drawn into the conflict. On the other were those who saw the war as a foreign disaster to be avoided at all costs.

With the debate on everyone's mind, the country was obviously ripe for a filmed comment on warfare. But still the producers refused to act. Perhaps speaking truthfully – or perhaps disguising their wish to avoid the budgets and craftsmanship needed to stage mock battles – they held that audiences in droves would boycott war pieces; people attended the movies, so the argument went, not to face reality but to be entertained; they wanted not bloody death up there on the screen but laughter and romance. It was a completely false view that was shattered in 1915.

Wielding the hammer blow was a failed stage actor of nicely chiseled features who had turned to film work in 1907 out of the need to eat steadily – David Wark Griffith. By 1915, the US motion picture business, now increasingly leaving its East Coast birthplace in favor of the more helpful Southern California climate, was growing into a major industry whose products were distributed and welcomed world-wide; further, American pictures were now telling stories and telling them not only in one and two reels but in feature lengths of a quality that challenged the best work done by those full-length giants, Italy and France. By 1915, the term 'movie star' was firmly implanted in the international vocabulary and such American luminaries as 'Bronco Billy' Anderson, Mary Pickford and the Gish sisters, Lillian and Dorothy, were known wherever a projector, screen and piano could be set up. In a nutshell, by 1915, the US was well on its way to becoming the world's ranking producer of filmfare. And, in a nutshell, by 1915, David Wark Griffith had risen from the ranks of the writers and players at the Biograph studio to become the nation's leading filmmaker – the man who had just written (with Frank E Woods and Thomas Dixon Jr) and directed what was to remain one of the greatest war epics of all time, *The Birth of a Nation*.

Set in the Civil War and the Reconstruction Era, *Birth of a Nation* touched an open nerve in a war-jittery contemporary public. The film was an instant commercial success. By 1915 standards, it had cost a fortune to produce –

Opposite top: A captured Mary Pickford in *The Little American* (1917).
Opposite below: A terrified Lew Ayres in *All Quiet on the Western Front* (1930).
Below: Charlie Chaplin (left) as one of the doughboys in *Shoulder Arms* (1918).

$100,000. More important, by some production standards that apply even today, it reaped a king's ransom at the box office – $15 million in a matter of months. Reserved seats for showings went for the unheard-of price of $2.

Even if the country hadn't been preoccupied with war, *Birth* undoubtedly would have done quite as well. With a running time of approximately three hours, it was a masterpiece of filmmaking. Solid professionals all, Lillian Gish, Henry B Walthall, Mae Marsh and Ralph Lewis gave sensitive performances as members of the two long-friendly families that are placed on opposing sides in the split between the states. Featured were fine cameos of historical figures, among them Donald Crisp's General Grant and Joseph Henabery's Abraham Lincoln. Griffith's direction and G W 'Billy' Bitzer's photography, effective throughout, were at their best in the film's most memorable sequences – the Battle of Petersburg, Virginia, and the burning of Atlanta – with the former capturing both the horror and glory of battle, and the latter impressive for its shots of

roadways clogged with terrified refugees.

When viewed today, the Petersburg scenes have a comic, herky-jerky look to them because they are run through a projector at sound speed (24 frames per second). In the early 1980s, however, as part of the ceremonies marking The American Film Institute's Life Achievement Award to Lillian Gish, a special projector was used to show segments of *Birth* – including the Petersburg sequence – at their intended silent speed (in Griffith's day, film speed varied from 12 to 20 fps). Gone instantly was that peculiar look. In its place, all beautifully coordinated, were troop movements, gun flashes and exploding cannon, plus adeptly-timed intercuts between hand-to-hand combat and the full vista of the struggle, with all played beneath the rolling pall of smoke that overlies any battleground. When the fighting rages into the night, the dark is split with the uneven rhythms of flaring rifle and cannon bursts. Then, introduced by the subtitle, 'War's Peace,' all ends with a somber shot of a trench and its littered dead; raised above the corpses in a

gesture of frozen supplication is a dead
soldier's arm. In all, the Petersburg
sequence is one that can hold its own
against any of the more lavish battles
expertly staged in later years with more
sophisticated gear, among them even
the Normandy landings in Darryl
Zanuck's *The Longest Day* (1962).

Though critically acclaimed for
much of its content and though a un-
precedented money-maker, *Birth of a
Nation* caused a national scandal and
saw Griffith, a Southerner whose family
had lost its home in the Civil War,
branded a racist. The trouble centered
on the Reconstruction Era scenes. In
one, the young white girl, Flora

Above: German fighters attack in *Battle of Britain* (1969).
Left: The landing of *The Big Red One* (1979).
Opposite far left: Warren Beatty as radical journalist John Reed in *Reds* (1981).
Opposite center: Elliott Gould (left) and Donald Sutherland as two of the manic surgeons in *M/A/S/H* (1970).

Cameron (Mae Marsh), leaps to her death from a cliff to avoid being raped by a black man (played in blackface by George Siegman; only a handful of blacks were used in the picture, in small roles and as extras). In another scene, a black-faced Elmo Lincoln, Hollywood's first Tarzan, attacks Wallace Reid. Added to these sequences – and intensifying the scandal – was Griffith's treatment of the Ku Klux Klan as the heroic defenders of the South against rampaging former slaves.

And a genuine scandal it was. The National Association for the Advancement of Colored People, helped by an assortment of liberal white organizations, called for the picture to be taken off the market. Riots broke out in front of theaters when it was shown in Chicago, Boston and New York. Word of its alleged racism reached Europe soon after the Armistice and it was barred from several countries out of sympathy for black Allied soldiers who had fought there. It was not seen in France until 1921 and then only after it had been severely edited. The film was never allowed in Russia.

The scandal notwithstanding, *Birth of a Nation* made cinema history. It was filmed in southern California (the Petersburg scenes were done on open land later to be occupied by the Universal Studios) and capped Hollywood's emergence as the film capital of the nation and then the world. Further, it accelerated the continued emergence of the US feature-length film and, for once and for all, put an end to the widespread feeling among producers that unsophisticated Americans

couldn't concentrate on pictures running longer than 15 or 20 minutes.

And, most important for the purposes of this book, it firmly established war as a viable film theme. Here was an early example of what is now a film and television axiom – always imitate a good thing. One look at those receipts mounting steadily toward the $15 million-mark convinced producers of how badly they had misjudged their customers. People *were* willing to be entertained and moved by bloodshed and death. Immediately, several producers, among them Thomas Ince and Griffith himself, threw themselves into the debate over the country's neutrality, turning out features that called for preparedness and damned all war.

When the US ended its neutrality in 1917, war emerged as a major film theme, but one that, as in Europe, served the single propaganda idea that 'our side' was noble and brave and the enemy brutish; it was a service that would be performed in every war to

come. The era following the Armistice, however, saw cinematic war take a major step; it developed into a genre, a type of film capable of handling a variety of themes and as capable of attracting audiences in peacetime as in wartime. Pioneering this advance were the writers, directors, and producers who had fought in France and who now wanted to drive home not the propagandized 'glories' of the battlefield but the unendurable realities that men somehow endured there.

As a genre, a thing molded by human skills and tastes, film war has done all that a genre cannot help but do – given us everything from the very worst to the very best of fare. It has, in every war since 1917, handed us the most blatant of propaganda nonsense, all the way from Mary Pickford's unflinching bravery when captured by the vile 'Huns' in *The Little American* (1917) to the defiance of flier Dana Andrews and his crew as fanatical Japanese try them

Above: The D-Day Invasion in *The Longest Day* (1962).
Left: Alec Guinness defends his bridge from a commando raid in *The Bridge on the River Kwai* (1957).

for war crimes in *The Purple Heart* (1944). But, at the other end of the scale, its propaganda message has been skillfully voiced in *Air Force* (1943) and splendidly in *In Which We Serve* (1942). It has, on the one hand, shown us silly heroics in *Desperate Journey* (1942) and at the start of *The Lost Squadron* (1932), but, on the other, has accurately depicted the genuine, bowel-loosening

John Wayne (left) in *The Green Berets* (1968), a Vietnam War film.

horror of battle in *The Big Parade* (1925), *The Bridge* (1959) and *The Victors* (1963). It's larded itself with unnecessary violence in *Attack* (1956), but has sensitively tuned violence to the exact right pitch in *All Quiet on the Western Front* (1930). It has been historically silly in *M*A*S*H* (1970), with characters who depict men of the 1950s but who anachronistically talk, behave, and think in the frenzied style of the '60s; historically competent in *Battleground* (1949); and splendid in *Napoleon* (1929) and *Battle of Britain* (1969), to name but a few.

Again and again, almost ad nauseam, it has given us the same old stock characters – James Cagney's tough guy who mends his ways and dies selflessly in *The Fighting 69th* (1939) and *Captains of the Clouds* (1942), Sonny Tuft's shy innocent in *So Proudly We Hail* (1942), John Garfield's cocky big city boy in *Destination Tokyo* (1944) and John Wayne's dedicated hero in anything from the sprightly *The Fighting*

Seabees (1944) to the impressive *The Sands of Iwo Jima* (1949) and the ultra-hawkish *The Green Berets* (1968). But its also come up with some very valid portraits of amateur and professional fighting men – in the squad that takes *A Walk in the Sun* (1946), in Burt Lancaster's cooly efficient sergeant on 7 December 1941 in *From Here to Eternity* (1952) and especially in the characterizations of Robert Mitchum and Curt Jurgens as experienced commanders playing out a cat-and-mouse dual between an American destroyer and a German submarine in *The Enemy Below* (1957). And it has etched such complex portraits as Gregory Peck's lonely and pressured Air Force general in *Twelve O'Clock High* (1949) and Alec Guinness' enigmatic colonel in *The Bridge on the River Kwai* (1957).

It has tried to be funny, failing in *What Did You Do in the War, Daddy?* (1967) and succeeding in Charlie Chaplin's *Shoulder Arms* (1918). It has tried to be haunting and symbolic, failing in *Castle Keep* (1969) and succeeding in *Forbidden Games/Les Jeux Interdits* (1952). It has spoken out

against war, both excellently and ineptly in *Apocalypse Now* (1979) – excellently in Robert Duvall's quite mad characterization and ineptly in Marlon Brando's pretentious and mumbled performance – and perhaps most eloquently of all in the quiet, measured horror of *Johnny Got His Gun* (1971).

In total, warfare as a film genre has written a varied history over the years since *The Birth of a Nation*, a history of varied themes, of varied successes and failures, and of the varied talents behind those successes and failures – the talents that produced the failures because they knew nothing of the heart of what they were filming or cared only for the quick dollar to be had from blatant flag-waving and cynically unharnessed violence, and the talents that produced the successes, including genuine works of art, because they understood and could communicate what war and the constant companionship with death can do to ennoble or debase the human spirit.

It's time now to look at that history. The house lights go down and the film begins to roll.

WORLD WAR I

Up from the Trenches

The Birth of a Nation was given its premier showing on Tuesday, 2 March 1915, at the Liberty Theater in New York City. On that night, the United States was almost exactly 25 months away from its entry into World War I.

With the film's success abruptly awakening producers to the box office pull of a war theme, those 25 months saw a succession of pictures on the nation's pro- and anti-war debate. Three feature-length offerings emerged as the chief representatives of the anti-war side. All issued in 1916, they were *Intolerance*, *Civilization*, and *War Brides*.

In *Intolerance*, producer-director D W Griffith mingled stories from four

Previous spread: The Germans charge in a remake of *All Quiet on the Western Front.* Below: The Babylonian battle from D W Griffith's *Intolerance* (1916).

widely separated periods – Christ's lifetime, the medieval era, the year of ancient Babylon's fall, and modern times. In the elements of the Babylonian and modern stories – respectively, an invasion and a desperately fought labor strike – Griffith spoke out against violence and suggested a pacifist attitude for the nation.

Producer Thomas Ince, in *Civilization*, did not match Griffith's subtlety. His film dealt with an evil king who plunged his country into war to satisfy his personal lust for power. He was opposed by a pure-hearted pacifist and a secret band of courageous women who vowed to frustrate the king's ambitions by producing no more children for the slaughter. Ince, however, sensitive to the countless Americans who were calling for preparedness against Germany, managed to straddle the debate fence by having the soldiers in his film

resemble German troops.

The idea of rebellious women served not as a partial theme but as the very basis of *War Brides*. Produced by Lewis Selznick (the father of *Gone with the Wind*'s David O Selznick) and starring Alla Nazimova, the film was set in an imaginary kingdom and told the story of the youthful Joan whose husband is killed when the kingdom goes to war. Despondent, Joan thinks first of committing suicide and then, for the sake of her unborn child, decides to go on living, only to hear the king decree that young married women must mate with soldiers leaving for the front. Angered that she and her kind are being forced to bear future cannon fodder, Joan calls for the women around her to disobey the edict. She is arrested and condemned to death, with her sentence then changed to imprisonment when her pregnancy is discovered. In the final sequences, Joan escapes from her cell and marshals the women to protest the war when the king makes a public appearance.

With fine performances by Nazimova, Richard Barthelmess and a solid supporting cast, *War Brides* was both a financial and critical success and was much praised for its idealism. The only sour critical note centered on its slow plot development, a problem caused by the fact that it was based on a 15-minute stage play and so, to come up with a screen time of 80 minutes, had been considerably padded. Because of its anti-war sentiments, it was immediately withdrawn from circulation when the United States ended its neutrality in the spring of 1917.

Completely opposite in theme were the era's two major all-for-preparedness offerings, *The Battle Cry of Peace* (1915) and *The Fall of a Nation* (1916). The first was the work of that transplanted Englishman, J Stuart Blackton, who had filmed himself tearing down the Spanish flag atop the Morse Building back in 1898. *The Battle Cry of Peace*, said to have been made at the urging of former president Theodore Roosevelt, passed itself off as an anti-war appeal by showing the Germans as sadistic 'Huns' and arguing that the US could best protect its people against an extension of the European disaster by arming itself to the teeth.

The Fall of a Nation presented, in the character of the Honorable Plato Barker, a thinly disguised, satiric portrait of fundamentalist orator and erstwhile presidential candidate William

Above: After the war – a scene from Thomas Ince's *Civilization* (1916).
Right: Alla Nazimova protects a young object of lust in *War Brides* (1916).

Jennings Bryan, one of the foremost pacifists of the day. Barker successfully talks the country into a state of ill-preparedness that opens the way to an invasion by an army in German-style uniforms. When Barker and his fellow peace leaders come out to greet and emotionally disarm the invaders with flowers and messages of love, they are taken prisoner and made to peel potatoes for the conquering general's soup.

An invading army likewise plays a part in *The Battle Cry of Peace*. This time, a confederation of European armies – again, in German-style battle dress – comes ashore. At one point, the invaders execute, by firing squad, two defiant Civil War veterans.

By 6 April 1917, public reaction to the debate pictures had thoroughly convinced producers that film was an awesome propaganda tool. America's entry into the fighting on that day ended the debate itself and Hollywood's participation in it. Now, propaganda in the name of the war effort quickly took over. It was a propaganda of a viciousness that many film historians think was rarely matched again, not even at the height of World War II. Taking their lead from British and French reports of German atrocities, producers began turning out fare that pictured German troops as baby-bayoneting sadists and their officers – chiefly in the persons of

Lon Chaney, Walter Long, George Siegman (the blackface rapist in *The Birth of a Nation*) and German-born Erich von Stroheim – as the personifications of arrogance, cruelty, and lust.

Just look at what those heathens in gray uniforms and spiked helmets did:
● They took 'Our Mary' Pickford prisoner in *The Little American* (1917) and threatened her with death.
● They captured noble American spy Rita Jolivet and stood her up in front of a firing squad in *Lest We Forget* (1918). To her everlasting credit, Rita quietly snubbed a blindfold.

● When Lillian Gish fell into German hands in D W Griffith's *Hearts of the World* (1918), she was so in danger of a 'fate worse than death' at the hands of lecherous Erich von Stroheim that hero Robert Harran – to save her pain and, perhaps more importantly, to preserve her virtue – was ready to shoot her dead. (The film, admittedly, was propaganda well done and contained one especially poignant moment for the colleagues who understood how deeply Griffith had been wounded by the charges of racism stemming from *The Birth of a Nation* and who, as Lillin Gish points out in her book, *The Movies, Mr Griffith and Me*, knew him to be a deeply sensitive and humane man. In one battle sequence, the director took the time to show a white soldier gently kissing a stricken black comrade.)

● In *The Eagle's Eye* (1918), which had the science-fiction smack of a late 1930s serial, evil German scientists prepared a paste containing infantile paralysis germs. Their plan was to infect thousands of house flies with the disease by dropping them onto the paste, after which the flies would be turned loose to cripple the enemy nations.

Joining the 1917-18 parade – with their titles all indicating their propaganda content – were such now-forgotten epics as *The Kaiser's Finish, To Hell with the Kaiser, The Woman The Germans Shot* (based on the Edith Cavell spy case), *Lafayette, We Come* and *The Beast of Berlin. The Beast of Berlin* took some well deserved kidding in a parody called *The Geezer of Berlin.*

Two scenes from *Shoulder Arms* (1918). Right: Chaplin and two comrades share the fate of all soldiers in all wars – boredom. Below: Chaplin disguised as a tree fights the Hun.

All this is not to say that audiences were fed a steady diet of nationalistic nonsense between April 1917 and mid-November 1918. Running contrary to the usual fare were Universal-Jewels' sensitive – at least, in great part – *The Heart of Humanity* (shot in 1918 but released in February 1919) and Charlie Chaplin's hilarious yet thoughtful *Shoulder Arms* (1918). Each, in its own way, was an anti-war testament.

Starring Dorothy Phillips in what today is her best remembered film, and directed by her husband, Allen Holubar, *The Heart of Humanity* tells the story of a young Canadian wife, Nanette, and her involvement with some French children left orphaned by the war. When her flier husband goes to France, Nanette follows as a Red Cross nurse. She soon finds herself caring for the children in a convent. Then German troops take over the convent and she encounters the cruel and arrogant Lieutenant von Eberhard (Erich von Stroheim) who had once attempted to romance her back in pre-war Canada. He now sets about claiming her by force, only to be stopped by the nick-of-time arrival of the flier husband. At war's end, husband and wife return to Canada with five refugee children.

Though *Humanity*'s basic story was quickly recognized as trite, the film was highly regarded as a fine wartime offering and an anti-war tract because of its concern for the young and blameless victims of the fighting and because of its touching comparisons between the battlefields of France and the peaceful rural areas of Canada. Its concern for the young, however, has not gone without criticism over the years; today, the scenes involving the children are regarded as emotionally overdone. Stroheim has been panned through the years for painting a caricature of German officerdom and making no more than a tracing of his earlier characterization in *Hearts of the World*. But, even by today's standards, the film's battle sequences are considered to be excellent.

Humanity suffered at the box office because of its post-war release. But not Chaplin's *Shoulder Arms*, which was first shown just before the Armistice. It was a tremendous draw for months after peace was declared – as it well deserved to be with its blend of high comedy, realism and lyric fancy, all of them adding up to a memorable satire on war. In his book, *My Autobiography*, Chaplin remarked with pride that the picture

was a great favorite with soldiers.

In a mere two reels that had been planned as five, Chaplin joins the Army, sees the horror of mud-filled trenches, camouflages himself as a tree to rescue a French girl (a scene that caused him great physical discomfort because it was shot in intense summer heat) and single-handedly ends the war by capturing the Kaiser, the Crown Prince and a German general. The entire film has a dream-like quality, a quality that makes sense when everything, indeed, does turn out to be a dream.

In the original ending, the dreaming Chaplin is feted by the Allied leaders – Poincaré, King George V, and Woodrow Wilson. He repays their homage by stealing their buttons as souvenirs. As a result, the audience watches them go skipping off into the distance, their dignity in a shambles as they attempt to hold up their trousers. It was irreverent humor such as this that frightened Chaplin's producer, First National, and caused the film to be trimmed from its intended five reels to a safer two.

For quite different reasons, Chaplin had his own fears about *Shoulder Arms*. Sharing the uncertainty that so many creative spirits have felt about what

Mary Pickford was one of the most hard-working sellers of Liberty Bonds during World War I. Here she addresses a rally.

later turned out to be some of their best work, he admitted in his autobiography that he did not like the film, apparently finding it not very funny. Ready, as he wrote, to relegate it to an ash can, he called on his close friend, Douglas Fairbanks Sr, for an opinion. At a private showing, Fairbanks did nothing but laugh through the picture's 2100 feet of film. Chaplin immediately forgot about abandoning the project and agreed to its release. It was a happy decision, with many Chaplin admirers ranking *Shoulder Arms*, which was made at the height of one of his greatest creative periods, among the 'Little Tramp's' genuine masterpieces. Chaplin would not again tackle a war theme until *The Great Dictator* (1940).

The months of 1917-18 also brought to audiences a type of film that would be perfected in World War II – the documentary. Arriving on US screens in late 1917, the first documentaries were disappointments – and not just because they were not filled with the villainy and derring-do heroics of the day's propaganda fare. They simply presented empty views of the war and revealed nothing of what was really going on. Their concentration – as illustrated by one of the most widely circulated of their number, *America's Answer* (1917) – was focused on troops moving about behind the lines and being served coffee at YMCA canteens. All that can be said is that they were the anemic forebearers of a film type that would be masterfully brought to maturity some two decades in the future.

Incidentally, D W Griffith, in *Hearts of Humanity*, invented a technique that would become practice in later war films, especially those of World War II. He shot parts of the picture in France and punctuated the final print with on-the-spot documentary scenes.

Yet another technique destined to be much imitated and honed to a fine point in World War II was introduced during the months of fighting – government-Hollywood cooperation. Out of the studios came such government-sponsored propaganda pieces as *The Common Cause*, a J Stuart Blackton attempt at symbolism; *Fit to Fight* with Paul Kelly; and *War Relief*, a Liberty Bond sales pitch boasting the diverse talents of William S Hart, Mary Pickford and Douglas Fairbanks Sr.

A town in France after a battle in *The Four Horsemen of the Apocalypse* (1921).

As demonstrated by *The Heart of Humanity*'s ill-fortune at the box office because of its 1919 release, audience interest in war pictures declined sharply with the Armistice. The decline was to be expected after a steady diet – mostly bad – of let's pretend warfare and months of very real wartime tensions. Yet, some interest remained and a number of producers were quick to take advantage of it. The next few years were marked with their fare, efforts that met with varying degrees of financial success and that were almost uniformly routine. Representative of what the early post-war period saw were such potboilers as *The Girl Who Stayed Home* (1919); *Shootin' for Love* (1923), with Hoot Gibson as 'Fighting Duke Travis,' a not-to-be-trifled-with warrior who single-handedly forces a trenchful of German soldiers into submission; and *Find Your Man* (1924), with Rin Tin Tin starring as a faithful battlefield rescue dog.

At odds with such fare was the most successful war film of the day – *The Four Horsemen of the Apocalypse* (1921). A screen adaptation of the Vincente Blasco Ibáñez novel, it made an instant star of Rudolph Valentino in the role of the young Argentinian who, awakening to his duty to his father's native France, crosses the Atlantic to join the fighting. Though Valentino captured the public

fancy not with his acting but with his sultriness and his ability to dance the tango, the picture was hailed as an artistic masterpiece for its scope and especially for the symbolism evident in the scenes in which the 'Four Horsemen' (War, Death, Famine and Plague) ride triumphantly above the battlefields of France. The film, however, has never been regarded as a realistic war piece. In this respect, it in no way differed from the day's mundane efforts.

Then came the mid-decade and the beginning of a change. It was a change that saw the public given solidly good war pictures and that started what had principally been a propaganda theme on the way to becoming a film genre. Behind this development were men such as writers Laurence Stallings and John Monk Saunders, and directors William 'Wild Bill' Wellman and Howard Hawks. They were men who had fought in the war – Stallings on the ground, and Wellman, Hawks, and Saunders in the air – and they now set about replacing the propaganda nonsense of the past with hard looks at what they knew to be the terrible realities and sorrows of battle. In the forefront with them was young director King Vidor who, though not himself a veteran, had the skill and the sensitivity necessary for responsible war work. Their output

in the 1920s gave moviegoers war-wise scripts, believable soldiers and highly knowledgeable stagings of combat sequences. Altogether, a standard was set for filmed warfare that, while frequently matched in the subsequent years, has been but rarely ever surpassed.

The change began in 1925 with King Vidor's filming of the Stallings script, *The Big Parade*. Basically, the story at hand was a simple one. It told of a young American (John Gilbert) who, filled with visions of glory, enlists in the Army, travels overseas, meets and falls in love with a peasant girl (Renée Adorée), participates in the fighting, is wounded and at last marries his sweetheart. Where the story differs from the wartime propaganda fare is seen in its attention to the growing affection among the men who share death together, in its attention to their varied expressions in their varied moments of fear, pain, anger and boredom, and in its attention to their personalities.

Gilbert was praised for a characterization that took him from a glory-struck

Above: Renée Adorée says goodbye to John Gilbert in *The Big Parade* (1925).
Left: Adorée comforts Gilbert in the film.

youth to a disillusioned and wounded combat veteran. The film made a star of its comic mainstay, the gangly mobile-featured Karl Dane in the role of a tobacco chewing doughboy. Fresh from Denmark, he had worked in *To Hell with the Kaiser* back in 1917, but had done little since. Now, as would the already well established Gilbert, he was to be a box office favorite for the remainder of the decade, counting among his successes the 1927 war comedy, *Rookies*.

Both Gilbert and Dane, however, were destined for tragic fates. Neither was able to make a successful transition to sound. For Dane, his thick accent proved to be the deterrent. Likewise, an inadequate voice was long thought to be at fault in Gilbert's downfall, but recent stories hold that mogul Louis B Mayer, after some altercation between the two, sabotaged the actor's career. Gilbert's failure led him to heavy drinking in his last years; he died of a heart attack in 1936 at age 41. Dane, after trying to earn a living as carpenter and mechanic, ended up working at a hotdog stand when he was 48. He shot himself to death in 1934.

As good as *The Big Parade*'s characterizations were, the film's greatest triumphs were scored in its depiction of the battle of the Argonne. On his first major directorial assignment, the 31-year-old King Vidor, with the thorough craftsmanship that was to mark his future films, took the time to study Signal Corps and newsreel combat footage before shooting the battle scenes. He noted that a battle often begins with a frenzied rush and then, when the tension begins to exhaust the troops, steadies itself to a slogging pace. It was a rhythm that he took pains to capture on film. Additionally, he hired veterans of the Argonne to do the mock fighting and went so far as have a former German soldier point out the precise locations of enemy machine-gun nests. In the end, Vidor's care and his grasp of a battle's rhythms gave the fighting a memorable reality, while to the audience went a sense of participation rarely matched in the years since.

On top of all else, *The Big Parade* communicated the fact that it was neither a pro- nor an anti-war commentary. It was, simply, a study of individual spirits caught in and reacting to a tragic reality and to those who were as much its helpless victims as they.

With *The Big Parade* setting the tone, the next years saw a brief spate of

Corinne Calvet raises morale in the 1952 remake of *What Price Glory?*

realistic war films. In 1926, the word 'Glory' went up on marquees everywhere. There was, first, young Howard Hawks' directorial debut, *The Road to Glory*, and then the film adaptation of writer Stallings' anti-war play, *What Price Glory?*, by then a long-running and, thanks to its profane dialogue, shocking Broadway hit.

The Road to Glory, which ex-flying officer Hawks had written and sold to Fox the year before on the condition that he would direct it, was a wartime romance starring May McAvoy, Leslie Fenton and Ford Sterling. It proved

Edmund Lowe (left) and Victor McLaglen in *What Price Glory?* – the original (1926).

inviting at the box office and launched the versatile Hawks on a career that would see him direct films in every genre, from comedies (*Bringing Up Baby*, 1937) to gangster fare (*Scarface*, 1932) to musicals (*Gentlemen Prefer Blondes*, 1952) to westerns (*Red River*, 1948), and on to solid productions on all phases of warfare – land warfare in *Sergeant York* (1941), air warfare in *Air Force* (1943) and naval warfare in *Corvette K-225* (also 1943).

As a title, *The Road to Glory* has had a somewhat confusing history. It has often been mistaken for *Paths of Glory*, an excellent Kirk Douglas film of 1962. Hawks directed a picture called *The Road to Glory* in 1936, but it was in no way a relative of his initial production. Rather, it was a remake of a powerful French film, *Les Croix de Bois* (1932). The 1936 Hawks' film is a melodrama centering on the relationships and tensions in a French regiment during its times at and away from the front, with the most interesting relationship being that between the commander (Warner Baxter) and his aged private-soldier father (Lionel Barrymore). On the other hand, *Les Croix de Bois* is a story of almost unrelenting trench warfare and is realistically performed by ex-servicemen. Its awesome power can be

seen in the fact that, when it was shown on French television in 1962, some 30 years after its initial release, it aroused such awful memories in a World War I veteran that he attempted suicide.

The filmed adaptation of Stallings' *What Price Glory?* cast Victor McLaglen and Edmund Lowe in the leading roles of Captain Flagg and Sergeant Quirt. As matters turned out, the picture seemed to concentrate less on the writer's anti-war message than on the Flagg-Quirt duo's lusty romancing of their leading lady. But still the message was there, especially in the well-remembered dugout scene, when after a battle, McLaglen and Lowe grimly count their dead and, with gentle roughness, tend their wounded.

The film and the two characters proved such a success that Lowe and McLaglen made several follow-ups. All were successful, with *The Cockeyed World* (1929) being the biggest box office winner of the lot. *What Price Glory?* itself was remade in 1952. The result was a picture that had a stagey

look and oddly – considering that it was directed by John Ford and spiced with energetic, fast-talking performances by James Cagney as Flagg and Dan Dailey as Quirt – gave the impression of having no real vitality.

The charge of listlessness has never been leveled against the most unusual of the war pictures seen in the late 1920s – director William Wellman's *Wings*. It was unusual because it dealt not with trench warfare but with air fighting, a topic that had sometimes played a background role (in *The Heart of Humanity*, for example) but had not yet served as basic subject matter. The film's popularity not only added an exciting page to the history of a theme fast becoming a genre but also started another theme – aviation – on its way to becoming itself a genre.

As was the case with its fellow war films, *Wings* told a simple story. Two energetic and innocent young Americans (Charles 'Buddy' Rogers and Richard Arlen) join the American Air Service, go to France, romance an

attractive Red Cross nurse (Clara Bow) and suffer the emotional corrosion that comes with flying out to meet and challenge death each day. Arlen is captured by the Germans, but manages an escape in one of their aircraft, only to be mistakenly shot down and killed by Rogers.

A tremendous box office success when it was released by Paramount, first as a silent in 1927 and then with sound added in 1928, *Wings* has earned two distinct and conflicting reactions over the years. On the one hand, its acting has been criticized as shallow, with the principal charge being that Rogers and Arlen continue to exude a much-too-boyish charm as they are tempered into battle-hardened veterans. On the other, no one has ever faulted the aerial and battle sequences. They have a sweep and reality that can yet thrill today.

Especially good are the scenes depicting the battle of St Mihiel. They are photographed from both the ground and the air, with the ground shots showing the little fighter planes sweeping low over the heads of charging infantrymen. The aerial shots take in the full panorama of the battlefield. The audience view is from above the low-flying planes. Stretched out below are the ravaged ground, the broken cottages, the bursting shells and the almost dance-like patterns of the infantry movements.

In all the air sequences, the audience is given a clear view of the pilots, and it is quickly apparent that the actors are not sitting in mock cockpits against a studio sky but are actually up there handling their own planes. Credit for the startling shots must go to director Wellman, a one-time pilot with the Lafayette Escadrille. In common with *The Big Parade*'s Vidor, he was 31 years old at the time and out to make the most of his first major directorial assignment. He insisted that his performers all do their own flying so that he could bring his cameras in closer than would be possible if doubles were used.

Wellman's demands caused no problem for Richard Arlen, who had flown with the Canadians during the war. But Buddy Rogers was another matter. He was no pilot and so, on arriving at Kelly Field, Texas, with the *Wings* crew to film the air sequences, he was handed over to a slightly-built second lieuten-

Charles 'Buddy' Rogers and Clara Bow in *Wings* (1927).

ant. Known simply as 'Van' to everyone on the picture, the young officer took Rogers aloft and taught him how to handle the controls. When actual shooting began, 'Van' would maneuver the plane into position for a shot and then hunker down out of sight while Rogers did a few minutes worth of flying. The second lieutenant became General Hoyt Vandenburg of World War II fame.

Though it was his first major directorial assignment, *Wings* was Wellman's twelfth film. Before his retirement in the late 1950s, he directed more than 70 pictures, ranging from dramas (the original *A Star is Born*, 1937) and comedies (*Lady of Burlesque*, 1943) to gangster stories (*The Public Enemy*, 1931), westerns (*Yellow Sky*, 1948) and contemporary action pieces (*Blood Alley*, 1955). Despite the reputation earned for *Wings*, fewer than a dozen of his subsequent works had military backgrounds. Chief among them were two superior efforts – *The Story of GI Joe* (1945, with Burgess Meredith his usual excellent self in the role of correspondent Ernie Pyle, and Robert Mitchum superb in an early showing of his acting skill as the exhausted and doomed young infantry officer) and *Battleground* (1949).

In addition to Wellman and his stars, three other names must be mentioned when speaking of *Wings* – Gary Cooper, Dick Grace and the picture's writer,

John Monk Saunders.

The Montana-born Cooper, with a drawl and an unsophisticated manner that belied his early schooling in England, had been in California since 1924, at first hoping to become a cartoonist for a Los Angeles newspaper and then drifting into pictures when friends touted him to casting directors as a natural for cowboy parts. He had played small roles in several westerns and then had scored as the second lead in the Ronald Colman-Vilma Banky vehicle, *The Winning of Barbara Worth* (1926). He had yet to become a major star, however. It was a small role in *Wings* that truly launched his career.

Cooper appeared in just one scene. On screen it ran less than two minutes, but, in that time, he made a deep impression on audiences with his portrayal of a humorous but fatalistic pilot who then flies off to his death. In the biography, *Gary Cooper*, writer Hector Arce tells the story of how Cooper was distressed when an apparently satisfied Wellman let the scene go with just one take. Cooper said that he had ruined things by picking his nose in the middle of the proceedings and asked for a retake – to which Wellman, who would become famous for his blunt and tough ways, profanely advised Cooper to keep on picking his nose and he would one day be a major star.

Wellman was dead right. Cooper,

dispensing with nose-picking, yes, but never losing his charming hominess, went from *Wings* to the war romance, *Lilac Time* (1928), and then on to a career that made him an international star and an American institution. Along the way, he played diverse roles, but showed his greatest strength in western and military features. Among the best of the latter were *A Farewell to Arms* (1932), *Lives of a Bengal Lancer* (1935), *Beau Geste* and *The Real Glory* (both 1939), *Task Force* (1949) and *The Court-Martial of Billy Mitchell* (1955). His greatest triumph in uniform was scored in the title role in *Sergeant York* (1941), for which he won the best actor Academy Award and the New York Film Critics Award.

Dick Grace served as the stunt flier on *Wings* and a series of aviation films that it immediately inspired. His feats were awesome and, to many an audience, beyond belief. For *Wings* and its followers he flew into mid-air collisions, crashed into trees and slammed nose-first into the ground. In one of his finest stunts, he dove a plane into a rooftop. He emerged with a painfully broken neck.

Former journalist John Monk Saunders, after establishing himself with *Wings*, put to paper the most entertaining aviation war features seen in the late '20s and early '30s. From his typewriter came the stories for *Legion of the Condemned* (1928), *The Dawn Patrol* (1930), *The Eagle and the Hawk* (1933), *Devil Dogs of the Air* and *West Point of the Air* (both 1935). *The Dawn Patrol* was remade in 1938, just two years before Saunders' death.

Just as D W Griffith invented the widely used technique of inserting documentary footage into feature films, so did Saunders come up with an idea that has since become a tradition. When he first approached Paramount with the story of *Wings*, the studio liked what it saw, but feared that the costs of mounting and filming the aerial and battle sequences would be prohibitive. Saunders suggested that the company turn to the War Department for help, with the result that the Department, recognizing the publicity value involved, lent Paramount several million dollars worth of gear, facilities and uniforms.

Left: Gary Cooper in the trial scene from *The Court-Marshal of Billy Mitchell* (1955).
Opposite: A publicity collage from *The Dawn Patrol* (1930) – American flyers in France in World War I.

Above: The grim face of war, from *Westfront 1918* (1930) – G W Pabst's triumph.
Right: A soldier, now a double-amputee, returns home in Alexander Dovzhenko's *Arsenal* (1929).

tively in two post-World War II successes, *Command Decision* (1948) and *Twelve O'Clock High* (1949).

With the somewhat abbreviated title, *Dawn Patrol*, the film was remade in 1938 as an Errol Flynn-David Niven vehicle. The remake suffered by comparison because it glamorized the two leading characters, though Basil Rathbone was applauded for the tension he brought to his role as the original squadron commander. Footage from the 1930 production was used for some of the aerial sequences.

As fine as *Wings* and *The Dawn Patrol* were, they were far surpassed by three films on ground warfare – Russia's *Arsenal*, Universal's haunting *All Quiet on the Western Front*, and Germany's *Westfront 1918*.

Directed by Alexander Dovzhenko, *Arsenal* (1929) genuinely fits the des-

Begun was the tradition of government-studio cooperation that is still seen today in the production of films with military settings; government cooperation has always been based on the understanding that the US military will be presented in a good light. Even with the Department's help, *Wings* cost $2 million dollars to make, a staggering sum at that time.

As clearly shown above by Saunders' story credits, *Wings* marked the start of several years worth of World War I aviation pictures. They were all entertaining and exciting, with the most outstanding of their number being 1930's *The Dawn Patrol*. Set in the France of 1915, it dealt with a squadron of volunteer American fliers who hate their commander (Neil Hamilton) because he must send them on missions that too often end in death. When the commander is assigned elsewhere, his place is taken by the pilot (Richard Barthelmess) who has been his most outspoken critic and who now quickly learns that death is inevitable and that commanding officers are helpless to shelter their men from it. He is then criticized by his closest friend (Douglas Fairbanks Jr). The film ends with Fairbanks taking command of the squadron and learning the terrible truth for himself.

Directed by Howard Hawks and marked with virile performances, *The Dawn Patrol* was more than exciting filmfare. It was an unusual offering because of its basic theme, a theme that Hollywood had not fully undertaken before but that had been recently explored on the stage in *Journey's End* – the loneliness and the draining responsibilities that go with command. It was a theme that the genre would use again in the coming years, perhaps most effec- cription undeservedly and routinely assigned by studio publicists to so many films – sprawling. The film matches in brilliance Dovzhenko's more heralded treatise on the Russian peasantry, *Earth*, or as it is also known, *Soil* (1930). *Arsenal*, looking at a Russia in turmoil because of the fighting in 1914, covers the horrors at the front, the miseries of peasant life in the torn countryside, and the political and labor upheavals that cause rioting in the cities. The film takes its title from the setting for a strike that provides the film with its climactic action – a munitions center.

All Quiet on the Western Front (1930) was not only haunting but unique as well. Its uniqueness came of the fact that it was the first US film to deal sympathetically with the Germans and their side of the fighting. Making the picture possible was, in turn, the fact that the national passions of 1917-18 were calming and softening into memories. That process was unmistakably seen in the widespread American welcome give to the book by the German novelist Erich Maria Remarque on which the film was based.

As directed by Lewis Milestone from a script by two of the American theater's finer talents, Maxwell Anderson and George Abbott (with Dell Andrews), *All Quiet on the Western Front* was a sensitive account of how the experiences of war – everything from the horror of battle to the quiet but deeply-felt joys of comradeship, the boredom of a soldier's life behind the lines and the fleeting excitement and forgetfulness to be had in trysts with village girls – turned a group of idealistic schoolboys into hardened but many-faceted adults. The hardening is described not through a detailed narrative of each soldier's life but in distinct episodes that reveal character development and send the audience through experiences recognizable to anyone who has ever been in a war.

For instance, the military's familiar hurry-up-and-wait syndrome is seen as the troops are herded to the front and then made to stand about idly because their food is slow in coming. There is the delicious moment of revenge when, under the cover of darkness, several young soldiers thrash the sadistic corporal who has made their lives miserable by ordering them to crawl about under tables and fall face forward in the mud; the score is more than settled when he is left behind in a pool of stagnant water, with sack tied over his head. Conversely, there is the terrible moment when, during a bombardment, a dugout is ripped apart and the screams of the injured and dying can be heard between the explosions. Then the moment (it seems to come in every war) when a soldier asks to have the fine boots of a fallen comrade now that the comrade will no longer need them.

Basil Rathbone (left) and Errol Flynn in the remake of *Dawn Patrol* (1938).

Then, in one of the attack sequences, that awful glimpse of a severed hand hanging from a barbed wire entanglement after a shell burst. And, finally, the film's closing moment – that instant of sad carelessness when the young and now battle-wise Paul (Lew Ayres) forgets his safety and reaches out to a butterfly from his trench shelter, only to die of a sniper's bullet. As we watch the slowly moving hand, a shot rings out. The fingers stiffen and then relax as life and the tensions of a too-long endured nightmare drain out of them.

For many, however, *All Quiet*'s finest scene – though some critics thought it a trifle long – is played out in a water-filled shell hole. Taking refuge there during an attack, the terrified Paul finds himself face-to-face with a French soldier as frightened as he. In his fear, the youth stabs his enemy. Then, as the Frenchman slowly dies, Paul is able neither to escape the shell hole nor the realization of his shared humanity with his victim. In a series of very human

actions, he reveals and endures the feelings of remorse and guilt for what he has done. At one point, he gathers up some of the dirty water at his feet and moistens the doomed man's lips. At another, he tries to explain his sorrow, somehow hoping that he will be heard and forgiven by someone who is now beyond hearing and forgiving. At still another, he removes a wallet from a pocket of the bloodied uniform and stares at a photograph of the man's wife and children.

In one of the most effective bit roles ever filmed, the former comedian, Raymond Griffith (no relation to D W Griffith), played the fatally wounded Frenchman. He gave a splendid performance and did so without saying a word. Griffith himself could speak only in a hoarse whisper, having damaged his vocal cords while yelling in a stage

melodrama some years earlier. A favorite in both comic and dramatic early silents, he was a man whose intelligence and talents enabled him to switch to production when sound ended his on-screen career. Among the films on which he worked as producer or associate producer before his retirement in 1940 were *Cardinal Richelieu* (1934), Shirley Temple's *Heidi* (1937), and *Drums Along the Mohawk* (1939).

Griffith's, however, was not the only outstanding performance on view in *All Quiet on the Western Front*. The cast was uniformly excellent, especially Louis Wolheim as the young soldiers' tough

Opposite: Pat O'Brien, James Cagney and George Brent in *The Fighting 69th* (1940). Below: British troops charge a German trench in *All Quiet on the Western Front* (1930).

but compassionate mentor, the philosophic Sergeant Katczinsky; John Wray as the sadistic Corporal Himmelstoss; Slim Summerville as the humorously cynical Tjaden, a radical departure from the comedian's usual rustic characterizations; and, of course, Lew Ayres as the sensitive, brutalized Paul.

Ayres, a deeply spiritual man, may have been keenly affected by his portrayal and the film itself. Early in World War II, he declared himself a conscientious objector and refused to don a uniform. There was widespread indignation over his stand, but it began to evaporate when he enlisted for non-combatant service in the medical corps. It disappeared with word of how Ayres distinguished himself under fire.

All Quiet on the Western Front was singly Hollywood's greatest achievement in 1930, one that received its just critical and financial due. Its excellence, however, was matched that year by Germany's *Westfront 1918*. Also known by three other titles – *Shame of a Nation*, *Four from the Infantry*, and *Comrades of 1918* – the film deals with the life and death of four young infantrymen assigned to the same company on the French front in the last months of the war. In following each soldier to his

Opposite: Gary Cooper, as the wounded World War I ambulance driver, and Helen Hayes, as the nurse who tends him when he is wounded, share a romantic moment in *A Farewell to Arms* (1932).
Below: A grim scene from *Oh! What a Lovely War* (1969).

death, director G W Pabst presents his audiences with a series of frightening and memorable images – men being buried alive in a bombardment, the wounded spread out over the floor in a church, an officer going insane, and – in sharp counterpoint – the first gentle meeting that leads to one young soldier's love for a French girl. In one especially powerful scene – a sequence reminiscent of *All Quiet* – a soldier

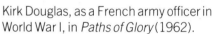

Kirk Douglas, as a French army officer in World War I, in *Paths of Glory* (1962).

meets his death at the hands of a wounded enemy.

In the opinion of some reviewers of the day – France's Georges Sadoul among them – *Westfront* not only matched *All Quiet*'s excellence but surpassed it as an indictment of the stupidity of the war. Whatever the case may be, both were masterworks that marked the highest points ever achieved by films set in World War I. In fact, it can be said that the years 1925-30 marked a golden age for World War I pictures and that *All Quiet* and *Westfront* brought the era to a stunning close.

In their wake came a decade of entertaining but, in the main, routine offerings. Buster Keaton enjoyed a few scenes of high comedy in the otherwise disappointing *Doughboys* (1930). On the air front, there were the already mentioned *The Eagle and the Hawk* and the 1938 encore of *The Dawn Patrol*. Some producers, searching for a new aerial approach, tried a post-war theme that inventively retained the all-important dog-fighting scenes; they came up with the likes of *The Lost Squadron* (1932) and *Lucky Devils* (1933), both of which told of ex-aces reliving past glories by working as stunt pilots on war

pictures. Producer Howard Hughes also tried for 'something different' and succeeded when he put an attacking German dirigible to use in *Hell's Angels* (1930), a hit attraction at the time but a film chiefly remembered today for turning Jean Harlow into a star. Possibly the most unusual effort of the decade was Britain's now-forgotten *Brown on Resolution* (1935), with a young John Mills cast as a seaman who holds the crew of a German warship at bay with a rifle; the picture was later retitled *Forever England* for domestic consumption and was shown in the United States as *Born for Glory*. More conventional fare was at hand with the filming of R C Sheriff's play, *Journey's End* (1930) and two novels of post-war Germany by *All Quiet*'s Erich Maria Remarque – *The Road Back* (1937) and *Three Comrades* (1938)

Set for the most part in a dug-out, *Journey's End* proved stiff and, suffering from the primitive sound equipment of the day, not the moving and interesting drama it had been on the London and New York stage. Both *The Road Back* and *Three Comrades* dealt with the problems of soldiers trying to resettle themselves in a torn country, with the former impressive and the latter an anti-Nazi testament that missed the mark as such but whose stars – Robert Taylor, Margaret Sullavan, Franchot Tone, and Robert Young – made its more emotional sequences memorable, especially its climactic graveyard scene.

All was not action and political treatise, however. In the area of pure romance, a wounded American ambulance driver on the Italian front, Gary Cooper, fell in love with nurse Helen Hayes in a 1932 filming of Ernest Hemingway's novel, *A Farewell to Arms*; the picture was unsuccessfully remade with Rock Hudson and Jennifer Jones in 1957 (so unsuccessfully, in fact, that producer David O Selznick decided to retire soon after its release). In 1937, James Stewart, though badly miscast, managed a touching portrait of a Parisian laborer who falls in love with a street waif (Simone Simone) and goes off to war to be blinded in *Seventh Heaven*, a remake of the 10-year-old Janet Gaynor-Charles Farrell hit.

The 1940s opened with the slambang *The Fighting 69th* (1940) and

Omar Sharif, playing the title role in *Doctor Zhivago* (1965), tends the wounded as Julie Christie (Lara) looks on.

Sergeant York (1941), both from Warner Brothers. We'll talk only of the former here, saving a description of *Sergeant York* for a later chapter on military biography.

The Fighting 69th was a highly entertaining mixture of action and sentimentality presented at the brisk pace that marked virtually all Warner Brothers products. On view was a fictionalized tribute to the famous New York regiment, complete with portrayals of its leading figures – Pat O'Brien's Father Duffy, George Brent's dignified Colonel Bill Donovan, and Jeffrey Lynn's poet Joyce Kilmer. But the picture belonged to James Cagney's fictional doughboy. In his unerring style, Cagney strutted, chopped out his dialogue in true tough-guy style, tried to hide his fears behind a street bravado, endangered his comrades with his carelessness, and finally, in one of those last-minute demonstra-

Above: Timothy Bottoms in *Johnny Got His Gun* (1971).
Below: A wounded George Peppard in *The Blue Max* (1966).

tions of decency that so often marked his characters, heroically sacrificed his life for his fellow soldiers.

By 1940, however, America had a new war on the horizon (undoubtedly, both *The 69th* and *Sergeant York* were, at least in part, filmed in response to the widespread interest and nervousness) and the first of this century's great conflicts was about to become a thing of the past as a film theme. It was revived sporadically, sometimes for its nostalgia value and sometimes as a vehicle for anti-war statements, in later decades in:

William Wellman's disappointing recollection of his wartime squadron, *Lafayette Escadrille* (1957).

Paths of Glory (1962), a thoughtful court-martial drama with Kirk Douglas as the attorney defending three French soldiers deliberately picked for trial and execution as object lessons when their unit fails to advance under a heavy artillery barrage.

Above: German pilot and falconer John Phillip Law in *Von Richthofen and Brown* (1971).
Right: Robert Redford as *The Great Waldo Pepper* (1975) – the former ace turned barnstormer.

Director David Lean's superb *Lawrence of Arabia* (1962), the story of the complex Englishman who mustered the Arabs to the Allied cause.

Doctor Zhivago (1965), another David Lean triumph, this one based on Boris Pasternak's novel of the revolution that took Russia out of the war in 1917 and changed the course of her history and destiny.

The Blue Max (1966) with its entertaining melodrama, its believable portraits of German officers by James Mason and Karl Michael Vogler, and its splendid aerial histrionics; the air sequences reach their zenith when rivals George Peppard and Jeremy Kemp engage in a stunt-flying contest that ends when the latter, challenged beyond his capacities, crashes and dies.

Oh What a Lovely War (1969), Britain's odd musical fantasia on the war, with an all-star cast that included Ralph Richardson, John Gielgud, Laurence Olivier, John Mills, Maggie Smith and Michael Redgrave.

Von Richthofen and Brown (1971), a pallid (except for its air sequences) tale of the German air ace and the Canadian who finally brought him down.

Johnny Got His Gun (1971), a perhaps too slowly moving and too talky picture that nevertheless – in its story of a soldier's terrible isolation after he has lost his arms, legs, sight and hearing – must stand as one of the most eloquent anti-war statements ever filmed.

Robert Redford's *The Great Waldo Pepper* (1975), so reminiscent of *The Lost Squadron* in its story of wartime pilots turned barnstormers and Hollywood stuntmen, but so much more haunting, especially in the movie dog-fight that turns into a battle-to-the-death between two ex-enemy aces who see no point in living because their lives are without purpose now that the era of flying for the joy of it is giving way to the stolidity of commercial aviation.

WORLD WAR II

On Land, on Sea and In the Air

In the mid-1930s, as Hitler came to power and started the world on its way to a new war, US film history repeated itself. In imitation of what had occurred just two decades earlier, producers ignored the themes to be had in the developing European tragedy, preferring instead to concentrate on the money-makers of the day – all the musicals, westerns, screwball comedies and romances that provided a few fleeting moments of escape from the hardships of the Great Depression. There was some social comment, granted, but it concerned itself not with Europe's headlong rush to destruction but usually, as it did in King Vidor's *Our Daily Bread* (1934), with the economic crisis at home.

The blindness, however, was not solely an American failing. British filmmakers managed to ignore what was happening just across the Channel and put their talents to such entertaining fare as *The Man Who Could Work Miracles* (1936) and such impressive historical offerings as Robert Stevenson's *Tudor Rose/Nine Days a Queen* (1936) and Alexander Korda's *Fire Over England* (1937); when they touched on war, they usually placed it

Previous spread: Marines attack the Japanese in *Sands of Iwo Jima* (1949). Below: *Things to Come* (1936).

Above: Laurence Olivier about to be knocked unconscious by spies who want his test aircraft in *Q Planes* (1939).

within a science-fiction context, as did Korda in *Things to Come* (1936). In France, where social comment was to be had in Jean Renoir's *Toni* (1935) and *Le Crime de Monsieur Lange* (1936), war was rarely considered, with its most effective handling being on view in Renoir's *La Grande Illusion/Grand Illusion* (1937), the story of the friendship between the commandant of a WWI German prisoner-of-war camp and the aristocratic French officer who is his prisoner. Only in Germany itself, in Leni Riefenstahl's worshipful and meticulously rehearsed documentaries on the Hitler regime – chief among them *Triumph des Willens/Triumph of the Will (1935) and Olympische Spiele* (1938) – were there filmed accounts of the disaster taking shape. *Triumph of the Will* was a masterful record of the Nazi congress held at Nuremberg in 1934; *Olympische Spiele* offered an explanation of Nazi ideology.

The blindness began to lift late in the decade. With that disaster now unmistakably just a matter of months away, contemporary war themes could no longer be ignored. In the US, the German-born and politically alert Walter Wanger released *Blockade* in 1938. In the same year, Britain put *Q Planes* and Carol Reed's *Night Train to Munich* into production, releasing the former a year later and the latter in 1940. *Q Planes* was issued in the US as *Clouds Over Europe*. The Reed picture has been known variously as *Gestapo* and, simply, *Night Train*.

Blockade, much publicized – and

Filmsonor présente:

VERSION INTEGRALE!

* JEAN GABIN
* PIERRE FRESNAY
* ERIC VON STROHEIM

DANS UN FILM DE JEAN RENOIR

LA GRANDE ILLUSION

SCENARIO et DIALOGUES de CHARLES SPAAK et JEAN RENOIR avec DITA PARLO · DALIO · CARETTE

VOLLEDIGE VERSIE!

DE GROTE BEGOOCHELING

Above: A poster for *La Grande Illusion*. Erich Von Stroheim was the commandant of a German prison camp during WWI.
Left: Henry Fonda was an American fighting in the Spanish Civil War in *Blockade* (1938).

respected – as Hollywood's first serious comment on the international situation, was a slow-moving yet effective drama about a young farmer (Henry Fonda) who hopes to defend his land by taking up arms in the Spanish Civil War. The picture was seriously damaged by the unlikely romance between the peasant Fonda and the sophisticated Madeleine Carroll, with the theater-trained Fonda enunciating his lines so impeccably that he himself seemed too sophisticated for his character. *Q Planes* and Reed's *Night Train* – the former about the theft of test aircraft, and the latter concerning itself with sneaking a secret formula

Young vehicle, was based on the Phyllis Bottome novel of a 1930s German family split by Nazism. Both pictures, as well as sharing a common theme, shared a common critical praise.

A greater praise went to Hitchcock's *Foreign Correspondent*, which was produced by Walter Wanger. The success of the director's *The Lady Vanishes* (1938) had obviously served as the inspiration for *Night Train*, and now he came up with a suspenseful tale of espionage and romance set against a background of a Europe on the brink of war. He brought all the good fun to a climax with, first, an enemy downing of an airliner crossing the Atlantic to the safety of the US, following it with a scene in which the young correspondent (Joel McCrea), standing in a London radio studio, broadcasts the news of the war's outbreak while bombs

Above: James Stewart, Margaret Sullavan and Robert Young in *The Mortal Storm* (1940).
Right: John Wayne, John Qualen and Thomas Mitchell look for enemy aircraft in *The Long Voyage Home* (1940). They played merchant seamen in World War II.

past German border guards – were highly entertaining comedy thrillers. They featured, respectively, lively performances by Laurence Olivier and Rex Harrison.

The Spanish conflict and the outbreak of the European war were more successfully handled in *Arise My Love* (1940), a stylish comedy-drama starring Ray Milland and Claudette Colbert. Especially good was Walter Abel as the harassed news editor. His line, 'I'm not happy. I'm not happy at all . . .' became a national saying that year.

Well before the release of *Arise My Love*, the blindness had completely lifted. With England's declaration of war in September 1939, the long-threatened European conflict became a reality. Filmed warfare was handed a topic that, whether it was to be given blind jingoistic or thoughtful treatment, would keep producers busy for years to come – in fact, right up to the present.

For Hollywood, the action truly began in 1940. In addition to *Arise My Love*, that year saw the studios gearing up for wartime production with five examples of the best that was to come – *The Long Voyage Home*, *Four Sons*, *The Mortal Storm*, Alfred Hitchcock's *Foreign Correspondent* and Charlie

Chaplin's 129-minute attack on Hitler and Nazism, *The Great Dictator*.

Based on a one-act play by Eugene O'Neill and directed by John Ford, the moodily photographed *The Long Voyage Home* focused on the daily lives, pleasures, and fears of a merchant crew sailing the Atlantic in the first days of the war. It featured a uniformly excellent cast that included Thomas Mitchell, Barry Fitzgerald, Ian Hunter and – in the first character portrayal of his career – a convincingly Swedish John Wayne.

Four Sons, starring Don Ameche and Eugenie Leontovich, told the story of a Czech family whose loyalties are divided with the coming of war. *The Mortal Storm*, a Margaret Sullavan-Robert

fall outside. The broadcast scene, called for by Wanger and written by Ben Hecht, was tacked on when, just before the picture's mid-year release, the air bombing of England became imminent (the original ending had McCrea and George Sanders flying to the US after surviving the downing of their airliner). As a hasty addition, it has, admittedly, the look of an after-thought, but, with McCrea urging his listeners to awaken to the fight against a common evil, it was quite effective at the time. Here was the sort of propaganda message with which so many films in the next years would close, prime examples being Randolph Scott's speech directly to the camera just before the final fade in *Gung Ho!* (1943) and all those promises of a

better day to come that Basil Rathbone's Sherlock Holmes made after he had solved each of his cases between 1942 and late 1945.

The year's most enthusiastic praise, however, was reserved for Charlie Chaplin's *The Great Dictator*, with critic Bosley Crowther, in *The New York Times* of 16 October 1940, calling it possibly the most significant film ever made. Chaplin, in tackling his first war theme since *Shoulder Arms*, without argument achieved the heights of satire by casting himself in the dual roles of dictator Adenoid Hynkel and the 'Little Tramp' Jewish barber and then expertly displaying, often by pantomime alone, their worlds-apart personalities, the splay-footed, bumbling but lovable creature on the one hand and the posturing, erratic, ludicrous tyrant on the other. His square mustache, internationally famous long before Hitler came on the scene (the people of the day never said that Chaplin had a Hitler mustache, but invariably described Hitler's mustache as Chaplinesque) made the imitation of the German dictator genuinely devastating. As Crowther saw things in the *Times*, Chaplin, in his two characters, beautifully symbolized the ancient problem of good versus evil.

First planned as early as 1935 and then revised three times before going before the camera, *The Great Dictator* centers on a little Jewish barber who loses his memory during World War I and awakens to find his country, Tomania, in the hands of dictator Hynkel. To his astonishment, he sees flags bearing the sign of the double cross, watches storm troopers patrolling the streets, learns that the Jews are being persecuted, has his barbershop burned by the state, and is himself sent to a concentration camp after he hides a friend (Reginald Gardiner) from the troopers. He flees the camp just as his identical look-alike, Hynkel, invades the neighboring country of Austerlich. The barber is mistaken for Hynkel and carried triumphantly to a celebration of the conquest. There, startling everyone, he gives an impassioned speech calling for peace and human kindness. Running six minutes, the speech, while regarded as more than eloquent, was considered over-long by some critics.

Though the main story line belongs to the little barber, Chaplin gives equal

Chaplin as Hynkel romancing his global balloon in *The Great Dictator* (1940).

time to his portrayal of Hynkel and, in so doing, provides the film with some of its most hilarious moments. Of them all, the critical consensus holds the best to be his ballet dance and his meeting with visiting tyrant, Napaloni (Jack Oakie), the dictator of Bacteria, a delicious send-up of Italy's Mussolini. In the former, he happily skips and pirouettes with a balloon representing a globe of the world, daintily spinning it on his fingertips, flicking it from hand to hand, and tossing it high, only to break into a frustrated child's tears when, plaything that it is, it finally bursts.

The scenes with Napaloni detail his attempts to intimidate Oakie by seating him in a chair much lower than his own and then conducting the visitor on a tour of the opulent Hynkel palace. Along the way, the two do their best to out-strut and outdo each other in displays of self-importance. Throughout, they work flawlessly as a team in playing off against each other the outlandish differences in their characters – Hynkel's assorted neuroses as opposed

to Napaloni's perennial bluffness. In the Napaloni role, Oakie, a popular but nevertheless much under-rated comedian, did the best work of his screen career, with most critics agreeing that his performance matched Chaplin's for excellence.

The Great Dictator, marking Chaplin's last appearance as the 'Little Tramp,' also featured fine performances by Paulette Goddard (Hannah, the barber's love) and an always-reliable duo, Henry Daniell (Minister of Propaganda Garbitsch) and Billy Gilbert (Minister of War Herring). The film was among the nominees for the 1940 best picture Academy Award, but unfortunately lost to Alfred Hitchcock's *Rebecca*, an entry that, while a fine and entertaining suspense effort, in no way matched the significance of its competitor. Both Chaplin and Oakie were nominated, respectively, as best actor and best supporting actor. Neither won.

The Academy's 1940 decisions can reasonably be suspected of having been made out of fear. *The Great Dictator*'s

release coincided with the same type of national debate over US neutrality that had marked the pre-1917 years. The Academy may well have been reacting to the widespread isolationist sentiment that was calling for the banning of a film treatise of so obvious an interventionist bent. Further, there was a growing personal dislike of Chaplin on the parts of many pro-isolationists because he had now been in the country for several decades without applying for citizenship.

Chaplin's later works – chief among them the bleakly funny *Monsieur Verdoux* (1947) and the poetic *Limelight* (1952) – were similarly ignored by the Academy, presumably over the scandalized feelings left by his paternity suit of the early 1940s and by the McCarthy-era hysteria over his suspected communist leanings. This most renowned of screen comedians was not duly honored by the Academy until the 1972 presentation of a special Oscar for 'the incalculable effect he has had on making motion pictures the art form of this century.'

The pro-isolationist outcry against *The Great Dictator* evaporated with the Japanese attack on Pearl Harbor and Franklin Roosevelt's declaration of war the following day. Having geared up for more than a year, Hollywood now plunged wholeheartedly into the business of filmed warfare. In 1942 alone, more than 80 war pictures came off the production line, to be followed by an endless stream in the subsequent years. In all, the pictures divided themselves into three types. There were (1) the early films of Americans preparing to go to war, both in the service and on the homefront, (2) the comedies and the musicals meant to lift everyone's morale and (3) the pictures dealing with the fighting in the Pacific and in Africa and Europe.

The first two types can be given but passing mention because the first had so few representatives and the second was intended as light-hearted entertainment to amuse and lift the spirits of everyone

Opposite: Robert Armstrong, Ralph Bellamy, Errol Flynn and Fred MacMurray in *Dive Bomber* (1941).
Right: Bud Abbott (left) and Lou Costello (center) are issued their uniforms in *Buck Privates* (1941).
Below: Stan Laurel (left) and Oliver Hardy (center) in *Air Raid Wardens* (1943) – one of their most disappointing pictures.

from draftee to defense worker. Chiefly remembered from the first category are *Dive Bomber* (1941), a tale of Navy doctors working to eliminate pilot blackouts; *I Wanted Wings* (1941), all about pilots in training under a tough Brian Donlevy; *The Navy Way* (1943), which sent an assortment of kids through basic training and turned them into dedicated warriors and *Wings for the Eagle* (1942), a modest something concerning aircraft workers at Lockheed's southern California plant. Nor should *Stage Door Canteen* (1943) be overlooked. A nonentity about how the theatrical luminaries of the day entertained and mothered war-bound ser-

vice personnel at the famous New York center, it featured a sequence in which a collection of buddies, just before being shipped abroad, are given passes to visit their girlfriends at the canteen. The whole idea had overseas servicemen, wise to the buttoned-up ways of all embarkation areas, rolling in the aisles.

The second category produced one forgettable comedy after another, though they were much enjoyed as fun ways to pass a few hours during some bad years. They ranged from Abbott and Costello's *Buck Privates* and Bob Hope's *Caught in the Draft* (both 1941 and both made before that year's fateful December to take advantage of public

interest in the recently inaugurated Selective Service System) to Joel McCrea's *The More the Merrier* (1943) and Robert Walker's *See Here, Private Hargrove* (1944). For Laurel and Hardy devotees, the era's two most disappointing comedies had to be *Great Guns* (1941) and *Air Raid Wardens* (1943). In the first, the two friends are servants who join the army with their young millionaire boss; in the second, after being turned down for military service and after becoming the world's most incompetent guardians of the homefront, they manage to capture a band of Nazi spies – by accident, of course. Both films were sadly unfunny and heralded the ultimate decline of the hitherto incomparable pair.

The bulk of the musicals, except for a moment here and there, were just as forgettable. Of those special moments, there are two that audiences of the day seem never to have forgotten – Alan Ladd, in *Star Spangled Rhythm* (1942), lampooning his dead-eyed killer of *This Gun For Hire* as he disposes of an adversary by firing off a toy bow and arrow;

and Bette Davis, in *Thank Your Lucky Stars* (1943), singing in ultra-sophisticated fashion the love lament of homefront women, 'They're Either Too Young or Too Old.' Both sequences came in revue-type pictures, the first from Paramount and the second from Warner Brothers, in which each studio dragged all its acting personnel before the cameras for cameo appearances. The best musical of the era was *Yankee Doodle Dandy* (1942), a James Cagney singing-and-dancing tour de force that

had little to do with the war but that raised everyone's spirits high. Running close on its heels so far as grandeur is concerned – and highlighted by 17 Irving Berlin songs – was *This Is the Army* (1943).

The films that took the actual fighting as their themes, of course, far outnumbered all the others. Regardless of where their make-believe skirmishes and battles occurred, they shared two characteristics in common. First, they all carried, directly or indirectly, pro-

paganda messages to rouse service and homefront pride in and dedication to the Allied cause. On screen, frightened though they well might be, Allied fighters were courageous, honorable, and patriotic. The message couldn't be missed: all others must match these qualities. It was not until well after the war that such human traits as self-interest and cruelty were to be closely explored in 'our guys' – the self-interest (subsequently dropped) of George Peppard as he considers desertion in

Second, the films, while obviously overlooking the human failings in the Allied fighter, just as obviously overstated those in the enemy. They all drew venomous portraits, though, with a few exceptions, not quite so outrageous as those baby-bayoneting, lustful characterizations seen in World War I. Of the various Axis forces, the Japanese received the harshest treatment, with foot soldier and officer alike being pictured as sadistic and fanatical. As for the Germans, most of the angry con-

Above: Ronald Reagan and Joan Leslie in *This Is the Army* (1943) — a morale booster.

Irving Berlin sings 'Oh, How I Hate to Get Up in the Morning' in *This Is the Army*.

Opposite: The grand finale of *This Is the Army* (1943).

The Victors (1963); the combined self-interest and cruelty of Dean Martin and Montgomery Clift in *The Young Lions* (1958) as they deliberately let two sightseeing desk-jockey officers go in search of battleground souvenirs so that, when sniper fire kills the visitors, the telltale rifle flashes will give the enemy positions away.

centration was focused on the Nazi leaders, who were likewise painted as sadistic and fanatical, often legitimately, as was the case in John Carradine's Reinhard Heydrich in *Hitler's Madman* (1943). Officers, even in those fleeting glimpses of fighter and bomber pilots ready to attack, gave the traditional impression of arrogance; it was

Above: Maximilian Schell and Marlon
Brando as two German Army officers in *The
Young Lions* (1958).
Right: Otto Preminger, Monty Woolley, Anne
Baxter in *The Pied Piper* (1942).

an arrogance happily punctured when
the strutting brass suffered the humiliation of capture or, ironically, faced a
very human dilemma, as did Otto Preminger's colonel when, in *The Pied
Piper* (1942), he freed Monty Woolley
on the condition that his, Preminger's,
young niece would be allowed to join
the children being shepherded out of
France by Woolley to the safety of
England. The German infantryman
was rarely characterized but was
usually seen as a faceless, helmeted cog
in the enemy machinery. The Italian
soldier, because his nation collapsed so
early in the fighting, received little
attention. Both during and after the
war, he was likely to be depicted as
emotionally volatile and far more
interested in romantic than territorial
conquests.

The studios divided the films, almost equally, between the Pacific and the African-European fronts. In quality, they came up with an outpouring of work that ranged from the very best to the very worst. The quality, obviously, was much determined by the stature of the individual studios. Regardless of the virtues or faults of any given story line, such giants as MGM and 20th Century Fox backed their films – from the top-of-the-line fare to the least of the bottom-of-bill B pictures – with excellent photography, fine (usually) special effects, and (considering that many of the industry's most talented male personalities were away in the armed forces) good performances. The worst came from the so-called 'quickie' studios, the outfits that grew nervous when a picture didn't get 'from camera to can in two weeks.' It is impossible to report on these pictures of such varied quality in the order of their release without the confusion of hopping back and forth between the two fronts. And so we'll deal with each front individually, beginning with the Pacific.

Starting with Hawaii on 7 December 1941, Americans did their first actual fighting in the Pacific and it was here that their Hollywood imitators had their baptisms under fire. For the duration of the war, the imitators would fight battles in locations recognized by anyone who looked at a headline. To use some of the era's better films from the major studios as examples:

For Paramount, Brian Donlevy mustered his troops to defend against an enemy onslaught in *Wake Island* (1942).

MGM's Robert Taylor, Lloyd Nolan, Robert Walker and ten companions defended a bridge against the invading Japanese in *Bataan* (1943). In a film reminiscent of 1932's *The Lost Patrol* – a tale of British soldiers trapped in the desert and surrounded by enemy Arabs – all but one of the men died, leaving the lone survivor, Robert Taylor, to settle down behind a machine gun and await his own fate.

Aiming at the female audience and coming up with a very effective and exciting tearjerker, Paramount sent nurses Claudette Colbert, Paulette Goddard and their colleagues out to face an assortment of dangers, among them the torpedo sinking of their transport,

Right: Japanese troops assemble under the Rising Sun flag in *Gung Ho!* (1943).

in *So Proudly We Hail* (1943). Along the way, they met a shy but valiant Marine in the person of Sonny Tufts. The picture made a star of this ill-fated performer who was on tap for wartime work because a college football injury was keeping him out of the service and who was to become, in the years before his death in 1970, one of Hollywood's more pathetic figures, a victim of alcoholism. Likewise, *Bataan*'s Robert Walker eventually met a tragic end because of drinking and emotional problems, dying in 1951.

Warner Brothers ordered submarine commander Cary Grant and his crew deep into Tokyo harbor in *Destination Tokyo* (1943). The film was notable for the understated way in which it handled the very human fears of the officers and men alike. In this vein, one scene was particularly effective. John Ridgely, cast as an officer assigned to temporary duty aboard the submarine, is embarrassed by the terror he feels during a depth-charge attack. He sheepishly admits his fear to Grant, saying that the

expression on his face must surely be giving him away. Grant quietly replies that the man looks no different than anyone else on board.

In *Air Force* (1943), acclaimed as one of the finest US wartime efforts, Warners followed a Flying Fortress crew as it saw action in Hawaii, the Philippines and the Coral Sea. Directed by Howard Hawks, the picture featured fine characterizations by youngsters John Garfield, Gig Young and Arthur Kennedy and by character actors Stanley Ridges and Harry Carey.

For Twentieth Century Fox, Marines Preston Foster, Lloyd Nolan and William Bendix fought to secure a vital Pacific island base in *Guadacanal Diary* (1943). The picture, which was based on a best-selling book by newsman

Right: Richard Crane pulls his wounded gunner out of the turret of their strafed plane in *Wing and a Prayer* (1944).
Below: George Murphy (left) and Robert Taylor worry about the impending assault in *Bataan* (1943). Lee Bowman lies dead.

Richard Tregaskis, was high-lighted by some fine action sequences, but was generally regarded by a public growing accustomed to war films as a standard propaganda piece. A young Richard Jaeckel, formerly a delivery boy at Fox and today a highly respected character actor, scored well in this, his first feature.

Twentieth Century then took audiences to sea in *Wing and a Prayer* (1944) for a look at life aboard an aircraft carrier. The picture's title came from one of the day's more popular flag-waving songs. Though melodramatic at times, it had a solid feel of authenticity. Don Ameche, in a sharp departure from his usual nice-guy roles, was particularly effective as a martinet officer whose outer hardness masks a deep concern for his men.

Fox also seated audiences in a Japanese courtroom to watch flier Dana Andrews and his crew being tried as war criminals in *The Purple Heart* (1944). The picture, marked by fine performances, especially from Andrews, Sam Levene and Richard Loo, provided somber and effective propaganda throughout, but was marred for many viewers by its principal setting – a highly stylized and dramatically lighted courtroom that looked anything but Japanese.

MGM drew its *Thirty Seconds over Tokyo* (1944) from one of America's

Above: The evil Richard Loo gloats over his capture of American pilot Dana Andrews in *The Purple Heart* (1944).
Right: Spencer Tracy, as Colonel James Doolittle, exhorts his bomber crews in *Thirty Seconds Over Tokyo* (1944).

most famous headlines of the early war years – the first US air attack on the Japanese homeland. Featuring documentary footage and a brief appearance by Spencer Tracy in the role of the attack commander, Colonel (later General) James Doolittle, the film launched airmen Van Johnson and Robert Walker in secret from a carrier, sent them above Japan, and on to crash landings in China.

Tracy was not the only actor to portray an actual war-time figure. In *The Sullivans* (1944), Thomas Mitchell and Selena Royle gave beautiful performances as the parents who earned the nation's sympathy when their five sons were killed in the early Pacific naval fighting. At Paramount, producer-director Cecil B DeMille entrusted Gary Cooper with the title role in *The Story of Dr Wassell* (1944), the film biography of the naval physician who saved so many lives in the Pacific. The picture met with a mixed critical reaction, with some moviegoers finding it impressive and others saying that, though periodically compelling, it was, in common with some other DeMille productions, overly long.

These were some of the best from the best. At the opposite end of the scale stood an assortment of nonsense from the quickie studios. For instance:

There was Monogram's *Wings Over the Pacific*, a 1943 dandy that had Edward Norris take care of enemies east and west by disposing of a band of Nazi spies and then knocking off a Japanese landing party, all in the name of keeping a Pacific island safe for democracy. But let's face a fact: it was all good fun.

Or how about the heroic tomfoolery

in *Submarine Raiders* (1942) from Columbia, a 'poverty row' studio in the process of becoming a major operation. In this one, John Howard fails to warn Pearl Harbor of the coming December 7th attack. Then he battles a Japanese carrier on which – get this – his beloved (Marguerite Chapman) is being held prisoner. But again: it was all good fun.

Not all the low-budget fare can be dismissed as trivial, however. Director Edward Dmytryk's *Behind the Rising Sun* (1943) was quietly dramatic as it told the story of a young Japanese-American who participates in the Japanese invasion of China during the 1930s and is eventually disgusted by the conquerers' barbarity. J. Carroll Naish, who didn't know how to give an inadequate performance, appeared as the young man's father. Tom Neal, another of the wartime's ill-fated players, did well as the young man. Neal, who held a law degree from Harvard, saw his career falter in later years and eventually became a landscape gardener. In

Right: Another Japanese soldier mistreats one of the conquered Chinese in *Behind the Rising Sun* (1943).
Below right: Robert Ryan (left) and Randolph Scott at the controls in *Bombardier* (1943).
Below: Alan Ladd was a guerrilla who sacrificed himself in battle in *China* (1943).

1965, he was sentenced to prison for six years on a manslaughter charge in the death of his wife. He died of congestive heart failure in late 1972, just eight months after his release.

The small studios were not the only outfits to turn out inferior material. The big operations also had their misses, some of them almost farcical. For instance, Alan Ladd, every inch of him a hero, went to *China* (1943) for

Paramount. He played an oil salesman who joined a Chinese guerrilla band and then outwitted and outfought every enemy in sight, proving, by golly, that one deadpan American was better than an entire Japanese army. The picture, however, was tailored for his admittedly unique talents and was, because of his presence, a box office success.

Unlike other genres – for example, westerns and musicals – filmed warfare has never had performers that it could exclusively call its own. The years 1942-45, however, did come up with two stars who seemed born for command and who, when called to duty, performed so well that they have become strongly identified with war films. Not at all coincidentally, both are even more strongly identified with westerns –

Randolph Scott and John Wayne.

A man with chiseled, hawk-like features that many audiences found classically American, Scott's initial World War II assignment was *To the Shores of Tripoli* (1942), a film that never left its Marine training locale in San Diego, California. He next prepared young recruits for Pacific duty in *Bombardier* (1943), that same year going to sea as a Canadian officer in *Corvette K-225* (British title: *The Nelson Touch*), an exciting yarn of convoys struggling across the Atlantic in the face of submarine and air attacks. It was still 1943 when he returned to the Pacific for his most popular wartime role, that of the commander in *Gung Ho!* Based on fact, the picture followed the Marine unit, Carlsen's Raiders, from training

Above: John Wayne and Anna Lee in *Flying Tigers* (1942).
Left: Wayne leads Paul Fix in a charge in *Back to Bataan* (1945).
Opposite left: Wayne as a US Marine Sergeant in *Sands of Iwo Jima* (1949).
Opposite right: Wayne leads his troops in Vietnam in *The Green Berets* (1968).
Below: Wayne with Kirk Douglas in *Cast A Giant Shadow* (1966).

through the first major American offensive in the war: the retaking of Makin Island. *Gung Ho!*, with its title inspired by the unit's battle cry, is considered blatant jingoism by many moderns, but was a favorite in its day, principally because of its climactic battle sequence on Makin and the strict attention that was given to the fate of each Marine participant. At war's end, Scott put his uniform away and spent the remainder of his 42-year career in westerns, retiring in 1962 after a fine character performance as an aging gunman in *Ride the High Country*.

Wayne's military career in films was far more extensive that Scott's. With two exceptions (as the Swede in *The Long Voyage Home* and as a pilot in *Reunion in France* [1943]; British title: *Mademoiselle France*), Wayne spent the

war years in the Pacific – in the air with the *Flying Tigers* (1942), on an island as the boss of *The Fighting Seabees* (1944) and in the Philippines, first as a Marine colonel organizing early-war guerrilla resistance against the Japanese in *Back to Bataan* and then as a torpedo boat officer with Robert Montgomery in *They Were Expendable* (both 1945).

Of the lot, *They Were Expendable*, which was in production at the time both the European and Japanese wars ended, ranks as the best. Based on a book that William L White had written about General Douglas MacArthur's

PT-boat departure from the Philippines in early 1942, the picture was done in a low key, particularly so in the sequence – MacArthur's departure – that could have been easily overdramatized to the detriment of the entire effort. Actor Robert Barrat portrayed MacArthur.

Wayne remained in uniform, trading it off routinely for western garb, for the next two decades. He relived the Pacific war in *Sands of Iwo Jima* (1950), *Operation Pacific* (1951), *Flying Leathernecks* (also 1951) and the sprawling and melodramatic *In Harm's Way* (1965). In *The Sea Chase* (1955), he appeared in one of his most unusual roles, as a German merchant marine captain doggedly avoiding Allied pursuit as he sailed his freighter home across the Pacific and Atlantic at the start of the war. Wayne went to Europe for a brief – and too dramatically played – appearance as a paratroop commander in *The Longest Day* (1962). In

Top: Robert Mitchum (center) and Ray Danton plan their next move in the D-Day invasion in *The Longest Day* (1962).
Left: Robert Montgomery aboard a PT boat in *They Were Expendable* (1945).
Below: A Japanese attack from *In Harm's Way* (1965).

another brief appearance, he portrayed a US general sympathetic to the Israeli cause in the fine spectacular, *Cast a Giant Shadow* (1966). Unfortunately, while climaxing his career in westerns with his splendid Rooster Cogburn characterizations, Wayne's final military film was his salute to the Americans fighting in Vietnam, *The Green Berets* (1968), an overly long and at times poorly done (example: the enemy hideaway that is so obviously a house in the Georgia area where the picture was shot) statement of his arch-conservative views. It earned an increasingly widespread derision as a piece of jingoistic claptrap when the nation, as a whole, came to oppose the Vietnam conflict. Later, whatever had been lost of Wayne's reputation was regained with his Cogburn roles and with public awareness of how stoically he endured the cancer that took his life in 1979.

Eastward across the Atlantic, US troops did their first fighting in 1942, on the North African front. From there, in 1943, they crossed the Mediterranean to Sicily and then Italy. Of the films that took the fighting around the Mediterranean as their themes, the best were

Five Graves to Cairo, The Immortal Sergeant and *Sahara* (all 1943) and *The Story of GI Joe*, which was produced in 1944 but released just as the European war was ending in early 1945. And, of course, the list wouldn't be complete without the Warner Brothers classic, *Casablanca* (1943).

Film histories and filmographies are in dispute over Casablanca's release date, with some giving it as 1942 and others as 1943. The 1943 date is used here because, according to Clive Hirschhorn's book, *The Warner Brothers Story*, the picture was shown and reviewed in late 1942 (*The New York Times* review is dated 27 November) but was officially released in 1943.

Five Graves to Cairo, directed by Billy Wilder, was a taut adventure melodrama about British spies trying to cripple General Erwin Rommel's tank forces by destroying his secret supply dumps. Its star, Franchot Tone, did fine work in a category generally unfamiliar to him – the action film. But it was Erich Von Stroheim who captivated audiences with his portrayal of Rommel. The general was to be given a more rounded characterization by James Mason in *The Desert Fox* (1951),

Anne Baxter and Erich Von Stroheim in *Five Graves to Cairo* (1943).

but Stroheim at the least did not endow him with the lechery and sadism that marked the actor's World War I 'Huns,' but rather made him the efficient warrior that he actually was.

True to its title, *The Immortal Sergeant* told the story of a British non-commissioned officer who so inspired his men in the desert fighting that his memory promised to remain with them for a lifetime after his death. Henry Fonda was his usual excellent self as the sergeant.

A Humphrey Bogart feature, *Sahara*, dealt with a multi-national band of soldiers who, separated from their units in the desert, join with a lost American tank to survive and harass the German forces. Bogart played the sergeant in charge of the tank in what turned out to be a highly successful blend of action, drama and comedy.

As good as the three films were, they were far outclassed by *The Story of GI Joe*. Though it featured some good action sequences, the film was basically a sensitively-done character study of an infantry company in the slogging Italian

Gestapo's Conrad Veidt, enchanting audiences along the way with his instructions to 'Play it, Sam' (*it* being Dooley Wilson's piano rendition of the song 'As Time Goes By') before finally strolling off into the night fog with French policeman Claude Rains. On final fadeout, no one could doubt that the Germans were in for a bad time indeed from these two amusing blends of cynicism and sentimentality.

As critics and audiences alike saw things, *Casablanca* had everything that a wartime melodrama could wish for – romance, excitement, a dash of come-

campaign. The cast was headed by Burgess Meredith as front-line newsman Ernie Pyle (whose reports on the daily life and heroism of the ordinary soldier made him one of the most widely-read of the war's correspondents) and Robert Mitchum as the doomed lieutenant. For Mitchum, who had been in Hollywood since 1935 and had worked in 24 pictures of varying quality, the film meant instant stardom – and deservedly so. He was beautifully on the mark in an underplayed demonstration of exhaustion, disillusionment and deep care for his men.

The praise won by *GI Joe* was matched – but for quite different reasons – by that given what was undoubtedly the war's single most

Above: James Mason (on landing) played Erwin Rommel in *The Desert Fox* (1951). Behind him are Richard Boone and Jessica Tandy.
Top: Spencer Tracy played the ghost of a killed American pilot in *A Guy Named Joe* (1944).
Right: The climax of *Casablanca* (1942) – Claude Rains (in dark uniform), Paul Henreid, Humphrey Bogart, Ingrid Bergman.

popular film, *Casablanca*. Here, everything was solid good fun as that hard-bitten owner of Rick's Café Américain, Humphrey Bogart, helped his former love, Ingrid Bergman, and her underground leader husband (Paul Henreid) escape the oily clutches of the dy, some patriotic corn (remember the cafe habitues standing and lustily singing 'La Marseillaise' in defiance of the German customers?), excellent performances in even its most secondary roles (as witness the field day had by Peter Lorre and Sidney Greenstreet) and a string of Academy Awards – to the picture itself, to director Michael Curtiz, and to writers Julius J Epstein, Philip G Epstein, and Howard Koch. Bogart was nominated as best actor and Rains as best supporting actor. Both lost, Rains to Charles Coburn for *The More the Merrier*, and Bogart to Paul

Lukas for *Watch on the Rhine*, an excellent (mainly because of its performances) version of Lillian Hellman's stage drama about a German refugee family pursued to the United States by Nazi agents.

Casablanca was more than just a good picture. It was also a lucky one. While it was in production, the British were at last winning the fight in North Africa and, to help wrap things up, were planning with the Americans a landing on the continent's northwestern coast in late 1942. By the happiest of box office coincidences, the picture was ready for

screening just one week after US troops went ashore near Casablanca.

Though films such as these were well presented and popular (more than popular when the list gets to *Casablanca*), most of Hollywood's interest was centered to the north, in Hitler's Germany and the beleaguered nations surrounding it. But, here, when it came to incorporating American troops into story lines, the producers faced a problem. US ground forces would not be fully committed to the fighting until the Allied invasion of June 1944, with the European war then ending in a matter

made a star of the young and open-faced Glenn Ford.

Everyday British life was torn by the war in *Mrs Miniver* (1942), the Greer Garson-Walter Pidgeon vehicle that took the Academy Award's best picture honors for the year. One of its high points came with the depiction of how small private yachts so valiantly assisted in removing the tattered British forces from the beaches at Dunkirk, a rescue that saved the army from annihilation.

Norwegian fighters, helped by the British Navy, fought the enemy troops occupying their country in *The Commandos Strike at Dawn* (1942), a solid action feature shot in Newfoundland.

Russian villagers defended their

Left: Jon Hall and Eddie Albert (center) in *Eagle Squadron* (1942).
Below: Albert Basserman, John Carradine, Philip Dorn and Joan Crawford in *Reunion in France* (1943).

of months and leaving little or no time to plan, mount and film a story of American exploits. The problem was partly solved with films that used Air Force participation in the bombings of Germany as backgrounds, among them *Bomber's Moon* and Spencer Tracy's *A Guy Named Joe* (both 1943). Aside from such fare, most US wartime films about western and central Europe spun yarns about the people of the various nations besieged or occupied by the German forces. To cite just a few examples:

Refugees from Nazi Germany wandered from country to country in search of asylum and were often rebuffed in *So Ends Our Night* (1941), the film that

Left: Gene Kelly and Jean-Pierre Aumont in *The Cross of Lorraine* (1944).

homes against the invading Germans in *North Star* (1943).

A German family endured the fanaticism of its offspring in *Hitler's Children* (1943), an off-beat picture for its time because it did not portray all its Germans as stupid or cruel.

In 1944, French soldiers escaped a German prison camp and triggered a local uprising in *The Cross of Lorraine*. That same year, as did the people in *North Star*, Russian peasants stood up to invading Germans in *Days of Glory*, Gregory Peck's first picture. Peck didn't look at all Russian, but audiences seemed not to mind. He was firmly established as a star.

All this is not to say that the Holly-

wood war offerings didn't manage to insert Americans into the action. US heroes were ever-present to lend the beleaguered nations a needed hand. Tyrone Power joined the fighting to be near his girl friend and got into the action over Dunkirk in *A Yank in the RAF* (1941). That same year, a future American president, Ronald Reagan, signed up with the RAF in *International Squadron* and proved himself not a ne'er-do-well Yank but a responsible combat flier. In 1942, Robert Stack and several friends likewise enlisted with the RAF, their aim being to fly with that force's much publicized American volunteer group, the *Eagle Squadron*. A year later, in *Reunion in France* (*Mademoiselle France* in Britain), American airman John Wayne helped Parisian couturière Joan Crawford fight

the German occupation troops.

James Cagney, looking very American as he played a Canadian bush pilot, joined the RCAF in *Captains of the Clouds* (1942). In a reprise of his cocky doughboy of *The Fighting 69th*, he disgraced himself, saw the error of his ways and valiantly gave up his life by flying into a German fighter that was attacking a fleet of bombers being ferried to England. In all – classic Cagney.

Cagney was not alone in shepherding needed aircraft to the Allies. Women ferry command pilots got into the act in 1944, in *Ladies Courageous*.

Not all the action was in the air, however. Randolph Scott, remember, spent a part of 1942 protecting Atlantic convoys from attack in *Corvette K-225*. Americans Humphrey Bogart and Ray-

Greer Garson and Walter Pidgeon comfort their children during an air raid in *Mrs Miniver* (1942).

mond Massey defied those same U-boats as they sailed with a merchant convoy to Russia in the fast-paced and exciting *Action in the North Atlantic* (1943). Tallulah Bankhead and John Hodiak fought an arrogant U-boat commander after their ship had been torpedoed and they found themselves adrift in a *Lifeboat* (1944), a masterful Alfred Hitchcock experiment in filming within a confined space.

Poverty-row and B players were just as active and heroic as the big-studio stars. Because he couldn't be seen, Jon Hall proved a more-than-successful spy in *The Invisible Agent* (1942). Silent screen comic Bud Duncan exchanged

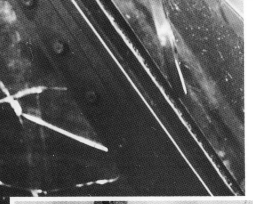

Opposite: James Cagney played a flippant Royal Canadian Air Force pilot during World War II in *Captains of the Clouds* (1942). Below: Eric Portman (left) and Leslie Howard (tied up) played the leads in *The Forty-Ninth Parallel* (1941).

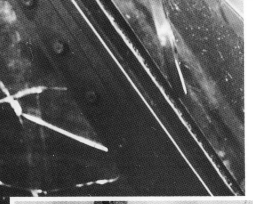

starred in a screen adaptation of the book in 1935.

This type of film was particularly well done in Howard's *Forty-Ninth Parallel* (1941). Shown as *The Invaders* in the US, it dealt with five U-boat men who, on being stranded in Canada, attempt to work their way into the US. En route, they kill several unsuspecting Canadians (Laurence Olivier and Finlay Currie among them) and see their own number dwindle until the lone survivor is bested by soldier Raymond Massey. Effective as members of the U-boat crew were Eric Portman and Niall MacGinnis.

Once the war had been declared, Britain concentrated mainly on films having to do with the fighting itself. The industry, however, shared a problem in common with Hollywood. At first, except for the North African campaign (which went badly in its opening stages) and the debacle at Dunkirk, there was no ground fighting on which themes could be constructed. Then, with the 1944 invasion, there was too little time for preparation and filming before peace was declared in May of the next year. Consequently, Britain's wartime attention went principally to air and sea films.

In the former category, *Dangerous Moonlight* (1941) ranks at the very top of the entries. Known to American audiences as *Suicide Squadron*, it mixes action, romance and drama in a quality tale of a Polish pianist (Anton Walbrook) who escapes the Nazis, joins the RAF and loses his sight in the Battle of Britain. Throughout, his patriotism is challenged by his sweetheart (Sally Gray) as she urges him to forget risking his life and concentrate on his music. Somberly photographed and splendidly acted, the film can still grip today. It was – and still is – famous for the composition, 'Warsaw Concerto,' which provided its musical background and contributed much to its mood and plot line.

The war at sea provided Britain with the theme for what many filmgoers and critics regard as the greatest of the wartime films made on either side of the Atlantic – *In Which We Serve* (1942). A drama set aboard the fictional destroyer, HMS *Torrin*, it was a superb accomplishment on all levels – as a propaganda hymn to the indomitable British spirit, as a documentary of shipboard life and as a sensitive portrait not only of the human beings who came from all walks of life to sail the nation's

his backwoods outfit for a uniform and made life miserable for the enemy in a picture with the war's most unforgettable title – *Hillbilly Blitzkreig* (1943). In 1944, Larry Parks, yet two years away from stardom in *The Jolson Story*, dropped into Germany with the aid of *The Black Parachute*, donned a Nazi uniform and made off with some mighty important secret information.

British producers were as busy as their Hollywood counterparts in the war years. Their earliest wartime themes centered mostly on British civilian heroes outwitting the German authorities, as did Rex Harrison's secret service agent when he helped save a scientific formula from the Nazis in *Night Train to Munich*. The tradition of such quiet derring-do continued throughout the war, a prime example being the heroics of Leslie Howard's deceptively mild-mannered professor as he smuggles political prisoners out of Germany in *Pimpernel Smith* (1942). The film, which was variously titled *Mister V* or *The Fighting Pimpernel* for US audiences, was a reworking of Baroness Orczy's *The Scarlet Pimpernel*, a 1905 novel of rescues in the French Revolution. Howard had

warships but of the families they left behind. Given equal attention in that portrait were men of all ranks – officers Noël Coward and Michael Wilding, non-commissioned officer Bernard Miles and young seamen John Mills and Richard Attenborough. As was to be expected because of their theater experience, all gave excellent performances, as did Celia Johnson as Coward's wife.

The story itself is simple. While on duty in the Mediterranean, the *Torrin* is torpedoed and sent to the bottom. The captain (Coward) and the few of his men yet surviving cling desperately to floating pieces of wreckage as they hope for rescue. In turn, the camera settles on each of the major characters and then dissolves into flashbacks of how each lived at home, entered the Navy and came to be aboard and cherish the *Torrin*. Some die there in the oily water while others last long enough to be saved.

Making *In Which We Serve* all the more impressive is the fact that it was, in the main, the creation of a single man, Coward himself. Using the loss of the destroyer, HMS *Kelly*, as his

Above: Noël Coward (right), the captain of HMS *Torrin*, during the torpedo attack in *In Which We Serve* (1942). ·
Right: RAF airmen in the ready room in *One of Our Aircraft Is Missing* (1941).

Below: The *Lifeboat* (1944) gang – Walter Slezak, Mary Anderson, Hume Cronyn, Tallulah Bankhead, John Hodiak, Henry Hull, Heather Angel, William Bendix and Canada Lee.

Opposite: Humphrey Bogart and Raymond Massey in *Action in the North Atlantic* (1943).

inspiration, Coward not only portrayed the captain but also wrote, produced, co-directed and scored the film. His work earned him a special 1942 Academy Award for 'outstanding production achievement.' The co-director was a young David 'Lean, working on his first major assignment behind the cameras. In future years, Lean would be responsible for three splendid war films – *The Bridge on the River Kwai* (1957), *Lawrence of Arabia* (1962), and *Dr Zhivago* (1964).

In the Coward biography, *A Talent to Amuse*, author Sheridan Morley writes that *In Which We Serve* came dangerously close to not being made. When Coward first submitted the story line to the authorities for government appro-

val, one high ranking minister turned it down because it dared to show a British warship being sunk, an affront in his view (despite the headlines of the day) to the Navy. Lord Louis Mountbatten, who had been the one to tell Coward of the *Kelly*'s fate, intervened and was instrumental in securing the needed government go-ahead.

Then, Morley goes on to report, Coward narrowly averted death during the filming. All the sea action was shot indoors, on sets that included a giant water tank and a full-sized replica of a destroyer. At one point, Coward was called to stand on a mock-up of the ship's bridge while tons of water crashed over him. Finding the rig too flimsy for his liking, he refused to do

the scene without a test of what would happen when the water was released from overhead tanks. He proved himself more than prudent here. The cascading water completely washed the bridge away and would have likely killed anyone standing there.

Britain surrounded *Dangerous Moonlight* and *In Which We Serve* – one an excellent film, the other a masterpiece – with wartime offerings of varying quality. Considered among the best were:

One of Our Aircraft Is Missing (1941), a somewhat slowly-moving story of British airmen being helped back to freedom by the Dutch underground after their bomber is downed.

Convoy (1941), which sees merchant

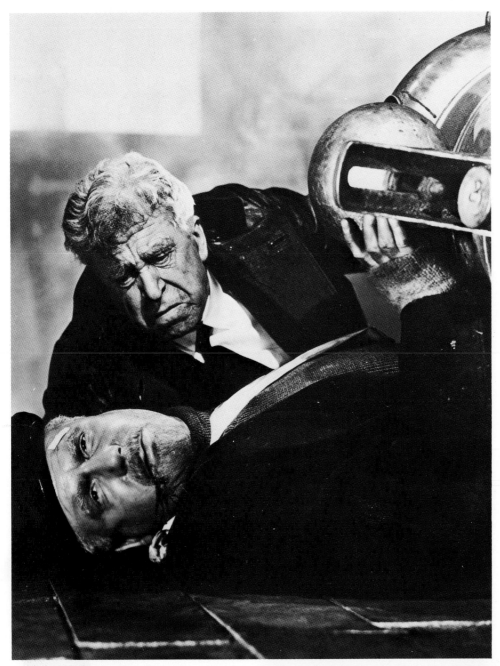

(Anton Walbrook).

David Niven's *The Way Ahead* (1944), a semi-documentary that follows an army unit from training through battle.

Receiving less enthusiastic welcomes were *The Big Blockade* (1941), a revue type film that, presenting sketches to show the importance of blockading Germany, ended up looking weak and uneven; the stilted *Secret Mission* (1942) which sent four British intelligence agents into occupied France to map the German defenses, and the ridiculous *Flying Fortress* (1942). Why ridiculous? How else can you describe a film whose climactic scenes have the hero climbing out to work on the damaged wing of an airplane in flight?

Considering the silliness inherent in propaganda, the US and Great Britain managed to turn out a goodly number of fine – and, on occasion, even brilliant – wartime films. But not even the best could match for drama and authenticity the documentaries of the period. Starting with Leni Riefenstahl's frightening *Triumph of the Will* in 1936, the anemic stepchild of World War I grew into a mature adult that, in the company of military and civilian cameramen, took audiences to wherever history was

Left: The officer lies dead during the attack in *Convoy* (1941).
Opposite: Hitler Youth in Leni Riefenstahl's *Triumph of the Will* (1936) – the official record of the Nuremberg Nazi Party Congress.
Below: A scene in the German extermination camp from *Night and Fog* (1955).

ships threatened by a German pocket battleship and climaxes with a merchant officer sacrificing his life to save his fellow seamen.

Next of Kin (1942), one of the war's more unusual films in that it was an instructional piece (about the harm done when civilians hear of secret military operations and then carelessly discuss them) that was so grippingly done that it became a favorite at home and abroad.

The Bells Go Down (1943), an energetic account of fire-fighters working at the height of the London blitz.

The Life and Death of Colonel Blimp (1943), an excellent character study of a British officer (Roger Livesey) working and loving his way through three wars; it also qualifies as an unusual entry because it draws a sympathetic portrait of the officer's lifelong German friend

being made and death encountered.

The war years saw Britain produce such excellent filmed commentaries as *The First Days* (1939); *London Can Take It* (1940), an eye-witness account of the Nazi bombings; *Target for Tonight* (1941), a report of the RAF attacks against German fortifications and industry on the continent; and *Western Approaches* (1944). From the Canadian National Film Board came *Churchill's Island* (1941). Within months after the attack on Pearl Harbor, US documentary units began to study every battle-

front on which the nation found itself. In 1943, *The Battle of the Beaches* followed American troops from one Pacific attack to another. *The Fighting Lady* (1944), photographed by Edward Streichen and narrated by Robert Taylor, dealt with life aboard a carrier in combat. *The Battle of San Pietro* (1944) placed audiences alongside US infantrymen in Italy. Joining these films were more than a dozen others, all with titles that explained their content. Among the most notable representatives were *US Navy, December 7* (1943),

The Life and Death of the USS Hornet (directed by John Ford), *With the Marines at Tarawa, Battle for the Marianas,* and *Attack! The Battle for New Britain* (all 1944). In 1945, Britain and the US joined to produce the story of the war, *The True Glory.*

One of the most heralded of the documenary works came from director Frank Capra. For the US Army, he supervised the production of the instructional series, *Why We Fight*. The series employed three directors – Anatole Litvak, Anthony Veiller and Capra himself. Its first entry, the Capra-directed *Prelude to War*, won the Academy Award for the best documentary of 1942. In 1943, Walt Disney released *Victory Through Air Power*, a full-length animated/live action feature that quickly placed itself among the year's great box office successes and among the war's greatest morale boosters.

Thus far, we've limited ourselves to a report on US and British films. But the other countries involved in the conflict were just as busy, at least until the war left them devastated. Russia produced films with general themes and even turned out some light fare for the homefront; her most notable war pictures included *She Defends Her Country* (1943, also known as *No Greater Love*) and several documentaries, among the most notable of which were *Leningrad in Combat* (1943), *Stalingrad* (1943), and *The People's Avengers* (also 1943). France, though occupied early on, continued its tradition of well produced films. The occupying Germans, however, apparently did not insist on a diet of propaganda and so the main offerings of the day were artistic and entertainment pieces, with France then moving to war productions in the post-war years and turning out such successes as Henri Cartier-Bresson's *Le Retour* (1946), Rene Clement's *La Bataille du Rail/The Battle of the Rails* (also 1946) and Alain Resnais' memorable outcry against the Nazi extermination camps, *Nuit et Brouillard/Night and Fog* (1955). In Germany, the accent was on propaganda, accompanied by some light entertainment fare for domestic relaxation. Japan, likewise, devoted much time to propaganda films, though the country rarely depicted its American enemies as harshly as its own people were portrayed by Hollywood. Japan's most successful wartime film was director Kimisaburo Yoshimura's *The Story of a Tank Commander* (1940).

THE BATTLES STILL RAGE

World War II Films of the Post-War Era

Previous spread: *Castle Keep* (1969).
Left: Dennis Morgan and Viveca Lindfors
confront the enemy in *To the Victor* (1948).
Below left: *The Best Years of Our Lives*
(1946).

Four decades have passed since World War II ended in 1945 with the grinding collapse of Germany and the sudden death that came to Japan with the atomic bombings of Hiroshima and Nagasaki. Yet, for moviegoers everywhere, that war continues unabated, kept alive over the years by a seemingly endless and – in quality and content, highly varied – stream of films, a stream that has just begun to run dry in the 1980s. No other modern war – and no conflict from any earlier period of history – has been granted anywhere near the same cinematic attention.

Though great in number and varied in content and quality, the films have tended to fit into four basic categories. What has been done over that span of four decades can be most easily discussed by looking at each of the categories in turn.

First, the end of hostilities saw producers in Europe and the United States quickly recognize the thematic material to be had in a matter of public preoccupation world-wide – the experiences and personal problems of living in the immediate post-war period. It was a theme bound to be of widespread interest for only the five years or so that the period lasted, but, in that time, it was put to varied use, serving as a backdrop in some films and as the central idea in others. For example, post-war Europe provided the background for such diverse pictures as the odd comedy romance, *A Foreign Affair* (1947); the Orsen Welles' thriller, *The Third Man* (1949); and the espionage yarn, *Diplomatic Courier* (1952).

As a central theme, life in the immediate post-war period began in 1945 with *A Bell for Adano*, an adaptation of the John Hersey novel and play. As book, play and film, *A Bell for Adano* appeared while the war was still raging, but can be said to have dealt with what were essentially post-war problems

because it was set in an Italian village once occupied by German troops but now at peace because the fighting has moved far to the north.

In the screen version, John Hodiak is cast as a US Army major whose occupation unit is assigned to Adano. Assisted by his sergeant – aptly played by William Bendix – the major is ready to supervise the village's recovery in any way possible and eager to replace the former German repressions with Allied democracy. He finds the townspeople suspicious of the newcomers and chiefly interested in one recovery project – the replacement of their church bell that the Germans have taken. To them, it is the symbol of both their own self-respect and the continuity of their village's history. From that point on, the film centers on Hodiak's search for a new bell and on the understandings and friendships that take shape between the villagers and the Americans as a result of his quest. The film ends as Hodiak and Bendix, ready to depart for a new assignment, listen to a bell ring in the church tower for the first time in years.

The picture, directed by Henry King, was universally well received. Both Hodiak and Bendix were critically applauded for their work, as was Gene Tierney, who, appearing as a young local woman, was following her success in the previous year's *Laura* with one of the better roles in her career. In all, *A Bell for Adano* provided a gentle comment on two cultures meeting and coming to know each other on very personal and human terms in the wake of man's most divisive enterprise. Critics called it dramatic, sensitive, moving and, in the words of least one, charming.

'Charming,' however, is not a word that can be applied to Italy's *Germania, Anno Zero* (1948; English title: *Germany Year Zero*). The work of writer-director Roberto Rossellini, here was a film that concentrated on the grimmest aspects of the European post-war period – the physical and emotional devastation, the struggle to survive in the midst of that devastation, and the moral dilemmas created by the daily actions necessary for survival. Basically, the story is that of a young boy who finds life so hideous that he at last poisons his ill father and then takes his own life. Within that framework, Rossellini provides the viewer with a constant flow of haunting and startling images of Berlin at the depths of her history. There are shots of deserted, blasted streets. There are cameos of broken and exhausted citizens. There is the memorable close-up of the phonograph in the wreckage of the once awesome Chancellery; the turntable spins and the sound track is filled with Hitler's ranting voice. And, even more memorable, there is the scene in which the boy dies in the ruins while the lonely sound of a passing tram is heard.

Germany Year Zero proved to be the final film in what is now known as Rossellini's 'War Trilogy.' The first film in the series had been *Roma, Cittá Aperta (1945; English titles: Open City; Rome, Open City)*, a study of the tyrannical German occupation of Rome as seen through the eyes of a group of local workers and their priest. Rossellini had then moved to *Paisa (1946; also known as Paisan)*, his account – told in six episodes – of the American invasion of Sicily and Italy.

On several counts, both films won for Rossellini an international acclaim. They were, first of all, solid interpretations of the war by an artist deeply affected by all that he had seen. Second, with one or two exceptions, Rossellini had used non-professional actors and had succeeded in drawing excellent performances from them. And, finally, there was an understanding of the difficult conditions under which the films had been produced. *Open City*, for example, had been planned during Rome's occupation and the filming had begun a mere two months after its liberation.

The two works brought the young writer-director to the forefront of the re-emerging Italian film industry, which had barely managed to survive the occupation and the fighting that came with the Allied invasion. Rossellini's straightforward manner of telling and filming a story was credited with generating the neo-realism of the international film world.

Germany Year Zero, which was financed by French interests and shot with the help of the East German Film Company, did not share in the acclaim bestowed on its predecessors. In great part, the negative reaction came from the intellectuals who had hailed Rossellini's neo-realism. He had given the picture a story line that they found contrived and at odds with the ideals of that neo-realism. It was a rejection that caused Rossellini to turn to other subject matter in his next films. Today, however, *Germany Year Zero* is widely regarded to have been the young film-maker's first mature work. Over the

Harold Russell, Dana Andrews and Fredric March come home in *The Best Years of Our Lives* (1946).

Three views of the attack on Pearl Harbor on 7 December 1941, from *Tora! Tora! Tora!* (1970). Battleships are sunk, sailors die and chaos reigns in Honolulu.

years until his death in 1977, Rossellini produced a series of sometimes criticized and sometimes highy-praised works. Among the latter is the splendid *Il Generale della Rovere* (1959; English title: *General della Rovere*), the tale of an opportunist, superbly played by Vittorio de Sica, who impersonates a general in World War II and becomes a hero despite himself.

Rossellini was not alone in commenting on immediate post-war problems. In 1948, the United States, in *To the Victor*, addressed two specific European problems – black marketeering and the fate suffered by the women who had collaborated with the Germans during the occupation of France. That same year, the United States and Switzerland joined forces to produce *The Search*, which, in telling the story of a lost and orphaned German boy, dealt with the tragedy of the millions left homeless and displaced by the war. Switzerland followed with the interesting and underplayed *Four in a Jeep* (1951). It detailed the work and relationships of four military policemen –

each representing an Allied power – who must patrol one of the occupation zones. Reflected at a very human level were the political tensions and competitions so clearly seen among the Allied nations with the arrival of peace – and the way in which four men, in their dealings with each other, lived with and, at times, ignored or overcame those problems.

The finest Hollywood comment on the immediate post-war era came in Samuel Goldwyn's *The Best Years of Our Lives* (1946). On a historical basis alone, it is a fascinating picture because, when contrasted with any of the above films, it points up the worlds-apart differences between the realities of post-war life in Europe and the United States. Seen here are not people existing and waiting to start afresh on a shattered continent but three US veterans re-establishing their lives in a country physically untouched by the war. At stake is not the question of basic survival but the much subtler matter of readjustment to business, social and especially family life – in all, an

emotional matter familiar to countless American families throughout the late 1940s.

Centering on the return of an aging Army master sergeant (Fredric March), an Air Force bombardier (Dana Andrews) and a sailor (Harold Russell) who has lost both hands in battle, the picture is excellent – even magnificent – throughout, as are all the performances. Of the trio, March makes the easiest transition, immediately reentering a loving family life as the head of household and then coping with a problem that would have been his had he never gone to war – his daughter's (Teresa Wright) love affair with Andrews. As for Andrews himself, he faces a humiliation that countless demobilized officers of the era actually did endure – the lowering of status that accompanied the

Opposite: Van Johnson (center) just before he takes over command of the ship from Humphrey Bogart (left) in *The Caine Mutiny* (1954).
Below: James Edwards, Lloyd Bridges and Frank Lovejoy in *Home of the Brave* (1949).

return to civilian employment; in Andrews' case, he had been a soda jerk before Pearl Harbor. Double amputee Russell must contend with the understandable embarrassments of a family that doesn't know yet how to treat a disabled son and with his own very understandable reluctance to marry his sweetheart (Cathy O'Donnell) and burden her with his handicap.

As directed by William Wyler, *The Best Years of Our Lives* is punctuated throughout with unforgettable moments. For one, there is the instant when March's unannounced arrival home surprises his wife (Myrna Loy) in the midst of housework and she can think of nothing to say except a joyful and thoroughly human 'I look terrible!' Another comes with the low but uncontrollable sob that breaks from Russell's mother when she first sees the steel prosthetic 'hook' devices that have replaced his hands. Still another: the haunting sequence in which the lonely and discouraged Andrews wanders through a junkyard of discarded and already rusting bombers, climbs aboard one and, as the roar of engines fills the sound track, sits in the bombardier's compartment and relives the glories now so quickly gone. And, set in sharp relief against the film's dramatic scenes, is the highly comic first-night-home binge on which March takes his

wife and daughter and which breaks the tensions atttendant to his return.

What is undoubtedly the finest scene of all involves Cathy O'Donnell and Russell, a non-professional actor who had actually lost both hands in the war. When O'Donnell insists that they should marry, Russell takes her aside to show her what the realities of life with his 'hooks' will be. He removes his shirt and quietly introduces her to the bandaged stubs where his lower arms had been, the strapped-on equipment that enables him to manipulate the prosthetic devices, and the devices themselves. She just as quietly touches and accepts them each in turn. It is a scene that, ending with their embrace and their understanding that they can spend their lives together, could have been ruined by the slightest discordant note of excess or feigned emotion. It was not. All the emotional impact of such an encounter is there, but held in perfect restraint by director Wyler and his two players.

Deservedly, *The Best Years of Our Lives* was the film most honored by the 1946 Academy Awards. To it went awards for: best picture, best director (Wyler), best actor (March), best supporting actor (Russell), best screenplay (Robert E Sherwood) and best musical score. In addition, Russell received a special award 'for bringing hope and

courage to his fellow veterans through his appearance' in the picture.

In 1946, the theme of readjustment also served as the basis for *Till the End of Time*, a modest and well done film that, likewise featuring three returning veterans, has been called a poor man's *Best Years*. A year earlier, Britain had used the theme in the thoroughly charming comedy-romance, *Perfect Partners* (US title: *Vacation from Marriage*). It detailed the lives of a dull-as-dishwater married couple (Robert Donat and Deborah Kerr) who enlist in the Navy and go their separate ways for several years, with each in that time blossoming and becoming a 'new person,' the husband a dashing officer, and the wife a beautiful and highly efficient WREN. As they prepare to meet again at war's end, each fears that the other will be as remembered, only to be happily – and passionately – surprised at what the years have done.

The second category brings us to the pictures that have depicted the war's combat as seen at the fighting man's level. Over the past four decades, literally dozens of such films have been released. In content, they have dealt with every situation that a modern war can produce – everything from infantry patrol actions, ground skirmishes, and commando-style raids to air attacks and

Clint Eastwood and Richard Burton (left) on their derring-do mission in *Where Eagles Dare* (1960).

full-scale land and sea battles.

In nature, they have been just as varied. Some, continuing the tradition established during the war years by the likes of *Desperate Journey*, have put the emphasis on pure action and adventure, as does the Richard Burton-Clint Eastwood vehicle, *Where Eagles Dare* (1969), with its acrobatic assault on a Bavarian castle to rescue a high-ranking officer. Some have been character studies, as is the excellent film dramatization of the Herman Wouk novel, *The Caine Mutiny* (1954), with its questions of whether the naval commander, Captain Queeg (Humphrey Bogart), truly deserves to be court-martialed for incompetence or is the victim of his subordinates' unsympathetic regard. Some have dealt with racial matters, as do both *Home of the Brave* (1949) and *Go For Broke* (1951); the former concerns the tensions lurking beneath a black-white friendship in a company of jungle fighters while the latter is one of the earliest post-war films to deal sym-

pathetically with the Japanese, doing so by tracing the European exploits of the 42nd Regimental Combat Team, a US Army unit manned by Americans of Japanese descent. Most have been highlighted by realistic combat sequences, though some have damaged themselves by giving in to moments of obviously gratuitous violence, as does *Attack* (1957) when it provides a close-up view of a tank running over a soldier's arm. The very best have, either throughout or in their greatest part, projected a genuine sense of what the war's fighting and the humans caught in it were like. In all, the category is the largest and most varied of the four – in fact, larger and more varied than its three companions put together.

It goes without saying that combat films have been inspired by the war's every theater of action. Early on, the Pacific gave us *Sands of Iwo Jima* (1949), a John Wayne piece that, though hampered by some cliché characterizations, features excellent combat sequences. They are made all the better by the adroit insertion of documentary footage of the Iwo Jima landings. So adroit is the inserting and

so carefully are the film's sets designed in accordance with the scenery on view in the documentary footage that it is difficult to tell where the real Iwo Jima ends and the studio one begins.

There are fine battle sequences – again, helped by the use of documentary footage – in three widely-spaced films of the Pacific sea fighting: *Task Force* (1949), *Operation Pacific* (1950), and *In Harm's Way* (1965). *Task Force* does not concern itself exclusively with the war, but is a story of the development of naval aviation; it features a solid performance by Gary Cooper and a memorable one by Walter Brennan as a

crusty, down-to-earth admiral. *Operation Pacific* pretends to be nothing more than a well-budgeted John Wayne action feature and, though criticized for being a shade too long, is entertaining throughout. *In Harm's Way* – another Wayne vehicle, this one with support from Kirk Douglas – suffers from its intricate soap-opera love stories and relationships. Though the battle sequences are well done, they are present

Two scenes from *A Bridge Too Far* (1977). Right: Sean Connery taking a break. Below: Robert Redford attacking.

not as testaments to the war but as backdrops for a highly complicated plot.

Some of the best combat scenes ever staged are to be seen in the December 7th attack on Hawaii's Schofield Barracks in *From Here to Eternity* (1953). No documentary footage is used here to detail the initial pandemonium and death and then the ragged efforts of the soldiers to fight back against the strafing Japanese Zeros. It is in these scenes that Burt Lancaster's conduct brings to its

highest point his characterization of the career soldier, the 'thirty-year man,' Sgt Milton Warden. In his self control, his reactions to danger, and his command of the men about him, he comes across as the truly committed and professional soldier, a man at last in his own element.

From Here to Eternity, adapted from the James Jones novel, is itself not a war picture, however, but a study of the peace-time army on the eve of disaster. As such, it gives solid insights into

barracks life, officer-enlisted soldier relations and the ideals and hopes of the various types of men – some stupid, some carefree, some bullying and some very capable – who can make up any nation's army. Under the direction of Fred Zinnemann, the film brings the book alive and is performed beautifully throughout – by Lancaster, by Montgomery Clift as Robert E Lee Prewitt, Frank Sinatra as Angelo Maggio, Ernest Borgnine as the cruel 'Fatso' Judson, Donna Reed as Lorene (an unlikely choice for the role of a prostitute because of her lady-like looks but nevertheless an excellent one because of her acting skills) and Deborah Kerr as the officer's wife who falls in love with

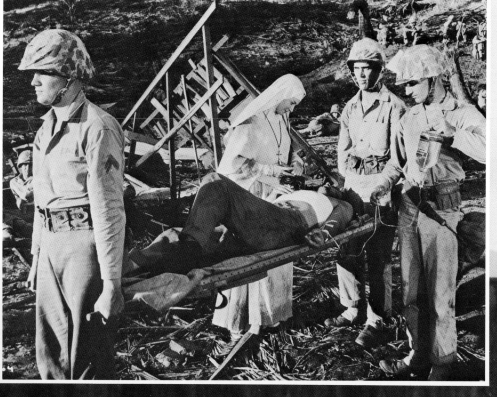

Left: Deborah Kerr looks fondly at Robert Mitchum as they are rescued in *Heaven Knows, Mr Allison* (1957).
Opposite top: Frank Sinatra (left) and Montgomery Clift in *From Here to Eternity* (1953).
Below: Burt Lancaster (center) in the attack on Schofield Barracks— . . . *Eternity* (1953).

Above: Americans on the German infantry in *The Devil's Brigade* (1968).
Right: Aldo Ray, Victor Millan, Tab Hunter and James Whitmore as US Marines on Saipan in *Battle Cry* (1954).

Lancaster. The famous night-on-the-beach love scene between Lancaster and Kerr was considered torrid stuff in its day (by 1980s' standards, it seems pretty tame) and has always run the risk of looking silly, especially at the point where the surf washes up about the two embracing players. It is kept from being so by the pair's talents and by the sense of loneliness and marital frustration that Kerr gives to her character.

Miss Kerr is equally effective in an altogether different role in *Heaven Knows, Mr Allison* (1957), an implausible film in which she is cast as a gentle Catholic nun who finds herself marooned on a Japanese-held island with tough Marine corporal Robert Mitchum. Their relationship is at first antagonistic; but they come to know and admire each other as they hide from the enemy and then help an invading American force take the island. The

skillful work of the two performers creates an interesting character study out of what could have easily been no more than a titillating question of will-he-or-won't-he-seduce-her.

Three other novels of the Pacific war joined *From Here to Eternity* on the screen in the 1950s – Leon Uris' *Battle Cry* (1955), Pierre Boulle's *The Bridge on the River Kwai* (1957), and Norman Mailer's *The Naked and the Dead* (1958). Both *Battle Cry* and *The Naked*

and the Dead emerged as flawed pieces. *Battle Cry*, which features some impressive sequences of its Marine company in action, is damaged by several stock characterizations and a predictable soldier-prostitute romance. *The Naked and the Dead* concentrates much on the tensions between the officers and men in a platoon; it was ill-received by most critics, who found it a routine action film given second-rate direction and performances.

As for *The Bridge on the River Kwai*, many audiences and critics yet consider it to be the best film ever made about World War II. Set in Burma (the photography was done in Sri Lanka), the picture is divided into two separate stories that eventually mesh – the building of a strategic bridge for the Japanese by British prisoners of war and the efforts of an Allied assault team to blow it up. The action sequences – the assault team's struggle through the jungle to the bridge site and then the detonating of the structure as a train crosses it – are splendidly directed by David Lean and just as splendidly performed by Jack Hawkins as a stern British commando and William Holden as his reluctant American companion.

But the film's most memorable moments are to be had in its character study of the stiff-lipped and militarily impeccable senior British prisoner, Colonel Nicholson (Alec Guinness). It is a study that begins with a contest of wills between Nicholson and the prison camp's Japanese commandant (Sessue Hayakawa). The colonel stubbornly endures starvation and torture when, insisting on the observance of military legalities, he rejects the commandant's demand that he and his officers work as manual laborers on the proposed bridge. On at last winning his point, however, Nicholson takes an odd turn and agrees that he and his officers will supervise the British enlisted prisoners in the construction project, apparently in the belief that the troops need the discipline of labor to keep their minds and bodies from rotting. Then, in yet another odd turn, he so comes to love the completed bridge that he attempts to stop the commando team from destroying it, only to bring it down in ruins himself when he is shot by the team, and falls across their detonator.

As fashioned by Guinness and novelist Boulle (who also wrote the screenplay), Colonel Nicholson remains one of the most enigmatic characters ever filmed. Why does the officer endure torture in defense of one military point and then ignore another of greater import – the prohibition against cooperating with the enemy – by allowing the enlisted troops to build the bridge and he and his officers to act as supervisors? Does he really believe that the discipline of work is necessary for the

Two scenes from *The Bridge on the River Kwai* (1957). Right: The bridge is completed.
Below: William Holden tries to stop Alec Guinness from reporting the explosives.

prisoners' physical and mental well being? Or does he undertake the project to quiet some restiveness in himself? Or does he wish to embarrass the Japanese commander by showing off the skills of the British? And how can he, even in his pride for both the completed project and the construction abilities of his men, so forget that the bridge is an enemy facility that he traitorously attempts to prevent its destruction? These are questions that fascinated audiences in 1957 and that remain unanswered among moviegoers more than a quarter-century later.

There was, however, no question then – as there is no question now – about the qualities of *The Bridge on the River Kwai*. It was honored by both the American and British Academy Awards, by the US National Board of Review, the New York Film Critics Circle, and the US Golden Globes. The honors given it are detailed in a forthcoming chapter.

Far more modest but quite as superior in its own way is the film that takes us now to the fighting east of the Atlantic, *A Walk in the Sun* (1945), whose release coincided with the close of the European war. Superbly directed by Lewis Milestone, it tells the story of a platoon of Texas infantrymen who must, on a splendid morning, march out and take an Italian farmhouse in which German troops are solidly entrenched. The film, though it climaxes with a realistic battle sequence, is mostly concerned with the individuals assigned to a meeting with death that fine day. The entire cast – headed by Dana Andrews and Richard Conte – give solid performances. The picture was praised not only by virtually every critic who saw it, with several calling it the most impressive combat film to emerge in the immediate post-war period, but also by combat veterans.

The years since have seen the European and African fighting depicted in varied films. For example:

Battleground (1949) deals with the experiences of a paratroop company while their 101st Airborne Division is trapped at Bastogne, Belgium, during 1944's Battle of the Bulge. The locale, the weather and the tensions of being hemmed in by German troops that pull

Left: Dana Andrews comforts the battle-fatigued Herbert Rudley in *A Walk in the Sun* (1946).
Opposite: Chips Rafferty (left) and Richard Burton during the siege of Tobruk in *The Desert Rats* (1953).
Below: John Hodiak, Walter Pidgeon, Van Johnson, Charles Bickford and Clark Gable in *Command Decision* (1948).

sneak attacks dressed in American uniforms are expertly evoked, but the picture suffers dramatically from some stock characterizations – among them, Jerome Courtland's innocent farm boy – and historically from a marching song that was never heard in the Bulge itself that grim winter. On the other hand, there has only been praise through the years for James Whitmore's grizzled and battle-wise sergeant. The picture made a star of the actor who, some three decades later, would charm theater audiences with his one-man stage characterization of the nation's president at war's end, Harry Truman.

Both *Twelve O'Clock High* (1949) and its immediate predecessor, *Command Decision* (1948), feature Air Force generals as their protagonists and concentrate on the pressures and loneliness of high command. The former stars Gregory Peck as a commander who finally cracks under the ceaseless demands imposed on his bomber squad-

ron; in the latter, Clark Gable is a commander facing a humiliating reassignment. Both films are principally character studies and contain little battle action. *Twelve O'Clock* does have a well done bombing sequence. A single aerial sequence highlights *Command Decision* – the crash of a damaged bomber as Gable, microphone in hand, tries to 'talk down' to a landing the young gunner who has taken over the controls because he is the crew's only survivor.

The Desert Rats (1953) tells the story of an Australian company's participation in the attack on Africa's Tobruk and a personal encounter with German commander, General Erwin Rommel. That encounter, in the eyes of most critics, weakened the impact of a film with good characterizations and well done action sequences. The producing company, Twentieth Century Fox, was suspected of inserting the meeting to take box-office advantage of the studio's

then-current big hit, *The Desert Fox* (British title: *Rommel, the Desert Fox*), a filmed biography of the German officer with James Mason in the title role.

The Enemy Below (1957) is a fine character study of two naval officers – an American destroyer captain (Robert Mitchum) and a German submarine commander (Curt Jurgens) – in a personal duel in the Atlantic. Both performers, working with a script that sounds as if it understands battle psychology and tactics, turn in excellent portrayals of two professionals trying to outwit each other and coming to a mutual respect as they do so. The picture features fine special effects in its depiction of the sub withstanding depth charge attacks and in the collision of the two vessels that gives the story its climactic scenes.

The Young Lions (1958) is the somewhat uneven but yet effective adaptation of the Irwin Shaw novel that viewed the men on both sides of the

suspenseful but nevertheless energetic *Force Ten From Navarone* (1978).

The Great Escape (1963) likewise puts the emphasis on action and adventure as it describes the efforts of Allied POWs to dig their way out of a German prison camp. There are fine performances from an international cast headed by the British Richard Attenborough and Donald Pleasance, and Americans James Garner and Steve McQueen. The same theme – but in reverse – is used in *The McKenzie Break* (1970), a tale of German prisoners escaping from a Scottish camp. Other films with prisoner-of-war themes include the comedy-drama, *Stalag 17* (1953), for which William Holden's portrayal of an opportunistic inmate won him an Academy Award for Best Actor; Britain's *The Colditz Story* (1954), which took its inspiration from the notorious

Left: Robert Mitchum played an American destroyer commander in *The Enemy Below* (1957).
Opposite: Anthony Quinn and Gregory Peck scout the territory in *The Guns of Navarone* (1961).
Below: Steve McQueen had plenty of time in solitary confinement to think about *The Great Escape* (1963).

African and European fighting. Giving fine performances are Marlon Brando as the German officer, Christian, and Montgomery Clift as the American Jew, Noah. Excellent, too, in one of his earliest dramatic appearances, is Dean Martin as the opportunistic yet patriotic Michael.

The Bridge (1959), a superb drama from West German director Bernhard Wicki, concerns a group of 16-year-old schoolboys mustered into service and given the suicidal job of defending a river crossing against an Allied tank attack as the German Army collapses in the spring of 1945. The film, in its depiction of youth being sacrificed to a defeated country's war machine, has been called a latter-day *All Quiet on the Western Front*. Its attack sequences, photographed in brilliant sunshine and accompanied by one of the few sound tracks ever to capture fully the distinc-

tive metallic crash of rifle and cannon fire, are frighteningly real.

The Guns of Navarone (1961), an adaptation of the Alistair Maclean novel, puts the emphasis on rip-roaring action and adventure as it sends a team of saboteurs onto an Aegean island to destroy two giant German guns. The saboteurs are all one-dimensional characters, but are brought alive through the spirited playing of Gregory Peck, David Niven, Anthony Quinn, Stanley Baker and James Darren. In common with the Maclean novel, the film has a little bit of everything – double crosses, captures by and escapes from the Germans, guerrilla fighting and, at last, the spectacle of the guns being exploded from their emplacements high in the face of a cliff and tumbling end over end into the sea. Throughout, the picture is solid good fun and inspired a sequel, the far less

Peppard) who deserts to live in comfort with a cafe owner (Melina Mecouri) and then finds himself unable to remain hidden while his friends go marching into combat. The film is notable for its irony, especially in two sequences: the wintertime execution of a young American deserter against a sound track of Christmas music, and the deaths of two former Allies – an American (George Hamilton) and a Russian (Albert Finney) – when their national competitiveness drives them to fight over who shall be the first to cross a plank bridge in a muddy post-war Berlin street.

The Dirty Dozen (1967), which ranks as one of the most violent war films ever made, tells the story of 12 convicts being reprieved from their life sentences so that they can be trained for a commando attack on a German stronghold. With a cast that includes Lee Marvin, Charles Bronson, George Kennedy, Ernest Borgnine, and Robert Ryan, the film is punctuated with

Left: Trevor Howard used Raffaella Carra in the escape in *Von Ryan's Express* (1965). Opposite top: George Segal in the title role as the scheming corporal in the Singapore prisoner of war camp in *King Rat* (1965). Opposite bottom: William Holden (right) in *Stalag 17* (1953). Below: Brian Keith supervises the British guards using fire hoses to quell a riot of German prisoners of war in *The McKenzie Break* (1970).

German maximum security facility in Saxony; *Von Ryan's Express* (1965), starring Frank Sinatra as a tough American colonel who leads a mass prison-camp break with the aid of a train, and *Victory* (1981), with Michael Caine coaching a group of POWs forced into a soccer match with German players.

The Victors (1963), writer-director Carl Foreman's sprawling and episodic commentary on the foolishness of war, follows an infantry company from the Italian campaign to the fall of Germany and the immediate post-war period in shattered Berlin. At each step along the way, it singles out one of its leading characters for attention – the private (Vince Edwards) who falls in love with an Italian woman, the sergeant (Eli Wallach) who tenderly shelters a French woman during an artillery bombardment, the opportunist (George

highly entertaining moments, among them the comic sequence in which the criminal team captures 'enemy headquarters' during troop maneuvers and, of course, the spectacular climactic attack on the German stronghold. A dash across a courtyard by American professional-football-player-turned-actor, Jim Brown, as explosions tear the stronghold apart, puts the cap on the climactic sequence. The film, a box-office winner, inspired several imitations, chief among them William Holden's *The Devil's Brigade* (1968).

Castle Keep (1969), the filmed adaptation of William Eastlake's fantastic novel, features Burt Lancaster as the leader of six war-weary American soldiers who take possession of a tenth century Bavarian castle, find it crammed with art treasures, and then die defending it. Their strange behavior bewilders the viewer until one question becomes paramount: are the men dying in defense of the castle or have they been dead all along? It's a question that is never answered in what has long been regarded as one of the strangest war yarns ever filmed.

The Big Red One (1979) takes its title from the US 1st Division's shoulder patch and provides a grim look at five battle-wise veterans surviving endless days of combat while the 'wet-behind-the-ears' replacements assigned to their squad die soon after arrival at the front. Lee Marvin is especially good as the nameless sergeant. The film is directed by Samuel Fuller and equals in quality his *The Steel Helmet* (1952), long regarded as one of the best of the pictures on the Korean war.

The third category brings us to films that are dramatizations of actual war-time events. They are films that share three characteristics. First, they attempt to recount history accurately and objectively, a job that, when successfully done, can make them look like documentaries. Second, they handle subject matter ranging from obscure – at times, hitherto unknown – operations to the war's most sprawling and decisive battles. Finally, they are markedly different from such previously mentioned combat films as *Sands of Iwo Jima* and *Battleground*, which

likewise deal with actual battles. The combat pieces involve fictional characters, but here fictional characters are mingled with actual wartime figures, with the emphasis often being on the actual figures.

The category, however, does not include such films as *The Gallant Hours* (1959), *Patton* (1970; British title: *Patton – Lust for Glory*) and *MacArthur* (1977). These are biographical films and will be discussed later in a separatre chapter.

Both the Pacific and European-African arenas have provided films for the category. Of the two, the Pacific fighting has attracted far less studio interest as a source of material over the years since 1945. In fact, it has been responsible for only three major offerings to date – *Above and Beyond* (1952), *Tora! Tora! Tora!* (1970) and *Midway* (1976).

Above and Beyond stars Robert Taylor as Colonel Paul Tibbetts in an account of the flight of the *Enola Gay*, the flight that climaxed in the atomic bombing of Hiroshima and not only

Opposite: Lee Marvin (center) during a break in the fighting in *The Big Red One* (1979).
Below: Telly Savalas, Charles Bronson and George Kennedy stop a jeep in *The Dirty Dozen* (1967).

ended the Japanese war but plunged the world into the nuclear age. Taylor gives an incisive portrait of Tibbetts and the film provides a chilling view of the Hiroshima bombing and the reactions of the *Enola Gay*'s crew to it, but the entire production is damaged by a tedious treatment of the pilot's domestic life.

Tora! Tora! Tora! is a minute-by-minute account of the events leading up to the 1941 attack on Pearl Harbor. Switching back and forth between the approaching Japanese fleet and the

targeted bases in Hawaii, it is a film punctuated with historically accurate details – the Navy's suspicion that an attack is imminent; the decision to send Admiral William F Halsey's ships to sea and thus safeguard them against the possibility of being bottled-up at Pearl Harbor; the commanding general's order that prevents the Army Air Corps from dispersing its fighter planes around the perimeter of Hickham Field and turns them into easy targets by requiring that they be parked together and close by for quick pilot access; the confusion that keeps a mountain listening post's warning of the approaching Japanese Zeros from being swiftly acted upon; and the surprise of the private pilot who, out for a Sunday morning flight, finds himself in the midst of those Zeros.

All these details are fine, but they pale in comparison to the depiction of the attack itself. Taking up much of the film's second half, the attack is a brilliantly staged affair that combines the use of documentary footage, full-scale sets and models. It is so well done that the film's special effects unit was honored with an Academy Award for their work.

Midway recounts the 1942 sea battle that, fought a mere six months after Pearl Harbor, marked the beginning of Japan's ultimate defeat. The steps leading to the encounter are seen from both the American and Japanese viewpoints. The battle itself is vividly recreated through the use of studio sets and Navy footage shot on the scene in 1942, plus some footage from an unidentified Japanese production.

telling of the 1943 British air attack that destroyed the dams providing hydroelectric power for Germany's industrial Ruhr Valley. Detailed in a neatly underplayed style are all aspects of the operation – the testing of the 'bouncing bombs' meant to skip across the water and strike the concrete sides of the dams, creating fissures that will eventually cause the walls to collapse; the

Though the battle scenes are excellent, the film has been widely criticized as tiresome because of the excessive time its characters devote to discussions of strategy.

The lion's share of the category's attention has gone to the war with Germany. In fact, the entries here, when listed not in the order of their release but in the order of the events depicted, come close to providing a complete pictorial history of that war. Major efforts in the category have come principally from Britain and the United States. They include:

The Battle of the River Plate (1956), Britain's flawed but nevertheless accurate account of how the German pocket battleship, *Graf Spee*, was trapped and ultimately scuttled in Uruguay's Montevideo harbor in 1939. The picture has been severely criticized for its studio look and the confusing manner in which it stages its battle sequences. Also adding to the confusion is its excess of players in small and ill-defined roles.

Battle of Britain (1969), director Guy Hamilton's sprawling account of the German aerial attacks that sought to bring the nation to its knees in 1940 and ended with the RAF in control of the skies. Viewed from both the German and British sides, the attacks are graphically depicted, though with a shade too much gore (machine bullets

Above: Robert Taylor learns about the atomic bomb from Larry Gates, while James Whitmore (left) looks on in *Above and Beyond* (1952).
Right: American troops in Rome during the liberation of Italy in *Anzio* (1968).

routinely striking German pilots full in the face) so far as some critics are concerned. Much criticism, too, has been aimed at the film's fictional characters, with most commentators finding them hackneyed and one-dimensional. Featured in a cameo role is Laurence Olivier as Air Chief Marshal Sir Hugh Dowding.

Sink the Bismarck (1960), a tightly-knit British drama centered on the sea maneuvers that finally resulted in the 1941 destruction of Germany's mightiest battleship off the coast of Norway. Most of the film is set in the small center controlling the operation and is highlighted by Kenneth More's fine performance as a naval officer who must concentrate on the work at hand while living through a personal crisis – the possible loss of his son in battle. Excellent, too, is Karl Stepanek as the German admiral who, in the final battle sequence, cannot believe that his invincible ship is actually being destroyed. The scenes at sea, however, suffer from the use of obvious models in a just-as-obvious studio tank.

The Dam Busters (1954), a superb

training flights; the development of a handmade device that will see the bombs dropped from just the right height for effective 'bouncing' and the final mission itself. Michael Redgrave is excellent as the bomb's inventor, Dr Barnes Wallis. The same must be said for Richard Todd in the role of the flight's commander. The attack sequences are excitingly handled, their only flaw being the explosions as the dams are struck; the special effects work misses here, with the geysering water looking as if its been 'painted' on the screen.

Anzio (British: *The Battle for Anzio*, 1968), a disappointing Italian depiction of the American landings at Italy in 1944; the picture, which sees good work done by Robert Mitchum, Peter Falk and Arthur Kennedy, suffers from a script jammed with pretentious statements about why men go to war.

The Man Who Never Was (1955), a thoroughly entertaining account of a successful British effort to fool the Germans into thinking that the Second Front was to be launched at a point far distant from the intended Normandy landing sites. The effort – a brilliant

Above: Richard Todd (pointing) explains the plan to destroy the hydroelectric dams in Germany's Ruhr Valley in *The Dam Busters* (1954).
Left: The Allied troops land in France on D-Day in *The Longest Day* (1962).

exercise in espionage – involves finding the corpse of a recently-dead and anonymous male, equipping him with papers indicating the false landing spot, and then, as if he had been the victim of a plane crash, depositing him in the sea at a point where he will be washed ashore and found by the Germans. Clifton Webb is memorable as the gentlemanly naval officer who dreams up and then carries out the devilish scheme. Its intricacies, incidentally, cannot be fully grasped in the above brief explanation.

The Longest Day (1972), producer Darryl Zanuck's account of the D-Day landings along the beaches of Normandy. The film captures the many facets of the battle by concentrating on various individual actions – US paratroops dropping behind German lines in the dark hours before the full-scale assault; British forces coming ashore; American Rangers scaling a cliff to silence a much-feared German battery, only to find that it is not in place; an American demolition team destroying a concrete block that is impeding troop movements up from Omaha Beach. In addition, there are personal touches throughout – a general (Robert Mitchum) giving the demolition team's corporal a battlefield commission; a paratroop colonel (John Wayne) en-

raged at the sight of paratroopers killed by enemy fire as they dangled helplessly from the trees in which they had landed; a downed British airman (Richard Burton) whose split leg is being held together by a safety pin; and the German officer who sights the approaching enemy from his gun emplacement and then endures the frustration of being unable to convince his superiors that the long-expected attack is at last a reality. In all – in its movements between views of the overall assault, unit attacks and individual experiences – the film successsfully captures the day as it was lived and felt.

Is Paris Burning? (1965), on the surface a re-creation of the Allied liberation of Paris in August 1944, but at heart a sympathetic character study of the general commanding the German occupation forces there. Ordered by Hitler to destroy the city before the enemy arrives, he finds that his love for all that is Parisian renders him incapable of doing so. Gert Frobe is excellent as the general. Other acting assignments, though well played, are badly miscast, among them Kirk Douglas as

General George S Patton.

The closing months of 1944 are detailed in *A Bridge Too Far* (1977) and *Battle of the Bulge* (1965). The first is an account of the Allied defeat at Holland's Arnhem, while the latter deals with Germany's last major offensive of the war. *The Bridge at Remagen* (1968) details the early 1945 assault that saw

American units thrust their way across the Rhine River and into Germany itself. The final moments of the war are depicted in *Hitler – The Last Ten Days* (1973), with Alec Guinness as the decaying Führer relegated to the underground bunker in which he eventually took his own life. Years earlier, in 1949, Russia included Germany's collapse in *The Fall of Berlin*, a propaganda piece about a soldier who fights loyally for his flag throughout the war and is rewarded by a handshake from Premier Josef Stalin; see-sawing between the poor and excellent, the film is highlighted with caricature-like portrayals of the wartime leaders and magnificently staged battle sequences.

The fourth and final category is made up of the war comedies that have been filmed since 1945. As was mentioned in the preceding chapter, the comedy fare seen during the war years themselves was limited to such forgettable – though, at the time, pleasing – commodities as Abbott and Costello's *Buck Privates* and Bob Hope's *Caught in the Draft*, all intended to lift spirits on the home and service fronts. The era pro-

Opposite top: Peter Ustinov is confronted by an Afrika Korps officer in *Hotel Sahara* (1951).
Opposite below: Glenn Ford beginning to give in to the Okinawans in *The Teahouse of the August Moon* (1956). Marlon Brando is in rear center.
Right: James Garner confused in *The Americanization of Emily* (1964).
Below: Henry Fonda as Roberts, William Powell as Doc and Jack Lemmon as Ensign Pulver in *Mister Roberts* (1955).

duced but a few genuinely memorable comedies, chief among them Chaplin's *The Great Dictator*; the Joel McCrea-Jean Arthur romance, *The More the Merrier* (1943), a satire on wartime Washington's crowded housing conditions; and Britain's *Tawny Pipit* (1944), a wry and delightful tale of how some dedicated amateur ornithologists in an English village disrupt military activity for miles around as they protect a family of rare birds nesting in a meadow scheduled for troop maneuvers.

The years since 1945 have seen a fairly steady flow of war comedies of all types and of varying quality. Two of the very best came from Britain in the immediate post-war era – *Whisky Galore* (1948) and *Hotel Sahara* (1950). The first, which was released in the United States as *Tight Little Island*, dwells on the adventures of the hard-drinking folks on a small Hebridean island – and the problems of the local excise officer – when a ship loaded with whisky is wrecked just offshore and ends a war-induced shortage of alcohol. Seen today mainly in art houses and on

late-night television in the United States, the film continues to delight, featuring outstanding comedic performances by Basil Radford, Joan Greenwood and Gordon Jackson.

The title role in *Hotel Sahara* belongs to a broken-down hostelry that, caught in the middle of the North African fighting, must constantly adjust its loyalties as it bounces back and forth between British and German hands. Peter Ustinov is excellent as the harassed and cagey proprietor whose commitment to 'business as usual' makes him an ideological chameleon. Just as excellent is Yvonne De Carlo as the local woman who endures the passions of the officers on both sides. An underrated actress who was confined to roles as a seductive temptress in US films of the '40s, Miss De Carlo proved herself a fine comedienne in *Hotel Sahara* and then went on to one of her best portrayals – that of the sexy night-club singer who yearns to be a house-wife – in Alec Guinness' hilarious *The Captain's Paradise* (1953).

Since then, the majority of war

Above: An American soldier surrenders to German troops in *Battle of the Bulge* (1965).

Opposite: Ben Gazzara (left) and his comrades taking *The Bridge at Remagen* (1968).

comedies have been adapted from novels and stage plays. Adaptations of the latter were much on the scene in the 1950s. That was the decade that gave audiences *Stalag 17* (1953), the Donald Bevan-Edmund Trzinski amalgam of comedy, tragedy and mystery in a prisoner-of-war camp, with a fine dramatic performance by William Holden and excellent comedic work by Robert Strauss and Harvey Lembeck; *Mister Roberts* (1955), the Thomas

Heggen-Josh Logan study of a supply ship's crew enduring the boredom of daily life far away from the heart of the Pacific fighting; *The Teahouse of the August Moon* (1956), John Patrick's gentle story of an Okinawan (beautifully played by Marlon Brando) introducing American occupation forces to the ways of Oriental life; and *Operation Mad Ball* (1957), with the antic teamwork of Ernie Kovacs and Jack Lemmon worth the price of admission in Arthur Carter's yarn about a group of GIs planning their major contribution to the war effort – a forbidden dance with army nurses. Another fine acting twosome – Danny Kaye and Curt Jurgens – were to be seen in *Me and the*

Colonel (1958), Columbia's version of Franz Werfel's sentimental tale in which an anti-semitic Polish colonel (Jurgens) who must flee from the Germans with a Jewish refugee (Kaye).

Adaptations of novels were in vogue from the late '50s to 1970. MGM started things in 1957 with the release of William Brinkley's *Don't Go Near the Water*, a farcical treatise on military public relations activities; the target of the adept fun-poking here is Glenn Ford's bumbling navy PR team that drives senior officer Fred Clark out of his mind. With Filmways, the studio then transferred William Bradford Huie's comedy-drama, *The Americanization of Emily*, to the screen in 1964.

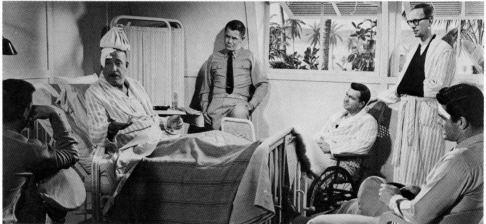

Above: Beginning the chore of hiding the wine. *The Secret of Santa Vittoria* (1969). Right: Commander Fred Clark in bed after one of his confrontations with Glenn Ford (leaning against the wall) in *Don't Go Near the Water* (1957).

Focusing itself on a self-serving naval officer who, as part of a Navy scheme for winning increased congressional appropriations, is sent to be the first man ashore on D-Day, the film turned out to be a well-done mingling of romance and bitter comment on the silliness of war. James Garner and Julie Andrews are excellent as the romantic partners – Garner as the self-serving but bluntly honest officer who admits that his love for life makes him a coward, and Miss Andrews (in a radical departure from her usual too-nice-for-words roles) as the starchy English widow who falls in love with him despite his objectionable Yankee ways. Likewise, Melvyn Douglas turns in a masterful performance as the admiral who dreams up the D-Day scheme while suffering a nervous breakdown.

Not so well done as *Emily*, however, were other adaptations of the '60s, a case in point being the fate of Howard Singer's *Wake Me When It's Over* (1960), which had a collection of GIs passing their time on a Pacific island by building a deluxe hotel; despite the zany presence of Ernie Kovacs, Dick Shawn and Don Knotts, the picture was critically declared a bore. Likewise, Britain's screen version of Patrick Ryan's *How I Won the War* (1967) proved to be built of inferior stuff.

Here, in the unending tribulations of a young officer, incisive black comedy was supposed to be lurking. Instead, the film emerged as an exercise in undisciplined nonsense. Two years later, Robert Crichton's *The Secret of Santa Vittoria* suffered much the same fate. It promised to be hilarious in its story of Italian villagers hiding their wine supply from German troopers, but was roundly criticized as being far too noisy, with all its characters overdrawn and talking at once. Matters improved

in 1970, however, when Alan Arkin, Martin Balsam and the entire cast brought vividly to life all the lunatic characters in Joseph Heller's marvelously bleak satire on the US Air Force, *Catch 22*.

Surrounding the adaptations through the years have been a number of come-

Above: Paul Newman and Silva Koscina in *The Secret War of Harry Frigg* (1967).
Top: Art Garfunkel (left) and Alan Arkin (right) in *Catch 22* (1970).
Left: The bomber lands in the La Brea Tar Pits in *1941* (1979).

dies designed especially for film use. Though their story lines have varied in quality, they have usually shared one characteristic in common – sparkling performances by some of the screen's most enduring talents.

In 1949, for instance, Cary Grant and Ann Sheridan romped through the amusing farce *I Was a Male War Bride* (British title: *You Can't Sleep Here*), with Grant playing a Free French officer who disguises himself as a woman so that he can accompany his WAC bride on her return to the US. Grant then went on to do two other enjoyable war comedies, both of which are set in the Pacific – *Operation Petticoat* (1959) and *Father Goose* (1964). In the former, he captains a submarine that must take aboard a disruptively beautiful contingent of nurses. The latter presents him as an unshaven recluse who shepherds a gaggle of French school children – and teacher Leslie Caron – through the dangers posed by surrounding Japanese troops.

Turning again to the comic talents that he had revealed in *Mr Deeds Goes to Town* (1936), Gary Cooper was effective as the '90-day-wonder' naval officer trying to command an experimental steam vessel in *You're in the Navy Now* (1951; British title: *USS Teakettle*). As was to be expected, Jack Lemmon turned in a fine performance as the harassed skipper of *The Wackiest Ship in the Army* (1960), a decrepit sailing vessel dispatched to operate in Japanese waters. And, again as was to be expected, Terry-Thomas delighted audiences as he mugged his way through France's *La Grande Vadrouille* (1966; English title: *Don't Look Now – We're Being Shot At!*), a far-fetched item about three members of the RAF who parachute into enemy territory from their damaged bomber and then make their way

Above: Cary Grant and Arthur O'Connell find that there are women aboard the submarine in *Operation Petticoat* (1959).
Below: Jack Lemmon in command of *The Wackiest Ship in the Army* (1960). Ricky Nelson, in costume, is seated at right.

to freedom by donning an assortment of quite mad disguises.

On the other hand, energetic performances by James Coburn and Dick Shawn could not save *What Did You Do in the War, Daddy?* (1966). The silliness and lame humor contained in the story of an Italian village willing to surrender to American troops on the proviso that its annual wine festival and football match be allowed were simply too much to rescue. Paul Newman faced the same problem – and was unable to salvage things, not even with expert help from James Gregory and Tom Bosley – in *The Secret War of Harry Frigg* (1967), a thoroughly implausible nothing about a con-man army private being dispatched behind German lines to rescue three captured generals and winning the love of aristocratic Sylva Koscina in the process.

Silly, too, was director Steven Spielberg's 1979 venture into comedy, *1941*. Though presenting an interesting idea – a Japanese invasion of the California coast in the days following Pearl Harbor – it turned out to be a crudish piece of too little wit and too much yelling, too many brawls and too much havoc wrought on buildings, vehicles and anything else that gets in the way of mad flier John Belushi. Belushi, Dan Aykroyd and Ned Beatty try their best to elicit laughs from the script and find it a

Above: Cary Grant sorts out his Scotch whiskey in *Father Goose* (1964).
Right: James Coburn (second from left) and Dick Shawn (right) enjoy themselves at the festival in *What Did You Do in the War, Daddy?* (1966).

hopeless assignment. But one thing must be said for *1941*, just as it must be said for every Spielberg work: though the destruction is excessive, the special effects are beautifully done (especially those of the beach amusement park going to pieces) and breath-taking to watch.

So far as productions for theater release are concerned, World War II films (and the films of any war) seem to have entered an eclipse in the 1980s, possibly caused by the widespread aversion to all matters military that was born during the Vietnam tragedy. Whatever the cause may be, little or nothing about the war – other than the prisoner-of-war drama, *Victory* (1981) and Germany's magnificent study of the men jammed together aboard a sub-

marine in combat, *Das Boot* (1982; English title: *The Boat*) – has been done in this latest decade. As a source for drama, comedy, character study, pure action, or historical exploration, the war is being kept alive in the US and elsewhere by television showings. No one can tell how long the eclipse will last (it may even be ending now in the United States, where there is a return-

ing pride in the nation's armed services). All that can be said with certainty is that, regardless of what the cinematic future holds for it, World War II will long rank as the conflict given the greatest amount of attention in motion picture history – a far greater attention than has gone, in total, to the hot and cold wars to which we now turn.

HOT & COLD WARS
WARS
From Korea To Vietnam

Pitting United Nations forces (chiefly US and South Korean troops) against those of North Korea and eventually China, the Korean War – or, to use the diplomatic euphemism of the day, Conflict – erupted in early 1950 and surged vainly back and forth across the 38th Parallel until the signing of the Panmunjom truce in July 1953. It was a war that saw the competing armies suffer a combined total of 3,500,000 casualties and that produced neither a clear-cut victor nor a peace treaty. And it was a war that was barely a year old when it bred its first motion pictures – *Fixed Bayonets* and *The Steel Helmet*.

Other than the war itself, the two films shared much in common. Each dealt with a small band of American soldiers – in *Fixed Bayonets*, a unit stubbornly fighting a rearguard action and, in *The Steel Helmet*, an infantry squad struggling to reach an artillery observation post in a Buddhist temple. Both were the work of director Samuel Fuller. Both were done on modest budgets – with *Helmet* being shot in ten days for a mere $105,000 – and both have been long praised for their grimly realistic portrayals of men in war. They are portrayals that make memorable two films with, admittedly, standard combat plots.

In the main, the praise has gone to Richard Basehart and Gene Evans – Basehart for his portrait of a corporal given the chance to be a hero in *Fixed Bayonets*, and Evans for the tough, cynical sergeant he etches in *The Steel Helmet*. Since both men turned in distinctive portraits, it is impossible to weigh their work against each other,

Previous spread: An attack in *The Killing Fields* (1984).

Opposite top: Relief troops come in in *Fixed Bayonets* (1951).
Below: Jeff Chandler visits his wounded in *Merrill's Marauders* (1962).

but the Evans characterization is today the better remembered of the two. And there can be no doubt that one of Hollywood's finer but most underrated performers did a quality job here. His character is introduced even as the opening credits are viewed, with the camera focusing on a helmet that rises slowly from broken ground to reveal, beneath its razor-like rim, Evans' face – hard, begrimed, narrow-eyed, and battle-wise. The character is set in that instant. Evans then never strays once from that character as he leads his squad, measures the enemy, survives as others fall and befriends a small Korean orphan boy.

Above: Gene Evans (left) and a North Korean captive in *The Steel Helmet* (1951). Richard Loo and James Edwards in center.

That such realistic characterizations are on view in the two films should come as no surprise to anyone acquainted with director Fuller's background. His experiences in World War II were on a par with those of the veterans of 1918 who, a quarter-century earlier, did such honest and accurate depictions of their war – director William A Wellman and writers Lawrence Stallings and John Monk Saunders. Fuller served in Africa and Europe with the 1st Infantry Division, along the way being awarded the Bronze Star, the Silver Star and the Purple Heart. He had 'been there' and was well able to communicate, in the characterizations he urged from his performers, the hard realities he had seen.

Fuller, who began directing in 1949, has made a career of action and suspense films. His output includes several war films, among them *China Gate* (1957), an action thriller about the French Foreign Legion during France's Vietnam troubles in the postwar '40s; *Merrill's Marauders* (1962), a memorable account of the crack US unit that operated in Burma during World War II and *The Big Red One* (1980), the director's very personal view of his old division's action in Africa and Europe.

Fixed Bayonets and *The Steel Helmet* marked an auspicious start for films played against a Korean backdrop. Unfortunately, those that came next

failed – by a very long shot – to match Fuller's standards. For example, 1952 saw the release of *Retreat, Hell!*, which detailed the fighting done by the US Marine's 1st Battalion. The picture was given some good battle sequences through a nicely-coordinated combination of studio sets and newsreel footage, but could claim to be nothing more than a standard combat yarn with standard heroics and more-than-standard cha-

racters, among them Frank Lovejoy's tough captain and Rusty (later Russ) Tamblyn's innocent youngster who wants to be a hero.

But, at the least, *Retreat* provided some good moments in its battle sequences. The two releases that joined it in 1952 – *Battle Circus* and *One Minute to Zero* – were critically mocked for not providing a single good moment throughout. *Battle Circus* came up with an unusual setting that would become all-too-familiar to the devotees of M*A*S*H (both the film and the television series) in the 1970s – an army

Left: Robert De Niro in the midst of the Vietnam War in *The Deer Hunter* (1978). Opposite: Elliott Gould (left) and Donald Sutherland (right) in *M*A*S*H* (1970). Below: Robert De Niro (left) and John Savage board a helicopter in *The Deer Hunter* (1978).

Above: Frank Lovejoy (left) talks to Richard Carlson (in ditch) in *Retreat, Hell* (1952). Right: Richard Widmark (right) confronts Karl Malden, who has stolen his girl, Elaine Stewart, in *Take the High Ground* (1953).

mobile hospital unit – but it surrounded that setting with the dullish story of an embittered army doctor falling in love with a bright-eyed, enthusiastic nurse. The picture was regarded as one of the year's great movie oddities because, though a grade-A effort from the prestigious MGM, it managed not only to have a phony studio look but also somehow contrived to draw only sodden performances from a stellar cast headed by Humphrey Bogart, June Allyson and Keenan Wynn. Contrary to all critical opinion, however, *Battle Circus* does have at least one good moment. It comes with the sick expression that crosses Bogart's face when Miss Allyson bubbles that the mobile tent hospital strikes her as being just like – and just as exciting as – a circus on the move.

One Minute to Zero was no better. Here, Robert Mitchum is a high-ranking officer (a colonel and then a briga-dier general) who evacuates Americans from the war zone while being annoyed by an intrusive, albeit attractive, United Nations representative in the person of Ann Blyth. He faces some terrible moments when he himself must bomb a group of refugees. Naturally, in the midst of everything, Mitchum and Miss Blyth fall in love. The film comes across as a flat, cliché-ridden (all sorts of statements about the futility and cruelty of war) melodrama. It is not even saved by its action sequences. In a picture with a $2 million budget, they should have been exciting, but were ruined by some artificial-looking special effects.

Matters, however, improved in 1953, the final year of the war. MGM atoned for *Battle Circus* by releasing *Take the High Ground*, a taut and interesting study of raw recruits being trained for Korean combat. Richard Widmark was praised for his work as a tough and dedicated training sergeant.

Equally as interesting that year was the one 'different' film to emerge from the war – *The Glory Brigade*. Accounting for its 'difference' is the fact that it deals with Greek troops fighting alongside the Americans as part of the overall United Nations Force. Modestly presented, it boasts solid character performances from Victor Mature, Lee Marvin and Richard Egan.

The years since the Panmunjom truce have seen but little cinematic in-

Right: Humphrey Bogart and June Allyson in *Battle Circus* (1952).
Below: Robert Mitchum listening to bad news in *One Minute to Zero* (1952).

terest in the Korean War. It has been conjectured that the scant interest can be traced to the outcome of the war itself – a frustrating stalemate rather than a triumphant victory. It is one thing to set battle films, especially the standard offerings with all their heroics, against a backdrop of what will eventually be triumphs, as were World Wars I and II. But it is quite another matter to set them against an eventual futility. Futility can play a role in war films – and has certainly done so in some of the best productions that the genre has produced. But it is too unpalatable a dish to be served audiences as a steady diet.

Inset below: Sidney Poitier gives blood in *All the Young Men* (1960).
Bottom inset: Richard Conte and Peggy Castle comfort the wounded in *Target Zero* (1955).

A helicopter discharges troops, including a medic, in *Apocalypse Now* (1979).

Whether all this be the actual case or not, the fact is that there have been no more than a smattering of Korean War films since Panmunjom. In quality and content, they have ranged from the average to the exceptional.

Target Zero (1955) ranks as one of the earliest examples of the average. With a cast headed by Richard Conte and Charles Bronson (who had changed his name from Charles Buchinsky the previous year), the film concerns an infantry patrol that works its way to the hoped-for safety of an isolated US outpost, only to find all the men there dead. Joining the patrol in its adventures are three members of a British tank crew, plus an attractive young lady (Peggy Castle) who has gotten herself stranded in the war zone and whose function in the plot is to romance Richard Conte. The film has its moments of suspense and action, but is flawed by its array of stereotyped characters.

An average plot is on hand in *A Hill in Korea* (1956), a British product about a small unit guarding a hillside against enemy intrusion. But the performances – as can be expected of a British cast – are well above average and do much to off-set the routine plot and the film's talkiness. Especially good is the work of Stanley Baker and Harry Andrews.

Sidney Poitier's performance and the story line should have made *All the Young Men* (1960) into a well-above-average film. But, in telling the story of a black officer's problems when he takes command of a white unit, the picture burdens itself with too many clichés – stereotype characters, platitudes about black-white tensions and misunderstandings, and standard battle heroics.

Above: Oscar Homolka (center), as a Russian officer, tries to get Ronald Reagan to give a propaganda broadcast from Korea in *Prisoner of War* (1954).
Right: Anne Francis, Paul Newman and Walter Pidgeon in *The Rack* (1956).

Above average throughout, however, is *Prisoner of War* (1954), an MGM feature that addressed a problem gaining international attention at the time – the torture of American prisoners-of-war by their North Korean captors. The film, directed by Andrew Marton and well acted by Ronald Reagan, Steve Forrest and Dewey Martin, is a grimly realistic offering that, apparently too harshly done for audiences of the 1950s, did not fare well at the box office. The mistreatment of POWs served as the basis for another above-average offering, *The Rack* (1956), an adaptation of an early US television drama about a young officer being court-martialed on charges of cooperating with his enemy captors because he can not bear the pain of torture. Paul Newman is effective as the young man, as is Walter Pidgeon as

his high-ranking officer father. Lee Marvin, seen in one of his best early roles, does superb work as a tough enlisted man who appears as a court-martial witness to explain how he himself was subjected to – and withstood – hours of torture.

Also in the above-average category are: *Men of the Fighting Lady* (1954), a

solid look at the attacks launched from an aircraft carrier off the Korean coast; *Men in War* (1957), with Robert Ryan, Aldo Ray and Nehemiah Persoff aptly sketching portraits of infantrymen who must attack an enemy position after their squad is cut off from its headquarters; and *War Hunt* (1962), a fine character study of an infantryman

(John Saxon) who finds himself growing to love the killing that he must do. Making his screen debut here – and winning critical praise as the troubled friend who sees what is happening to the infantryman – is Robert Redford.

At the very opposite end of the spectrum is what may well be the worst film made about the Korean War – *Marines Let's Go* (1961). This one's about some leathernecks who spend their leave in

is a compound of anti-war outrage and black comedy.

At heart, *Bridges* is the story of a reserve navy flier (William Holden) who is recalled to service, assigned to carrier duty off the Korean coast, and finally sent to bomb a complex of strategic bridges deep within the country. But, in a thoughtful rendering of the James E Michener novel on which it is based, the film surrounds this basic plot

line with a variety of themes. For one, it looks closely at the war's disruptive effects on the pilot, his wife (Grace Kelly) and their children. For another, it comments on the unlikely loyalties developed in wartime, doing so in its depiction of the stolid Holden's friendship with the flamboyant helicopter rescue pilot (Mickey Rooney) with whom he is destined for tragedy in the picture's final sequence. For yet another, in Rooney's character, it concerns itself with the military pride and daring that can be found lurking within the most outwardly carefree personalities, and, in the character and actions of the fleet admiral (Fredric March), the outlooks and problems of military command. And – in the well-remembered Tokyo bathhouse scene in which the American and Japanese families bathe together – it makes a passing but nonetheless effective comment on the basic human sameness that underlies the surface dissimilarities between the people of different cultures.

Photographed in color, *The Bridges at Toko-Ri* is highlighted with breathtaking sea and air sequences. One of the best focuses on a grinning Mickey Rooney as, sporting his lucky top hat, he transfers from one ship to another via a breeches buoy. Topping the action sequences is the attack on the complex of bridges, an attack that ends with

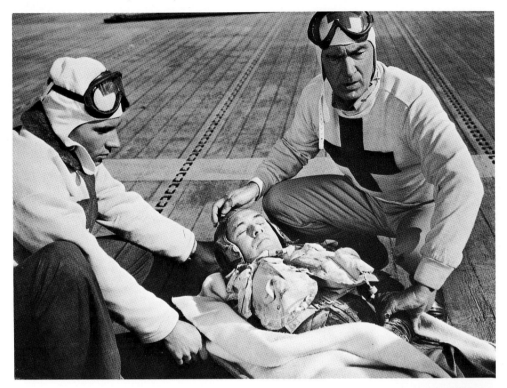

Above: Walter Pidgeon (right) in *Men of the Fighting Lady* (1954).
Right: An exhausted Robert Ryan in *Men in War* (1957) – a scene that seemed to recapitulate the terrible toll that war takes – even on the survivors.

Japan brawling and drinking and womanizing and brawling some more. Perhaps the whole thing is supposed to look like World War I's *What Price Glory*. If so, it fails miserably.

Three widely-separated productions stand as the most memorable of all the Korean offerings. They are *The Bridges at Toko-Ri* (1954), *Pork Chop Hill* (1959) and *M★A★S★H* (1970). Not only are they widely separated in their release dates but also in their themes, forming, when considered together, one of the most disparate trios in the history of war filming. *The Bridges at Toko-Ri* is the multi-faceted study of the Navy men who fought the war; *Pork Chop Hill* is a tough, straight-forward account of the infantry in battle; and *M★A★S★H*, set in – and drawing its title from – a mobile army surgical hospital,

Holden's plane being shot down. Rooney then attempts a helicopter rescue, only to be shot down himself. The film closes grimly with the two pilots – humanly terrified – meeting death as enemy ground troops close in on them.

In *Pork Chop Hill*, Gregory Peck is cast as an infantry officer whose unit, at the time the truce negotiators at Panmunjom are jockeying for positions of bargaining strength, takes a highly strategic enemy hill and then tries to hold it against repeated counterattacks. Peck is impressive as the quietly dedicated officer; he receives excellent supporting work from George Peppard, Rip Torn, Woody Strode and George Shibata. The combat sequences (particularly those done at night, with the darkness intermittently turned into shadowless day by shell bursts) are excellently staged; the dialogue is terse and realistic; and the grimness of battle is especially well evoked by the black-and-white photography.

Though not widely remembered and revered by the movie-going public, *Pork Chop Hill* has long been critically applauded as one of the best combat films ever made, in its own way on a par with such classics from other wars as *The Big Parade* and West Germany's *The Bridge*. Its effectiveness is no accident because the picture was in the hands of one of Hollywood's most experienced directors of war material – Lewis Milestone. By 1959, the Russian-born Milestone was nearing the end of a directorial career that had begun in 1925 and had reached an early zenith in 1930 with *Hell's Angels* (uncredited co-director with Howard Hughes) and the magnificent *All Quiet on the Western Front*. From there, he had gone on to *The General Died at Dawn* (1936), *Our Russian Front* (a 1943 documentary), *North Star* (also 1943; later released as *Armored Attack*) and *The Purple Heart* (1944), reaching still another zenith with *A Walk in the Sun* in 1946. Milestone's post-war work included *Halls of Montezuma* (1951) and Britain's *They Who Dare* (1954), both considered standard pieces. Following *Pork Chop Hill*, he worked on one more war feature – *PT 109* (1963) – but was

William Holden (left) and Mickey Rooney under attack in *The Bridges at Toko-Ri* (1954).

replaced in mid-production by Leslie Martinson and received no screen credit. Milestone, who was known for his realistic battle touches and fluid camera work, also devoted some of his time to general comedies and drama. His last years were spent directing episodes for several television series. Milestone died in 1980, at age 85.

In a trio of highly contrasting films, *M*A*S*H* is itself an exercise in sharp contrasts. In fact, in its plot development and especially its execution, this story of life in a tent hospital is a matter of exact opposites throughout. On the one hand, in the reactions of the doctors and nurses as the wounded come pouring in, it is (though it makes no critical statements about the military itself) an outraged shout against war; on the other, it devotes so much attention to the antics of the doctors and nurses that – even if those antics are viewed as needed releases from the daily horror – it seems far more interested in sexual comedy than in anti-war comment. At one extreme, it is harshly realistic in its operating-room sequences (much too realistic in the opinion of some critics who found the gore unnecessarily excessive), but, at the other extreme, laughably anachronistic in the characterizations of its three leading physicians (Donald Sutherland, Elliott

Gould and Tom Skerritt); supposedly men of the 1950s, they are portrayed as frenetic, openly irreverent and loudly anti-authoritarian – traits not widely seen in the 1950s but definitely on view for public shock and/or adulation in the social and behavioral upheavals that marked the late 1960s and early 1970s.

Nor do the contrasts stop here. The picture is touched with sharply etched hints of how the war's insanity has invaded the hospital – for example, all those weird announcements on the compound's public address system – but it falls apart in the prolonged and grotesquely played football game that seems intended to symbolize the ultimate insanity of war. Played between the M*A*S*H unit and a nearby evacuation hospital, it goes nowhere, says nothing, proves nothing and – though laced with some profanities that brought shocked giggles here and there in audiences – is quite unfunny.

Finally, the film is punctuated with moments of ironic humor, with one of the best occurring in the night scene when Head Nurse 'Hot Lips' Houlihan (Sally Kellerman) meets with several colleagues to divide the money won on the day's football game. A Jeep passes close by, bearing a corpse whose white shroud is a pale and somber gleam in the darkness. The group affords it no more than a momentary glance before gleefully getting back to the business at hand. The scene is a memorable one, but much greater chunks of time are devoted to a crudish humor of the dirty-stories-behind-the-barn variety, as witness the doctors' constant and juvenile questing after the nursing staff and the scene in which the side of the wash-room tent is made to collapse and reveal for the assembled personnel the nude and humiliated 'Hot Lips.'

Despite its flaws, *M*A*S*H* comes across as a powerful film, principally because of its sometimes bleak and sometimes funny touches and its unflinching depiction of a front-line surgery. The critics greeted it with mixed reactions and the American public gave it an unrestrained welcome. In great part the widespread US opposition to the nation's involvement in the Vietnam War accounted for that welcome. It was patently obvious that *M*A*S*H*, though set in Korea, had the frustrations and agonies of Vietnam on its mind, and dealt with them in a most unusual way.

The film became the basis of a successful television series that ran through the 1970s and that is presently syndicated internationally. The television offspring is critically regarded as a far more trenchant and sensitive anti-war statement than was the parent.

The troubles in Vietnam began to take shape as film themes in the 1950s. Among the earliest releases were two modest features – *Jump into Hell* (1955) and director Samuel Fuller's *China Gate* (1957). Serving as the background for both was the eviction of the country's long-time colonial overlord, France, by the guerrilla forces of Communist leader Ho Chi Minh.

Though modestly done, *Jump into Hell* set an ambitious goal for itself. In its story of four French paratroopers who drop in to assist their comrades in the besieged and doomed military outpost of Dienbienphu, it attempts to re-create the defeat that marked the end of French rule in Vietnam. Had the film been well done, it might have been an impressive historical offering. But, even though the insertion of newsreel footage provides it with some moments of hard reality, the picture fails to communicate the full scope of a battle that involved more than 12,000 troops. Rather, the impression is that the battle is fought by the film's four paratroop heroes – Jacques Sernas, Kurt Kaszner, Norman Trout and Peter Van Eyck.

China Gate, telling the story of an American who sniffs out a secret communist arms cache, pretends to be little more than an adventure story. Given standard heroic treatment are the French Foreign Legionnaires on duty in their country's final Vietnam days. Being what it is, the picture comes

Above: Gene Barry is comforted in *China Gate* (1957). The film also starred Angie Dickinson.
Left: A violent scene from the Indo-China War film, *Jump Into Hell* (1955) – the story of four French para-troopers.
Below: Marshall Thompson (left) is an interested onlooker as a spy is caught in *A Yank in Vietnam* (1964).

nowhere near matching the power and seriousness of Fuller's Korean films. It does achieve a certain uniqueness, though, by casting singer Nat King Cole as a Legionnaire. He comes across well in his role and adds to the film's overall enjoyment with his singing.

The years following Dienbienphu witnessed a succession of events that finally led to disaster for both the Vietnamese and the Americans. The Geneva Conference, faced with two opposing factions within the nation, partitioned the country at the 17th Parallel, awarding the northern half to the Communist faction and the southern half to the Nationalist faction, and declaring that a nation-wide referendum would permit the Vietnamese people to decide under which regime they would be reunited. Prior to the election, however, the Nationalists renounced the partition and established the southern area an independent republic. The Communist North replied by outfitting southern Communists – the Vietcong – for a guerrilla war against the new republic. The United States sided with the South Vietnamese government and began assisting it with military advisors. By the late 1960s, the US involvement had burgeoned – 'escalated' was the operative jargon of the day – until more than a half-million troops were committed to fighting the Vietcong.

The growing US involvement was early noted in *A Yank in Vietnam* (1964), a modestly budgeted tale of a Marine officer who assists a Vietnamese soldier in the rescue of a kidnapped doctor. The film, directed by its star, Marshall Thompson, actually has little to say about the American involvement but, photographed on Vietnamese locations, gave audiences of the mid-1960s a first-hand look at the country.

The Thompson film may have had little to say about the growing American involvement, but the same is not true of John Wayne's *The Green Berets* (1968). Produced and directed by Wayne and released at the time when the American public's opposition to that involvement was reaching its zenith, the film is an unabashed tribute to that involvement and an unquestioning acceptance of US policy – in all, an ultra-conservative actor's chauvinistic statement that ignores the complex questions then plaguing the world public. So subjective is the film's view and so hot were the passions of the day that it earned Wayne a ridicule he had never suffered

Above: In *Gordon's War* (1973), Paul Winfield is a veteran of the Vietnam War out for revenge.
Left: Henry Winkler (right) tries to shake some sense into his one-time Army buddy, Harrison Ford, who is still suffering from battle fatigue from the Vietnam War, in *Heroes* (1978).
Below: Stan Shaw (left) consoles Michael Lembeck as James Whitmore, Jr looks on in *The Boys in Company C* (1978), a story of the Marines in Vietnam.

before in a career that had seen him become not just a film star but a national institution. And to make matters worse, *The Green Berets*, aside from its political hue, is simply an unsophisticated piece of war filmmaking. All the Special Forces soldiers under Colonel Wayne's command are undiluted heroes, courageous, selfless and dedicated. All the enemy Vietcong are heartless savages who fight dirty and set up horrible booby traps for Wayne's men, one of which is a spiked affair that takes easygoing Jim Hutton's life. The propaganda abounds even more than it did in the worst of World War II's offerings. Further, the skirmishes and battles, though, in true Wayne fashion, well staged, have too much the smack of derring-do about them. And the settings are without the authenticity customary in big-budget productions; much of the film was shot in Georgia – and looks it.

1968, however, was saved by the release of a splendid documentary – *A Face of War*. Photographed two years earlier by Eugene S Jones, it recorded the front-line experiences of the Seventh Marine Regiment and, in so doing, gave audiences an unforgettable view of men living and dying in the horror that is battle. It does not comment on the rightness or wrongness of the American commitment. With the compassion of its photographer – who was twice injured during the filming – shining through at every step of the way, it simply shows what happens to men in battle. It needs do no more.

Anti-war activist Jane Fonda was responsible for two documentaries in the early 1970s – *FTA/Free the Army* (1972) and *Introduction to the Enemy* (1974). Miss Fonda's theatrical company, the Anti-War Troupe, which she formed with *M*A*S*H*'s Donald Sutherland, was the subject of *FTA*. The film recorded the company's tour of military bases in defiance of Pentagon opposition. *Introduction to the Enemy* reported on her controversial visit to North Vietnam near war's end. Miss Fonda served as producer on both films, with husband Tom Hayden and Haskell Webster joining her as co-producers on *Introduction to the Enemy*.

The 1970s saw the beginning of a cycle of films on the return of Vietnam veterans to civilian life. A cycle that has continued into the 1980s, its pictures have only occasionally dealt directly with the adjustment problems of the returnees. Rather, most have simply

employed the Vietnam experience as a background against which a character can be built for use in a comedy, a romance or a crime drama. *Gordon's War* (1973) serves as an early example of the shape that so many of these films have taken. A black veteran (Paul Winfield) returns to Harlem and is shattered to learn that his wife has died of a drug overdose. He immediately declares war on the area's drug lords and, using his combat skills learned in Vietnam, brings them all to violent and deserved ends. The film, spattered with gore throughout, is chiefly remembered for its excellent location photography in New York City.

One of the oddest films in the cycle, *Heroes* (1978), tried to combine comedy and romance with a commentary on veteran problems – and failed miserably. It tracks the adventures of a young soldier (Henry Winkler) who, mentally out-of-sync as a result of his combat experiences, escapes a Veterans Administration hospital and stumbles through a series of cross-country adven-

Burt Lancaster as a commander in the Vietnam War in *Go Tell the Spartans* (1978).

tures before his balance is restored (at least somewhat) and he settles down to civilian life. Judged tiresome and overlong, the film marked Winkler's major debut on theater screens (he had been seen earlier in two minor films, *Crazy Joe* and *The Lords of Flatbush* [both 1974]), and was intended to further the popularity he had won as the harmless delinquent, 'Fonzie,' in the long-running American television series, *Happy Days*. Though *Heroes* presented him with a few good scenes in which to display his wacky comic talents, it was an unfortunate debut. Sally Field, however, turned in a solid performance as the object of his daffy affections.

Coming Home (1978), a film that met with mixed critical reaction, was a serious attempt to comment on veterans' problems and, in that comment, to condemn the whole idea of war. In the opinion of some critics, it brilliantly

Opposite: Martin Sheen (on top of boat) on his way to assassinate Colonel Kurtz in *Apocalypse Now* (1979).
Below: The helicopters approach in *Apocalypse Now* (1979).

achieved its purpose, doing so in Jon Voight's poignant characterization of a paraplegic and in the glimpses of the wounded confined to a VA hospital with him. But, conversely, the film's basic story – the love affair between Voight and a Marine captain's wife (Jane Fonda) – was widely held to be little better than the fare seen on television soap operas.

Yet, despite the mixed critical reaction, there were no complaints about the Fonda-Voight performances, which were judged as sensitive and thoughtful. The Academy Awards Committee chose Voight and Miss Fonda as the year's best actor and actress. Nor did the mixed reaction damage the Academy's view of the film itself. *Coming Home* received the 1978 Oscar as the year's best picture.

Several combat films were on hand in the late decade. 1978 brought *The Boys in Company C*, director Sidney Furie's story of the effects of battle on a number of young Marines. The film gets off to an excellent start with sequences of the youngsters in boot training, but falls apart when it reaches Vietnam and begins a closer examination of the characters, all of whom turn out to be the stereotypes that have been on hand in war films since the 1930s. The film finally devolves into nonsense with the playing of a soccer match that can only be seen as a pale imitation of the football game in *M*A*S*H*. Though burdened with stereotypical characters, a cast of relative unknowns – Stan Shaw, Andrew Stevens and James Canning –

performs well. The best performance, however, is turned in by a complete unknown, Lee Ermey, as a boot-camp drill instructor. Ermey, himself an ex-drill instructor, was originally hired as a consultant on the picture, but was then invited to join the cast, after which he did an admirable job re-creating his former occupation.

1978 also brought *Go Tell the Spartans*, with Burt Lancaster starring as an experienced US commander whose raw troops help to defend a beleaguered South Vietnamese outpost. At bottom,

the film is an intelligent study of the early American advisers sent into Vietnam. Its sympathetic view of the military, however, did not sit well with the anti-war mood of the late 1970s and the picture fared poorly at the box office.

The decade closed with the two finest films produced to date on the Vietnam fighting – *The Deer Hunter* (1978) and *Apocalypse Now* (1979). Both are considered cinema masterworks. Many critics and moviegoers look on them not only as the top Vietnam entries but also

as deserving of being listed among the best war pictures ever made.

The first major work of director Michael Cimino (he had previously written and directed for Clint Eastwood), *The Deer Hunter* tells of how three young Pennsylvania steelworkers are emotionally and physically shattered by the horrors of their Vietnam experience. The film, however, does far more than view their personal tragedies (as if those tragedies are not sufficient dramatic material in themselves). It extends itself to the Vietnamese and shows how they, too, were devastated by the fighting. And, in a series of flashbacks – to a Pennsylvania deer hunt and the wedding of one of the young workers – it communicates the damage done to the American spirit and conscience by the war.

The film was named 1978's best picture – and Cimino the year's best director – by the Academy Award Committee. Excellent performances by Robert De Niro, Christopher Walken and Meryl Streep were also acknowledged by the Academy. De Niro was nominated as best actor (he lost to Jon Voight for *Coming Home*) and Walken received the Oscar for best supporting actor. A nomination for best supporting actress went to Miss Streep.

Apocalypse Now, a tailoring of Joseph Conrad's 1902 novel, *Heart of Darkness*, is the work of director Francis Ford Coppola. The picture follows a US intelligence officer (Martin Sheen) as he undertakes a river journey to locate and then execute one Colonel Kurtz (Marlon Brando), a once respected commander who has been driven mad by the war and is now living like a primitive king deep in the jungle. In his quest, Sheen has a series of experiences – among them a helicopter attack and a bizarre USO entertainment – that leave audiences in no doubt about the insanity not only of the Vietnam conflict but of all war. The helicopter attack is targeted against a village thought to be a Vietcong stronghold, while the USO show is noisily staged aboard a brilliantly lighted river boat deep in the bowels of enemy territory.

Long judged a flawed masterpiece, *Apocalypse Now* is magnificent in some of its moments and awful in others. It is at its best in the helicopter attack

Robert Duvall as the US Marine flyer who is a warrior without a war in *The Great Santini* (1980), which was the nickname he gave himself.

Above: The ethnic Pittsburgh wedding in *The Deer Hunter* (1978).
Left: Sam Waterston (right) in *The Killing Fields* (1984). He played the part of a newspaper correspondent who was helped by a native photographer during the Khmer Rouge takeover in Cambodia.

sequence. Combined here are excellent special effects and splendid photography. The attack is seen both from the air and the ground, with the aerial shots providing a frightening look down on the choppers as they cut their deadly way back and forth across the village. The ground scenes are played against a pall of black smoke that well communicates the horror of what has been done to the village.

Rounding out that horror is Robert Duvall's frightening and superb portrayal of the gung-ho and quite mad air cavalry officer in charge of the attack. Duvall, a stage actor who made his screen debut as the reclusive Boo

Radley in *To Kill a Mockingbird* (1963) and has since specialized in unique characterizations, was deservedly nominated by the Academy Awards for best supporting actor honors, but lost to Melvyn Douglas in *Being There*. A year later, Duvall again took an Academy nomination for a military role – this time as best actor for his work in *The Great Santini*, a fine character study of a Marine flier whose outer hardness reflects the inner frustrations of being, in his words, a warrior without a war. Again he lost, now to Robert De Niro in *Raging Bull*.

If *Apocalypse Now* is at its best in the helicopter attack sequence, it is certainly at its worst in its climactic scenes with Marlon Brando as the insane Colonel Kurtz. Brando manages to turn the Kurtz role into one of the most pretentious acting jobs ever seen. And, so far as communication with the audience is concerned, one of the most inexpert. At the least, he could have enunciated his lines so that they could be understood by someone other than a speech pathologist. At the least, director Coppola could have insisted that he do so.

Despite its overall quality *Apocalypse Now* was not a success at the Academy Awards in 1979, in great part because it had the misfortune to be released in the same year with *Kramer Vs. Kramer*, one of the most popular films in Hollywood history. Nominated as best picture and for best direction and screenplay (based on material from another medium), *Apocalypse* lost on all counts to *Kramer*.

Below: Gene Hackman performs a rescue mission in *Uncommon Valor* (1983).
Bottom: Chuck Norris and M Emmet Walsh fly over their enemies in *Missing in Action* (1984).

As is true of the Korean War, the years have seen but a few films produced on the Vietnam tragedy – and, in great part, for the same reason. Like Korea, Vietnam early showed itself to be a war that would end not in proud victory but in frustration and humiliation. Additionally, it eventually proved itself to be the most unpopular conflict in which the United States ever participated, triggering widespread public criticism both at home and abroad. Present here were factors that more than discouraged the production of the standard heroic fare that is the backbone of the war genre.

The mid-1980s have brought the beginnings of a change, however. During the Vietnam years and for some time thereafter, the feeling communicated on the screen was that the men who fought the war were either brutes (Duvall's air cavalry officer), nuts (Winkler's out-of-sync vet) or victims (Voight's paraplegic). Very few were heroes (Lancaster's commander in *Go Tell the Spartans*) and those who were went ignored at the box office. But time has been healing the wounds left by the opposition to the conflict, and the United States is showing signs of a returning pride in its military forces. What time has achieved can be seen in two mid-'80s productions that may well mark the beginnings of a cycle of Vietnam films – *Uncommon Valor* (1983) and *Missing in Action* (1984). Both feature competent fighting men – Gene Hackman and Chuck Norris respectively – who return to Vietnam to rescue soldiers listed officially as missing in combat but actually held captive by Communist Forces. Both feature heroic action, much of it criticized for its excessive violence.

The mid-decade has also seen the release of a serious and sensitive study of one aspect of the Vietnam experience. The highly praised *The Killing Fields* (1984) looks at the tragedy that befalls an American journalist and his

Indonesian photographer during the political and military upheavals in neighboring Cambodia following the end of the fighting in Vietnam. Excellent performances come from Sam Waterston as journalist Sydney Schanberg, and Dr Haing S Ngor (a nonprofessional actor) as the unfortunate Indonesian.

A scene of the war in Cambodia from *The Killing Fields* (1984).

Ever since the 1920s, the military in peacetime has served as a popular film theme. In 1926, for instance, Lon Chaney put aside his liking for grotesque characters and played a tough but underneath-it-all lovable sergeant in *Tell It to the Marines*. Clark Gable and Wallace Beery spent a part of 1931 as tough Navy airmen in *Hell Divers*, an adventure-romance that featured superb aerial sequences and a walk-on appearance by one of the future's most enduring stars, Robert Young. The mid-1930s saw James Cagney and Pat O'Brien embark on what would be, by the early 1940s, eight highly profitable co-starring ventures, two of which would be set in the peacetime military – *Here Comes the Navy* (1934) and *Devil Dogs of the Air* (1935). In the first, Cagney established his familiar tough-guy serviceman who alienates his buddies with his cockiness and then redeems himself with an act of heroism.

Devil Dogs of the Air, casting the Cagney-O'Brien duo as Marine pilots, was lauded for giving an accurate view of Marine air training and is remembered today chiefly for its top-notch aerial stunt sequences. O'Brien went on to help test a new underwater craft in *Submarine D-1* (1937). In 1939, with World War II looming on the horizon, *Wings of the Navy* had George Brent turning raw recruits into skilled fliers at Florida's Pensacola Naval Air Station.

Virtually all the military-in-peacetime films of the day were adventure-romances that used the drill field, the sea and the air as backdrops against which the action sequences that came between the romancing could be built. They were, in general, pretty lighthearted pieces that, while at times giving some insights into service life, did not seek to depict that life with the accuracy later seen in *From Here to Eternity*. The peacetime theme was so

lighthearted that it had room for musicals, chief among them the Astair-Rogers vehicle, *Follow the Fleet* (1936), and three Dick Powell efforts – *Flirtation Walk* (1934), *Shipmates Forever* (1935) and *The Singing Marine* (1937).

The peacetime service has proven as popular a theme in the years since World War II as it was in the 1930s. But, for one reason alone, it is a vastly changed theme, no longer the lighthearted thing it once was. For four decades now, it has been imbued with a social import and a dramatic impact unknown in the 1930s because it has been played out against the potentially lethal tensions of the East versus West Cold War.

Opposite: Rock Hudson commands Ernest Borgnine (left) and Tony Bill in *Ice Station Zebra* (1968).
Below: James Stewart (center) in *Strategic Air Command* (1955).

The Cold War pictures have divided themselves into several types over the years. For openers, the 1950s and 1960s produced a string of pictures emphasizing the military's readiness to respond in an instant to an enemy attack. The chief US examples here are *Strategic Air Command* (1955), with James Stewart cast as a professional baseball player who is recalled to active duty and participates in long-range bomber flights; *Bombers B52* (1957; British title: *No Sleep till Dawn*), a hymn to the efficiency of the aircraft for which the picture is named and to the sergeant (Karl Malden) who, when lured by a high paying civilian job, decides that he can best serve his country in uniform; and *A Gathering of Eagles* (1962), in which Colonel Rock Hudson works to lift a Strategic Air Command base to top efficiency. Britain's principal entry is

Left: Gregory Peck (center), aided by Buddy Ebsen, halts a Russian officer in Berlin in *The Night People* (1954).
Below: On board the American submarine in *On the Beach* (1959) – Fred Astaire (left), Gregory Peck (center standing), Anthony Perkins (center seated) discuss possible avenues of escape.

Above: Peter Sellers in the title role of *Dr Strangelove – or How I Learned to Stop Worrying and Love the Bomb* (1963), a black humor film about the eventual total destruction of the world.
Left: Jane Fonda, a married woman, falls in love with Jon Voight, a paraplegic war veteran, in *Coming Home* (1978).

High Flight (1956), an enjoyable yarn about cadets in training at the Royal Air Force College.

The second type consists of what can be called 'confrontation' pictures. The basic theme here calls for Americans and Russians to come face-to-face in an incident that could trigger a shooting war. Representative of the type are: *The Night People* (1954), with Gregory Peck as an American occupation officer in West Berlin who affects the rescue of a young soldier held prisoner in East Berlin; *The Bedford Incident* (1965), the story of a hard-nosed US destroyer captain (Richard Widmark) pursuing a Russian submarine in the Arctic and so intimidating a junior officer (James MacArthur) with his demand for efficiency that the nervous youngster accidentally triggers the ship's nuclear weapon, and *Ice Station Zebra* (1968), an adaptation of the Alistair Maclean novel in which American and Russian units compete in the Arctic search for a lost space capsule containing vital military information.

The confrontation theme has also provided audiences with the comedy, *The Russians Are Coming, The Russians Are Coming* (1966), the story of the panic – all of it hilarious – that takes hold of a small New England island when a group of sailors (headed by Alan Arkin) comes ashore from a grounded Russian submarine. In sharp contrast to its fellow types with their hard-eyed and dedicated warriors, everyone here is quite human, bumbling and afraid on both sides of the fence as the enemies of East and West alternately avoid and stumble into each other. In a sentimental close, the Americans and Russians are united in the rescue of a

Above: Alan Arkin (in cap) is captured by Carl Reiner in *The Russians Are Coming, The Russians Are Coming* (1966).

little boy from a church tower, after which the islanders man their boats and protectively surround the submarine as it returns to sea while US planes lurk threateningly overhead.

A constant public worry through the years has centered on the hot – and, with its nuclear weapons, perhaps final – war that has always threatened to erupt from the Cold War. Conflicts set in the future are usually the province of science fiction, but the decades of worry

have prompted a number of films that belong within the war genre. They have looked at the possibility of a future disaster with both a comic and dramatic eye – with a comic eye in director Stanley Kubrick's devastating satire, *Dr Strangelove – or How I Learned to Stop Worrying and Love the Bomb* (1963), the Peter Sellers-George C Scott-Slim Pickens film about a USAF

Above: President Henry Fonda in *Fail Safe* (1954).

Right: In *War Games*, a teenage computer genius almost destroys the world (1983).

Left: Charlie Sheen (left) and Patrick Swayze search for an escape route in *Red Dawn* (1984).

bomber ordered by a mad general to attack Moscow; and with a dramatic eye in such varied fare as *On the Beach* (1959), *Fail Safe* (1964), *War Games* (1983) and *Red Dawn* (1984). *On the Beach*, an adaptation of the Nevil Shute novel, is set in Australia and concerns the last people to die when the cloud born of an atomic blast poisons the world. *Fail Safe* is also an adaptation of a novel – this one by Eugene Burdick and Harvey Wheeler – and resembles *Dr Strangelove* in plot; it details a nuclear attack on Moscow when an electronics device in command headquarters malfunctions and turns a US training flight into a mission of destruction. Bordering on science-fiction, *War Games* takes as its hero a teenage computer genius who brings the world close to within seconds of catastrophic war by breaking into the US Defense Department's master computer. *Red Dawn*, another sign of America's changing view toward military heroics, is the story of a group of teenagers who valiantly defend their town when enemy forces invade the United States.

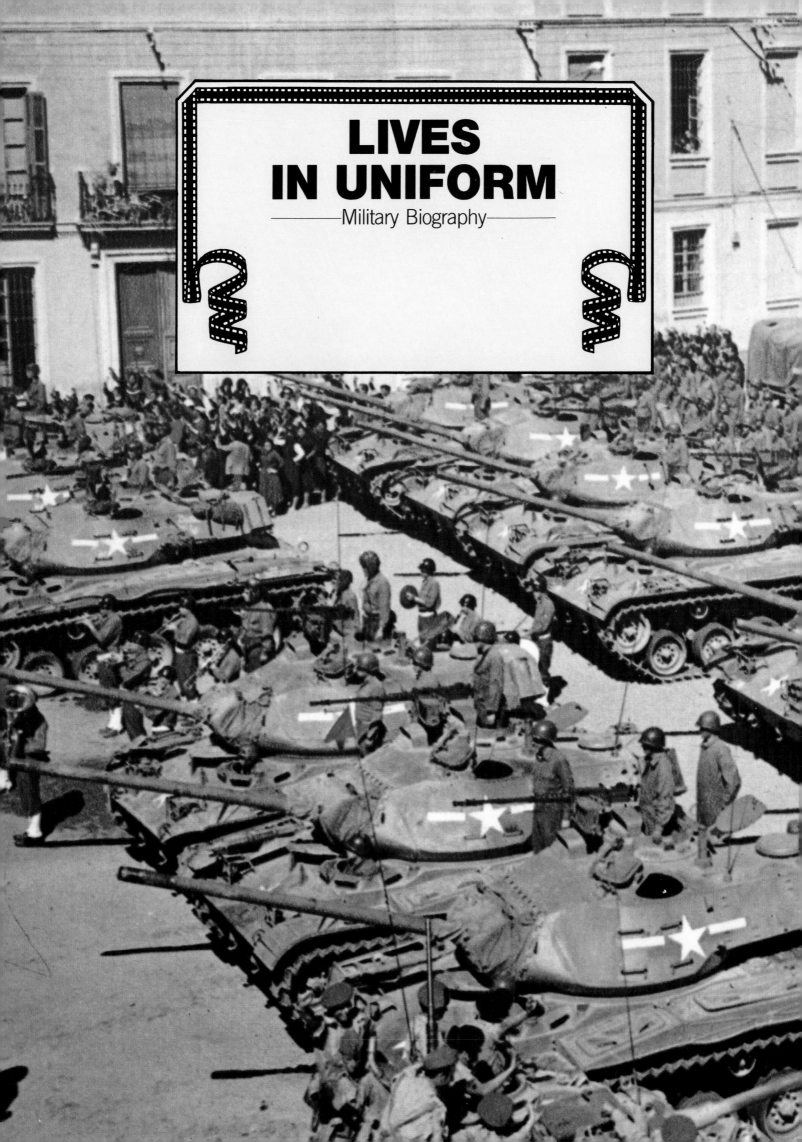

LIVES
IN UNIFORM
Military Biography

We come now to the smallest of the categories within the war genre – military biography. Its smallness has to do only with the number of films it has produced, little more, for example, than two dozen from the United States and Great Britain over the years since 1945. But, in content, it can claim to be one of the broadest categories in any film genre, with its subjects ranging from history's best- to least-known military figures – from *Napoleon* (1927) and *MacArthur* (1977) on the one hand to the blinded infantryman Al Schmid of *Pride of the Marines* (1945) and aging flier Robert Lee Scott of *God Is My Co-Pilot* (also 1945) on the other.

The category would be much larger were it to include all the military figures that producers have fictionalized or have cast – with some attempt at accurate characterization – in fictional pieces. A case in point is General George S Patton. He belongs within the category for George C Scott's *Patton* (1970), a serious study of the man's character and his World War II career. But, though the general may have been later depicted just as accurately by George Kennedy in *The Brass Target*

(1978), his effort simply cannot be placed in the category. *The Brass Target* is a highly imaginative fictional conjecture of how Patton met his death in the immediate post-war period.

This distinction must be kept in mind throughout this chapter for it is responsible for the omission of some highly respected films, among them Dustin Hoffman's *Little Big Man* (1970), a fictional piece that contains Robert Mulligan's satirical but highly effective portrait of America's Indian-fighting General George Custer and an excellent staging of the tragic battle at Little Big Horn.

Just as it has been responsible for the majority of combat films, so has World War II provided the inspiration for most of the genre's biographical works. Great Britain started the ball rolling in 1942 with *The First of the Few*. Cast here was Leslie Howard as R J Mitchell, the designer-inventor who, on seeing the inevitability of World War II, developed the Spitfire fighter plane. It was the aircraft credited with defeating the Germans in 1940's Battle of Britain.

The film, which was shown in the United States as *Spitfire*, was critically acclaimed for its quiet drama. Marking an auspicious start for the biographies born of the war, it was followed through the years by fare that ranged from the

Previous spread: A scene from *Patton* (1970).
Below: Advance forces of the Seventh Army landing on Sicily – July 1943 – from *Patton*.

Above: The Battle of the Little Big Horn from *Little Big Man* (1970). Left: Dustin Hoffman played the lone white survivor of the Little Big Horn in *Little Big Man*.

average to the superior and that, even in its worst moments, never showed itself as patently inferior. Here is what the years brought since 1945.

1945 itself proved a banner year for biographies, with Twentieth Century Fox responsible for *Captain Eddie*, and Warner Brothers for *God Is My Co-Pilot* and *Pride of the Marines*. Of the trio, *Captain Eddie* – with Fred Mac-Murray in the title role as Edward V Rickenbacker, the World War I flying ace who later became a US automotive and airline executive – proved to be the weakest of the lot. The film is set in 1942 and is played out during the long days when Rickenbacker and several companions were adrift in the Pacific after their plane had crashed while on a government mission. As the men are pitched about on a life raft and face starvation, a series of flashbacks take

Above: A scene of the campaign in North Africa from *Patton* (1970).
Left: Fred MacMurray (as Eddie Rickenbacker) and Lynn Bari in *Captain Eddie* (1945).

MacMurray back through the major incidents in his subject's life.

MacMurray is his customary solid self and gives a pleasing performance, as does Lynn Bari as Rickenbacker's wife. But the picture suffers from its sentimental treatment and idealization of Rickenbacker's character and life. It is at its best in its closing sequences when the screen Rickenbacker, as does the actual Rickenbacker in his 1967 autobiography, sees the hand of God in his Pacific trial and eventual rescue.

God Is My Co-Pilot ranks as slightly stronger fare. Starring Dennis Morgan, the picture tells the story of 34-year-old Colonel Robert Lee Scott who, on being dismissed by the Army as too ancient for combat service, became a hero in Burma with General Claire Chennault's Flying Tigers. The plot and the performances are on the pallid side, with the film making audiences sit

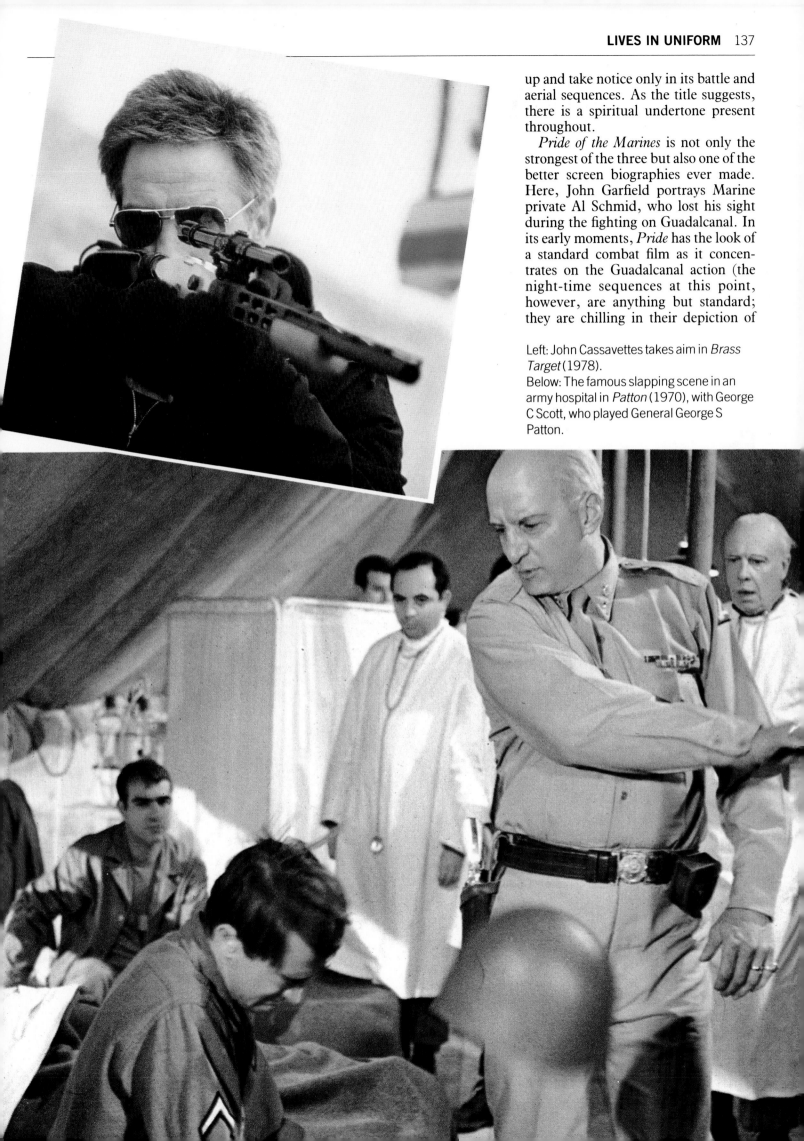

up and take notice only in its battle and aerial sequences. As the title suggests, there is a spiritual undertone present throughout.

Pride of the Marines is not only the strongest of the three but also one of the better screen biographies ever made. Here, John Garfield portrays Marine private Al Schmid, who lost his sight during the fighting on Guadalcanal. In its early moments, *Pride* has the look of a standard combat film as it concentrates on the Guadalcanal action (the night-time sequences at this point, however, are anything but standard; they are chilling in their depiction of

Left: John Cassavettes takes aim in *Brass Target* (1978).
Below: The famous slapping scene in an army hospital in *Patton* (1970), with George C Scott, who played General George S Patton.

tired, frightened soldiers staring into the darkness where an invisible enemy lurks). Once Garfield is wounded, the picture changes its direction and becomes the story of his experiences – in a hospital and then at home – in adjusting to his new life. That story, never once devolving into sentimentality, handles those experiences with intelligence and compassion. In the presence of these qualities, the film is reminiscent of the sensitivity on view a year later in the handling of Harold Russell's double-amputee sailor in *The Best Years of Our Lives*.

Pride of the Marines resembles *Best Years* on yet another count. Both films hit an optimistic, upbeat note in their treatment of adjustment problems. It is obvious that their producers understood that both could be of service to the several million veterans just beginning to endure, physically or psychologically, their own periods of adjustment to civilian life.

John Garfield, whose screen career had been built mainly of tough and cynical characterizations, did some of his finest work in *Pride of the Marines*.

Left: Rosemary de Camp and John Garfield in *Pride of the Marines* (1945), the story of the real life American war hero, Al Schmid.
Opposite: Front row: Richard Boone, James Mason, Walter Kingsford in *The Desert Fox* (1951).
Below: The United States Army Infantry advances in *To Hell and Back* (1955).

His innate toughness is present in his Al Schmid and enables him to meet the trials of his adjustment, but it never over-rides the hesitations, fears, angers and frustrations engendered by his handicap. Rounding out the emotional portrait is his tender concern for the woman facing his problem with him, his wife, beautifully played by Eleanor Parker with the sense of inner strength that has marked so many of her performances.

Both received fine supporting work from Dane Clark (as Schmid's best friend) and sensitive direction from Delmar Daves. Writer Albert Maltz's screenplay was nominated for an Academy Award. For reasons known only to those who dream up movie titles, the picture was shown in Great Britain as *Forever in Love*.

The 1950s and 1960s brought eight biographies of widely varied content.

The Desert Fox (1951) followed the career of Afrika Korps commander General Erwin Rommel from his Tobruk and El Alamein campaigns early in the war to his implication in the 1944 plot to assassinate Hitler. James Mason is excellent in his portrayal of a proud and brilliant officer who becomes increasingly disillusioned with the Nazi Regime and who, on being given the choice to stand trial or commit suicide after the failed assassination, ends his own life with poison.

To Hell and Back (1955) had Audie Murphy reliving the experiences that had made him America's most decorated soldier in World War II. The picture was underplayed throughout by Murphy, Charles Drake and Marshall Thompson. In commenting on its battle scenes, one critic remarked that he had the feeling of watching not actors at work but combat-wise veterans recalling their techniques of old.

Great Britain's *Reach for the Sky* (1956) told the story of Douglas Bader, the RAF pilot who lost both legs in a 1931 plane crash, learned to walk on artificial limbs, pestered his superiors into giving him a fighter assignment in 1940, and became one of Britain's leading aces of World War II. Kenneth More appears as Bader and comes through as a quietly colorful, tough, and humorous man who stubbornly refuses to be bested by his handicap. Without ever being maudlin, the film is inspirational throughout and is dotted with especially good moments: the half-conscious Bader drifting close to death at one point in the days following the amputations, only to be accidentally yanked back to life by a nurse's voice; the recovering Bader and several fellow amputees immensely enjoying a wild ride as they try to drive a car; an annoyed Bader getting up after every fall as he works to master his golf swing; the Luftwaffe allowing the RAF to drop a replacement limb for the one destroyed when Bader is shot down and captured and a frustrated but grudg-

PT 109 (1963) dealt with the World War II naval exploits of a young John F Kennedy. Cliff Robertson, who was selected for the role by the Kennedy family, portrayed the future president in a film that won him praise for his work but that was judged slow-moving and routine combat fare.

There is nothing routine, however, about the work that opened the 1970s – *Patton* (British title: *Patton – Lust for Glory*). Here is a film that seeks the goal of all serious biographical efforts: an honest scrutiny of its subject, warts and all. Winning for itself such critical descriptions as 'splendid,' 'magnificent' and 'monumental,' it achieves that goal in a 170-minute study of General George S Patton's career from Africa in 1942 to war's end in 1945. In all, *Patton* stands with Abel Gance's *Napoleon* (1927) as the finest and most ambitious biography that has been produced to date in any film.

As nothing more than a war film, *Patton* is an excellent piece of work, highlighted with realistic battle scenes, first in Africa, then in Sicily, then France and finally in the snow and ice of

Top left: *The Password is Courage* (1962).
Left: Cliff Robertson as John F Kennedy in *PT 109* (1963) – passing the coconut.
Below: US troops wage war in New Guinea in a scene from *MacArthur* (1977).

ingly admiring Luftwaffe officer taking the limb away when he then uses his mobility to attempt a series of escapes.

The Gallant Hours (1960) was producer-director (and former Navy lieutenant) Robert Montgomery's tribute to Admiral William F 'Bull' Halsey. James Cagney, in a departure from his usual screen characterizations, is quietly effective as Halsey in a film depicting several incidents in the admiral's World War II career.

Hitler (1961) starred Richard Basehart in an episodic and poorly-received psychological study of the Führer, tracing his life from his first activities with the Nazi Party to his death a quarter-century later in the Berlin bunker. Basehart, a fine character actor, especially in his later years, was judged an unconvincing Hitler.

The Password Is Courage (1962), a British production, cast Dirk Bogarde in the role of Charles Coward, a man who drove his Nazi captors to distraction with his repeated escape attempts. The film is painstakingly detailed in its account of several of the attempts.

Gregory Peck, as General Douglas MacArthur, wades ashore on the Philippines in 1945 – from *MacArthur* (1977).

the Battle of the Bulge. But it is George C Scott's portrayal of the colorful and hot-tempered general that lifts the film into the realm of the extraordinary. Guided by a beautifully crafted script (for which Francis Ford Coppola and Edmund H North won an Academy Award), Scott exposes all sides of the Patton character – the regal formality that sees him dress for his first African battle as though performing an age-old ritual; the violent temper that causes the much-publicized slap given a shell-shocked soldier; the sense of honor that is so violated when Eisenhower calls the

slap a 'despicable' action and orders an apology from Patton; the hard humor that is displayed in the giving of that apology to the hospital staff and, conversely, the gentle humor seen when his newly-purchased bull terrier proves to be a timid 'Willie' rather than a ferocious 'William the Conquerer'; his pride in his troops as he stands beside an icy road and watches them on their 48-hour forced march to the Bulge; his sorrow for those who die in battle and, at the same time, his understanding that he helplessly loves the horror that took those lives; his belief in reincarnation and his conviction, that, in previous lives, he has fought in the great battles of history.

Following one of the most unusual opening sequences in screen history – a

splendidly, almost ridiculously uni-formed Patton delivering a speech to his troops (literally, the audience) as he stands before a giant American flag – all these elements come across in a series of major and minor scenes. Underlying them throughout the film is Scott's evocation of the brilliance, toughness and arrogance that made Patton, in General Omar Bradley's opinion, the finest battlefield commander in the US Army. The performance won for Scott an Academy Award, which, for personal reasons, he declined.

Not unexpectedly, *Patton* emerged as the most honored film of 1970. To it went Academy Awards for best picture, best direction (Franklin J Schaffner), best screenplay (based on factual material or material not previously published), best sound and best art/set decoration. Karl Malden, though not acknowledged by the Academy and though not resembling his subject in the least, etched a fine down-to-earth portrayal of the 'soldier's general,' Omar Bradley.

Biographies of two other, perhaps even more consequential World War figures, were attempted later in the 1970s – in Italy's *Mussolini: Ultimo Atto* (1974) and Twentieth Century Fox's *MacArthur* (1977; also known as *MacArthur the Rebel General*). The first, which was titled variously as *The Last Four Days* and *Last Days of Mussolini* for English-speaking audiences, featured an energetic performance by Rod Steiger as the Italian dictator in a depiction of Mussolini's 1943 capture by the Allies, his rescue by the Germans, and his subsequent death at the hands of Italian partisans.

The latter, tracing General Mac-Arthur's career from the early days of the war to his farewell speech before Congress on being stripped of all his commands by President Harry Truman in 1951, is a work that, because of the similarity between the two subjects, has been consistently compared with *Patton* – and has always come off second best. Gregory Peck's interpretation of MacArthur catches the man's dignity and egocentric nature, but simply does not have the bite of Scott's characterization. Yet, Peck is a pleasure to watch throughout and the film is especially impressive in its re-creation of several events, chief among them the return to the Philippines in 1945, the signing of the Japanese surrender aboard the USS *Missouri* that same year, the Inchon landing in 1950, and the dispute with Truman that led to General Mac-Arthur's dismissal. Character actor Ed Flanders is excellent as President Harry S Truman.

MacArthur is one of a scant few biographical films to touch upon the Korean War. The other principal representatives are *The McConnell Story* (1955), *The Eternal Sea* (1955) and *Battle Hymn* (1957). In the first, Alan Ladd is cast as Captain Joseph McConnell, who served as a navigator aboard a B-17 in World War II, became a jet ace in Korea, and subsequently lost his life testing jet aircraft. *The Eternal Sea*, which is reminiscent of *Reach for the Sky*, features Sterling Hayden as

The rescue of a wounded man from a destroyer from *The Eternal Sea* (1955).

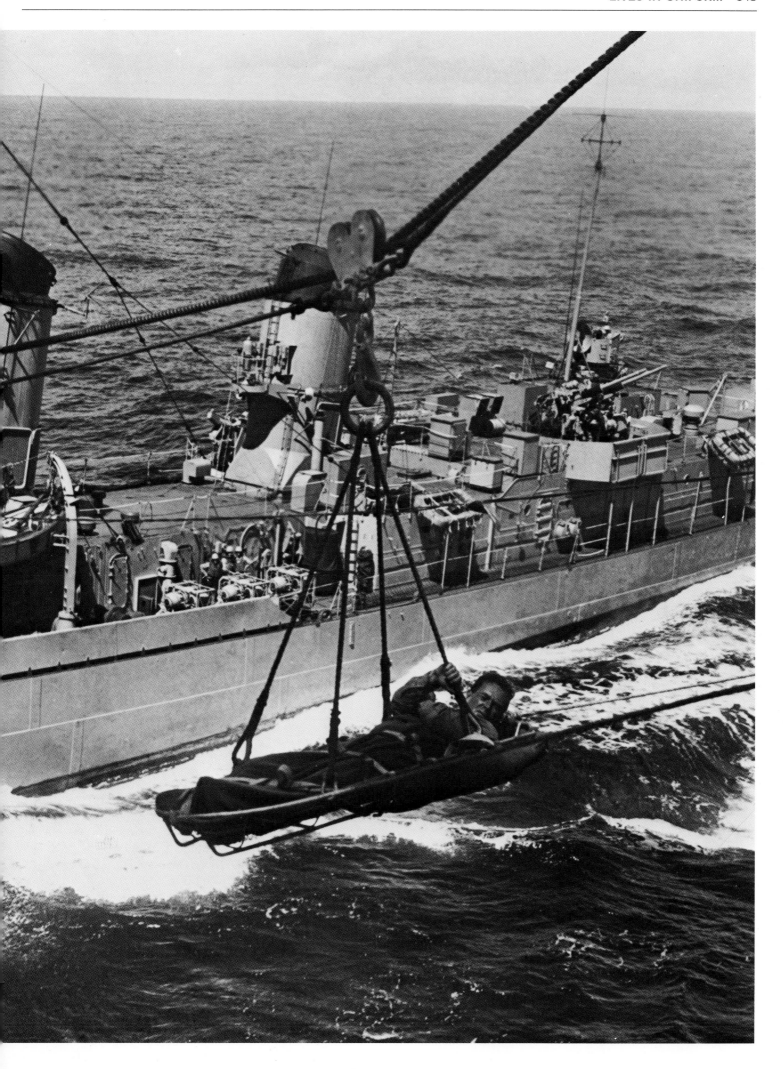

Above: Omar Sharif as Che Guevara, addresses his troops in *Che!* (1969).
Left: Sharif with American ammunition in *Che!*

Admiral John Hoskins who commanded an aircraft carrier in World War II and successfully returned to sea in the Korean War after losing a leg. *Battle Hymn*, a Rock Hudson vehicle, tells the story of a preacher, Dean Hess, who went to South Korea to help those left homeless by the war and eventually founded an orphanage there. The three films, which were intended as family fare, contain healthy streaks of sentimentality. *The McConnell Story*, which was released in Great Britain as *Tiger in the Sky*, is best remembered for its splendid aerial photography.

Though World War II has been responsible for the great bulk of screen biographies, some of the most interesting works seen through the years have dealt with figures from other wars.

Gary Cooper has performed effectively in two such offerings – *Sergeant*

York (1941) and *The Court-Martial of Billy Mitchell* (1955). To say that Cooper is effective in the former is an understatement, as is substantiated by the best-actor Academy Award he received for his impersonation of the Tennessee backwoodsman, Alvin York, who, single-handedly captured 132 German soldiers in the Argonne fighting of World War I.

As good as they are, the scenes of the capture are not the most memorable aspects of the film. Where the picture really hits home is in Cooper's portrayal

Rock Hudson and his orphans in *Battle Hymn* (1957).

of a simple man who, after a hell-raising youth, is transformed into a religious pacifist who must, in a wrenching conflict with his sense of patriotism, decide whether to enlist or stand as a conscientious objector. To that decision Cooper brings an unforgettable anguish that easily matches the anguish communicated in another, perhaps better remembered film that also brought him an Academy Award, *High Noon*.

Cooper's assignment to *Sergeant York* was not a studio decision. For years, the real-life York, whose 1918

feat had won him the Congressional Medal of Honor, steadfastly rejected every Hollywood application – including one from Cecil B DeMille – to film his story. When York at last agreed to a Warner Brothers request, it was with the proviso that he be allowed to supervise all aspects of the production and that Cooper be assigned to the title role.

Happily agreeing, Warners then turned out a film that was criticized for the studio sets meant to pass as the Tennessee backwoods, applauded for its realistic combat sequences, com-

mended for its patriotic ardor at a time when America was facing a new war, and applauded for its performances not only by Cooper but by three of Hollywood's best character players – Walter Brennan, Ward Bond and, in the role of York's mother, the superb Margaret Wycherly. Both Brennan and Miss Wycherly received Academy Award nominations for best supporting performances.

The Court-Martial of Billy Mitchell (titled *One Man Mutiny* for British audiences) saw Cooper's interpretation of the World War I flier and visionary Army general who, in the 1920s, urged the US to develop an air force independent of naval or army control. His broadly publicized view that the military was negligent and almost treasonable in its slow development of the nation's air power lead to his 1925 trial for insubordination and a suspension from military service for five years. Mitchell resigned from the Army in 1926 and worked in civilian aviation until his death in 1936.

Cooper gives a thoughtful performance as the troubled Mitchell who stubbornly pushes the cause of air power and, in the process, so incurs the wrath of a reactionary general (solidly played by Charles Bickford) that the court-martial results. Joining Cooper and Bickford with fine performances are Ralph Bellamy as a congressman sympathetic to Mitchell's cause, Rod Steiger as Mitchell's defense attorney, and James Daly as the prosecuting attorney. In all, though Mitchell's character is not as fully explored as York's had been 13 years earlier, the film adds up to an arresting and accurately-done courtroom drama.

American figures from earlier periods have been interpreted by George Arliss, Robert Stack, Richard Dix, Errol Flynn and Robert Shaw. To Arliss went the title role in *Alexander Hamilton* (1935), an account of the work done during and after the American Revolutionary War by the man destined to be the first US Secretary of the Treasury. Stack proved to be dour but effective in his portrayal of another Revolutionary War hero, *John Paul Jones* (1959). Dix was effective as a thoughtful Sam Houston freeing Texas from Mexico in *Man of Conquest* (1939). Both Flynn and Shaw were assigned the role of the Indian fighter, General George Custer, in two widely separated films – Flynn in *They Died with Their Boots On (1941)* and Shaw in *Custer of*

Above: Gary Cooper (right), with Ward Bond, contemplates joining the Army in *Sergeant York* (1941).
Right: Cooper as the embattled General Mitchell in *The Court-Martial of Billy Mitchell* (1955).

the West (1968). Both men gave energetic portrayals in offerings that took Custer from his cavalry exploits in the Civil War to his death at Little Big Horn, with the Flynn picture said to be the more historically accurate of the two. Both films were highlighted with exciting, well-staged battle sequences.

In one of the most off-beat of American military biographies, *The Long Gray Line* (1955), Tyrone Power was cast as Sergeant Marty Maher, the Irish immigrant who came penniless to the

United States in the late 1800s, joined the Army, and built a lifelong career for himself as an athletic trainer at the military academy at West Point. Based on Maher's book, *Bringing up the Brass*, the film deals with the sergeant's influence on students who were to become the country's military leaders in World War II, among them Dwight D Eisenhower. Power, Maureen O'Hara as his wife and Donald Crisp as his father give strong performances under John Ford's direction in a picture that is unabashedly sentimental and, though criticized as somewhat over-long, a pleasure to watch throughout.

If we turn from American figures, we find that the motion picture has gone from the earliest to the latest of times in search of subjects for its military biographies. From the earliest times have come the inspirations for Richard Burton's often brilliant characterization of *Alexander the Great* (1956), Victor Mature's muscular *Hannibal* (1959), Nikolai Cherkassov's heroic thirteenth

century soldier-prince in Russia's *Alexander Nevsky* (1938) and John Wayne's unlikely Genghis Khan in *The Conqueror* (1955). Wayne was badly miscast in the role, but the same cannot be said of Omar Sharif, who appeared effectively (at least, he looked the part) in the entertaining compound of saga and sex, *Genghis Khan* (1965). Later historical eras have given audiences George Arliss

as a dignified General Arthur Wellesley, the Duke of Wellington, in *The Iron Duke* (1935); Peter O'Toole's complex T E Lawrence in the excellent *Lawrence of Arabia* (1962), and Omar Sharif's doomed Cuban revolutionary, Che Guevara in *Che!* (1969).

Of all the military characters in history, Napoleon Bonaparte has received the most screen attention. Over

Two actors portraying General George Custer.
Above: Robert Shaw in *Custer of the West* (1968).
Left: Errol Flynn in *They Died With Their Boots On* (1941).

the years, he has been portrayed by Charles Boyer in *Conquest* (1937; British title: *Marie Walewska*), a Greta Garbo vehicle concerning the most enduring of the 'Little Corporal's' mistresses; Herbert Lom in *Young Mr Pitt* (1941); Marlon Brando in *Desirée* (1954), the biography of his ex-fiancée, later Queen of Sweden; and Rod Steiger in *Waterloo* (1970), the excellent Italian-USSR account of Napoleon's final battle and also of the series of events leading up to it.

Without doubt, the finest and most ambitious depiction of the man's life came from France's Abel Gance in 1927 – *Napoleon* or, as it is sometimes also called, *Napoleon vu par Abel Gance*. Begun two years earlier, this silent film astonished its premiere audience with its 28 reels that ran upwards of five hours and took Bonaparte from his Corsican childhood to the French Revolution and thence to his victory over the British at Toulon, his marriage to Josephine de Beauharnais, and his invasion of Italy in 1796. Starring in the title role is Albert Dieudonné.

Dieudonné does a fine impersonation of Napoleon, but it is Gance's directorial genius that is the star of the picture. Anticipating Cinerama by a quarter-century, Gance, one of the immortals of the French film industry,

Peter O'Toole as *Lawrence of Arabia* (1962).

shot portions of *Napoleon* with three synchronized cameras and showed the results simultaneously on a triple wide screen. It was a process that he called Polyvision and that gave the production a visual sweep never seen before on the screen. In addition – incorporating two other at-the-time experimental processes – he photographed several scenes

Richard Burton addresses his troops, in *Alexander the Great* (1956).

in color and 3-D. Deciding that the scenes might divert attention from the film's story line, he cut them prior to the premiere date.

Gance, who had begun acting in French films in 1909 and had been a

critically acclaimed director since 1917, was 36 years old when he began filming *Napoleon*. Into it, along with his Polyvision photography, went some of the most inventive camera techniques ever seen, before or since. At one point, to give added impact to a chase scene, he strapped a camera on a galloping horse. At another, to accentuate the rhythms of a folk dance, the camera was attached to a dancer's chest. At still another, to

Above: Charles Boyer (as Napoleon) and Greta Garbo (as his mistress, the Polish Countess Marie Walewska) in *Conquest* (1937).
Top: Marlon Brando (as Napoleon) and Jean Simmons in *Désirée* (1954).

communicate the violent rocking of a storm-tossed boat, the camera was affixed to a giant pendulum. In mob and battle scenes, Gance suspended the camera overhead from wires so that his hundreds of extras (sometimes several thousand) could be seen all at once.

Gance originally intended *Napoleon* to be first in a series of six pictures that would take Bonaparte through the battle of Waterloo to his final exile on the island of St Helena. It was a plan that never materialized because of financial problems. Gance did, however, add stereophonic sound effects to the film in 1934. Also added was a 12-minute prologue. The prologue was set in 1815, with the picture itself then serving as a giant flashback. Gance prepared a new version of the 1934 film in 1955, and then still another in 1971. The 1955 version, which runs 135 minutes, is titled *Napoleon-Bonaparte*. The 1971 version, released as *Bonaparte et la Revolution*, contains a new color sequence and runs 275 minutes.

Though shown in 28 reels for its premiere, Napoleon was cut to 17 for its Europe distribution. It was never seen in its entirety in the United States because MGM, on acquiring the American distribution rights for $400,000, felt that Gance's Polyvision might, in the expensive era of converting to sound, bring on yet another costly

Above: Albert Dieudonné as Napoleon in Abel Gance's *Napoleon* (1927).
Left: A scene from Gance's *Napoleon*.

technical revolution. US audiences were given only a disastrously cut version that they greeted with bewilderment and disdain.

Recently, after years of exhaustive research and recutting, English critic Kevin Brownlow presented *Napoleon* again. With a marvelous score by Carmine Coppolla, the picture was a tremendous success, playing in art houses across the United States. It is nice to report that Gance was still alive at the time, and after years of obscurity, saw *Napoleon* recognized for the masterpiece it was.

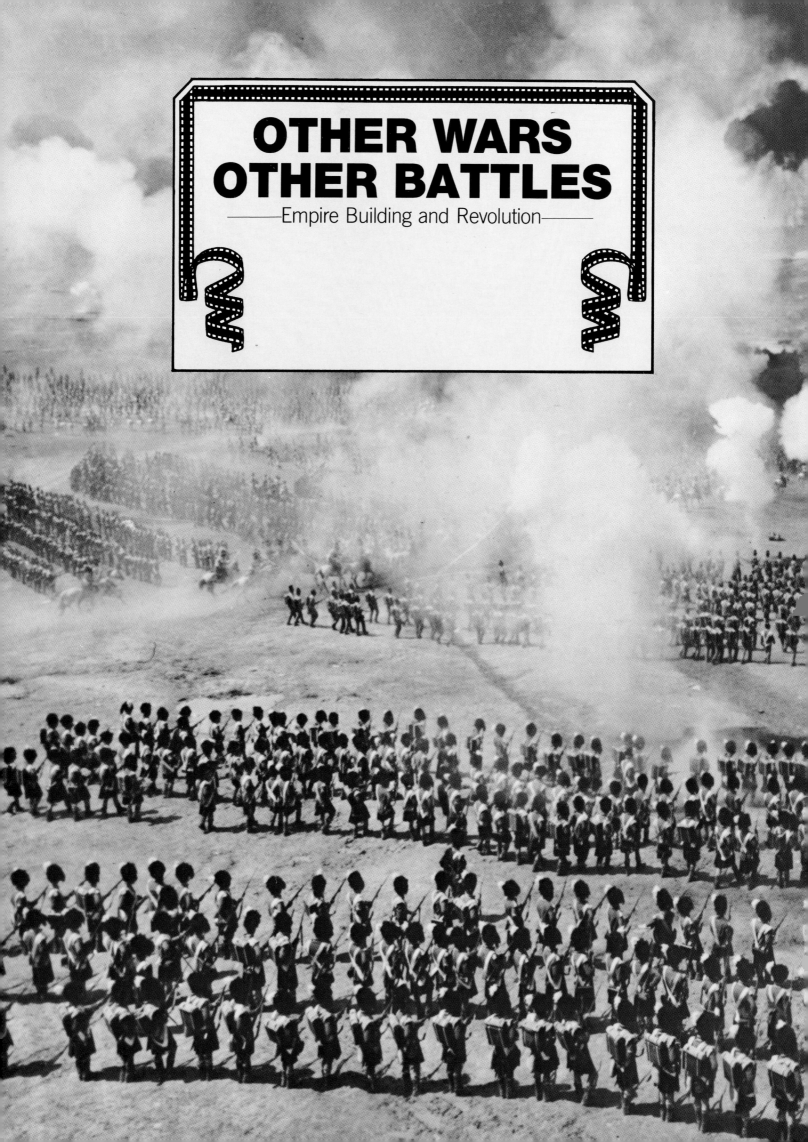

OTHER WARS OTHER BATTLES

Empire Building and Revolution

Thus far, we've dealt principally with the films devoted to the wars of the twentieth century. But, wherever there has been a war on a revolution in the course of history, the genre has turned in that direction for subject matter. Just how far back into history has it reached? Just how diverse have been the conflicts it has selected as topics? The following list should leave no doubt as to the answers:

In one of its major segments, D W Griffith's *Intolerance* (1916) travels back to 538 BC for the fall of Babylon to Cyrus the Persian.

The lively spectacle, *The 300 Spartans* (1962) is set in 480 BC and takes as its heroes the small band of rugged Greeks who held an invading Persian army at bay for three days at the pass of Thermopylae.

Previous spread: A panorama of *Waterloo* (1970) in which the British troops confront the French troops under Napoleon.
Below: The escape of the gladiators in *Spartacus* (1960).

Spartacus (1960), widely judged to be one of the best spectaculars ever made, sees Kirk Douglas as the rebel leader whose slave army revolted against the Roman Republic and captured all of southern Italy in the Gladiators' War of 73-71 BC.

Trading in his gladiator's rig for a fur jacket and leather shield, Douglas – joined by a one-handed Tony Curtis – heads a free-wheeling Norse invasion of 9th-century England in *The Vikings* (1958).

Sadly looking like what they are – model boats in a studio tank – the ships of the Spanish Armada attack England in 1588, only to run up against a dashing Laurence Olivier and *his* model fleet in *Fire Over England* (1936), an early (and unsuccessful) British attempt to compete with Hollywood in the spectacle market.

The White Angel and *The Charge of the Light Brigade* (both 1936) are Warner Brothers versions of the mid-nineteenth century Crimean War, with Kay Francis as nurse Florence Nightingale in the former, and Errol Flynn as a gallant

British officer fighting the battle of Balaclava in the latter. Both films are recognized as inaccurate depictions ('hokum' is the description often used) of the war, though *Angel* has been much praised for the realism of its hospital sequences, while *Brigade* has never been faulted for its action sequences, but which involved stunts which were subsequently banned as inhumane. A more accurate *Brigade* was produced in 1968, with a cast headed by Trevor Howard and with a script that transformed the tale of a century-old conflict into an effective modern and anti-war statement.

The Boer War of 1899 to 1902 serves as the backdrop for Australia's superb *Breaker Morant* (1980), a film that, while essentially a courtroom drama, includes field sequences showing the brutality of the fighting. Britain's *Young Winston* (1972), a biography of the wartime Prime Minister's youthful years, also features excellent sequences on the South African upheaval.

Military troubles in China early in this century provide the inspiration for

Above: The one-eyed Kirk Douglas accuses the one-handed Tony Curtis in *The Vikings* (1958).
Right: Edward Woodward as *Breaker Morant* (1980), a film about the Boer War in South Africa.

55 Days at Peking (1962) and *The Sand Pebbles* (1966). The former is a Charlton Heston-David Niven spectacle about the foreign legations under rebel siege for close to two months at the Chinese capital in the Boxer Rebellion of 1900. *The Sand Pebbles*, set in 1926 and based on Richard McKenna's best-selling novel, pits an American gunboat on the Yangtze River against some vicious Chinese warlords. The film won an Academy Award nomination as the year's best picture and a best-actor nomination for Steve McQueen. And, speaking of Chinese warlords, no moviegoer of the 1930s can forget the evil spun by the sinister Warner Oland

about Marlene Dietrich and Clive Brook in *Shanghai Express* (1932). Quite as wily is Akim Tamiroff as he tries to make life difficult for Gary Cooper and Madeleine Carroll in *The General Died at Dawn* (1936).

The Irish struggle for independence in the opening decades of this century is chronicled in *The Plough and the Stars* and *Beloved Enemy* (both 1936). Preston Foster leads a citizen army in the former, much to Barbara Stanwyck's worry, while in the latter Brian Aherne bargains for peace with the British and suffers the pains of a romance with Englishwoman Merle Oberon, his 'beloved enemy.'

Problems surrounding the Jewish state of Israel have likewise served as film themes. *Exodus* (1960), starring Paul Newman and adapted from Leon Uris' epic novel, depicts the fighting and the political struggles involved in the 1948 establishment of the state.

Above: Akim Tamiroff, as the general, is flanked by Gary Cooper and Madeleine Carroll in *The General Died at Dawn* (1936). Behind Cooper is the ubiquitous Richard Loo.
Left: Marlene Dietrich in trouble in *Shanghai Express* (1932).
Opposite: The *Exodus* embarks to Israel (1960).
Opposite inset: *Operation Thunderbolt* (1977).

Israel's *Operation Thunderbolt* (1977, also released as *Entebbe: Operation Thunderbolt*) is a tightly-knit account of the Israeli Army's commando attack to rescue 104 airline passengers held prisoner in Uganda in 1976. (That hostage crisis has also served as the basis for two major US television films – *Raid on Entebbe* and *Victory at Entebbe*.)

Though the conflicts of virtually every century since there was such a thing as history have served as themes for the genre, several have received such attention that they cannot be placed in the above list. They require special sections of their own.

Of the wars fought on US soil, the Civil War has always proved the most enticing to moviemakers. Earlier conflicts are recalled in no more than a handful of films – the French and Indian Wars in the fine Spencer Tracy-Robert Young action feature, *Northwest Passage* (1940), and the War of 1812 in *Old Ironsides* (1926); in *The Magnificent Doll* (1946), starring an apparently miscast but yet effective Ginger Rogers as Dolley Madison; in *The President's Lady* (1953), with Charlton Heston as Andrew Jackson defending New Orleans and then rising to the presidency; and in *The Buccaneer* and its remake (1938 and 1958), an entertaining yarn about French pirate Jean Lafitte assisting Jackson at New Orleans, with Lafitte played by Fredric March in the first edition, and Yul Brynner in the second. Texan efforts to break free of

country – the Revolutionary War – has received short shrift when compared to the fighting of 1860 to 1865. Representative of the few Revolutionary War films seen through the years have been *Betsy Ross* (1917), with Alice Brady in the title role; *The Howards of Virginia* (1940), a Cary Grant vehicle fashioned from Elizabeth Page's novel, *The Tree of Liberty*; the French-Italian *Lafayette* (1961) and, of all things, a musical – *1776* (1972), the screen version of the Broadway success.

As for the Civil War, it began its movie service as early as 1910 – in *A Dixie Mother* and the first adaptation of Harriet Beecher Stowe's nineteenth century abolitionist novel, *Uncle Tom's Cabin*. Both were produced by J Stuart Blackton's Vitagraph. *Uncle Tom's Cabin* was recycled by Universal in 1913, Peerless in 1914, and Paramount in 1918.

The very best early treatment given the war came in 1915, with D W Griffith's masterful *The Birth of a Nation*. In its story of two families split by the fighting and in its memorable Battle of Petersburg sequences, *Birth* is regarded by many critics as being not just the best early treatment but the best treatment ever seen of the conflict, surpassing even *Gone with the Wind*.

Left: Spencer Tracy surveys the destruction after raiding an Indian village in *Northwest Passage* (1940), the fictionalized version of the true story of Major Rogers' Rangers.
Below: David Niven, Burgess Meredith and Ginger Rogers in *The Magnificent Doll* (1946).

The feeling is that *Birth*, with its battle sequences, goes more deeply into the war itself than does *GWTW*, which, aside from the siege of Atlanta, remains behind the lines and sees the disaster through a woman's eyes.

But both pictures are superb, each in its own way, and so a comparison is not only odious but also useless. On its own, *The Birth of a Nation* ranks in many film histories as the single-most important work in the development of the American motion picture as an art (on this score, beating out even 1941's *Citizen Kane*). In its running time of close to three hours, it deftly uses and then advances beyond all the cinematic techniques known at the time. Further, in its scope, character relationships, varied settings and opposing armies of extras, it involves production complexities rarely dreamed of in Griffith's day. It is credited as the achievement most responsible for starting the US motion picture industry on the road to full maturity.

Griffith prepared and released an abbreviated version of the picture in 1930, equipping it with music and sound effects. He also added a brief prologue which saw him introduce the film in a conversation with Walter Huston.

Released simultaneously in 1915 with *The Birth of a Nation* was another Civil War offering, *The Warrens of Virginia*, the work of a 34-year-old director whose name would one day be more famous – but no more respected – than Griffith's, Cecil B DeMille. The picture is one that neatly sets romance

Opposite bottom: Charlton Heston (as Andrew Jackson) in *The President's Lady* (1953).

Mexico in the 1830s have been touched upon in Republic's modest *Man of Conquest* (1939) and John Wayne's flamboyant *The Alamo* (1960), with Wayne himself as Davy Crockett, Richard Widmark as James Bowie, and Laurence Harvey as William Travis. The nineteenth century wars with the Indian nations, while inspiring many a slam-bang western, have only occasionally been given genuinely serious treatments, among the better efforts being director John Ford's *Fort Apache* (1948) and Alan Ladd's *Drum Beat* (1954), a story of California's Modoc uprising.

Even the conflict that founded the

Above: Victor McLaglen (second from left),
John Wayne, Henry Fonda and George
O'Brien in *Fort Apache* (1948).
Right: Lillian Gish is given a soulful look by a
Union soldier in *The Birth of a Nation*
(1915).

and intrigue against the upheaval of
war. It begins as the young Southern
woman, Agatha (Blanche Sweet), and
her Northern sweetheart, Ned Burton
(House Peters), are separated at the
outbreak of hostilities. While Agatha,
the daughter of a general, works on the
Confederate homefront, Ned joins the
Union Army and fights bravely during
the next years, only to have his superiors order him to rejoin and spy on his
beloved's influential family for the
purpose of sabotaging a train with sup-
plies badly needed by the Confederate
Army. His efforts to this end see him
captured. Though sentenced to die,
Ned proudly rejects Agatha's plans for
his escape. Just as he is about to step
before a firing squad, word arrives of
Lee's surrender at Appomattox. The
young soldier is spared and reunited
with Agatha.

The Warrens of Virginia attracted little attention, both from critics and potential customers, undoubtedly because it stood so much in the shadow of *The Birth of a Nation*. This was unfortunate because, as Anthony Slide remarks in the book *Fifty Great American Silent Films, 1912-1920*, it features a compact plot and intelligent direction. Slide adds that DeMille's battle scenes are as well staged as Griffith's.

The next years saw moviemakers concentrating on films about World War I. Yet the Civil War did not go completely ignored. Benjamin Chapin starred in the *Lincoln Cycle* (1917). In *Hayfoot, Strawfoot* (1919), Charles Ray played a rural innocent who joins the Union Army. Lewis Stone (destined to become the head of MGM's Hardy family in 17 years) was effective as a captured Confederate officer in *Held by the Enemy* (1920), as was Jack Holt as his Union captor. Vitagraph put playwright David Belasco's stage success, *The Heart of Maryland*, before the cameras in 1921. Warner Brothers did a remake in 1927, with Jason Robards (Sr) and Dolores Costello as the young lovers (he from the North, she from the South) whose lives are made miserable by the war, but who nevertheless, in the name of romance, overcome all difficulties.

1927 marked the release of the decade's best Civil War picture, Buster Keaton's marvelously funny and just as marvelously exciting *The General*. Critical consensus holds it to be Keaton's finest comedy, his masterpiece.

In the film, which is based on an actual 1863 incident, Keaton plays railroad engineer Johnnie Grey who attempts to enlist in the Confederate Army immediately after the firing on Fort Sumter. Without being told the reason, he is turned down because the military recognizes his occupation to be an essential one to the Southern cause. His beloved Annabelle (Marion Mack), when he is unable to explain why he is still a civilian, jumps to the conclusion that he never even tried to enlist. She wants nothing to do with such a coward as he is.

As if Johnnie's life isn't complicated enough, some Union spies steal what is, along with Annabelle, his greatest love – his locomotive, *General*. Kidnapping Annabelle, they make their way north aboard the locomotive, their plan being

to destroy Confederate communications as they travel. Enraged – but with Keaton's world-famous 'stone face' letting that rage show only in his expressive eyes – Johnnie goes in pursuit, using first a handcar (it ends up in a river on encountering a section of uprooted track), then a thoroughly unwieldy bicycle, and finally a Confederate locomotive called *The Texas*. On at last overtaking the villains, he rescues both Annabelle and the *General* and heads for home, whereupon the spies board *The Texas* and begin a chase that ends with the picture's most memorable sequence.

That sequence comes when Johnnie crosses a wooden bridge, brings the *General* to a grinding halt, and dashes back to set the bridge afire. On arriving at the span, the leader of the spies decides that, though the bridge is weakening by the moment, it will support *The Texas*. The locomotive starts across, only to have the bridge give way at mid-span and send *The Texas* crashing into the river below. The scene was not done with trick photography, but with an actual locomotive and buckling bridge. Biographer Tom Dardis, in his excellent *Keaton*, remarks that the single take of the disaster reportedly cost $42,000 and was the most expensive shot made in films to that date.

Altogether, *The General*, which the comedian also directed (with Clyde Bruckman), is an amalgam of Keaton's comic and personal views. It is laced with one sight gag after another. It contains hair-raising stunts, long a hallmark of his work. It reveals the sad hilarity that, in common with Chaplin (*Modern Times*), Keaton sees in the machinery that is taking over life. And, again in common with Chaplin (*Shoulder Arms* and *The Great Dictator*), the horror that he sees in war and in its apparent inevitability.

Technically, the film was one of the most difficult ever undertaken by Keaton, a man who, as one glimpse of the monster windstorm sequence in *Steamboat Bill, Jr* (1928) will prove, loved technical challenges. For the sake of authenticity, he insisted on using single-gauge locomotives of Civil War vintage, going so far as to request the loan of the engine used in the actual 1863 incident, a request that Tennessee authorities, not liking the idea of a comedy about the war, refused. Then, unable to find usable narrow-gauge tracks still extant in neither Tennessee nor Georgia, he scouted other areas until he came up with an appropriate location in Oregon. To that spot, he brought his locomotives and 17 railroad cars jammed with equipment. Keaton

Right: Buster Keaton oils his beloved locomotive in *The General* (1926).

then hired 500 members of the Oregon National Guard to work as extras, garbed them in Confederate and Union uniforms, housed them in tourist cars provided by the Union Pacific Railroad, and rounded up 125 horses for them to ride. The film was shot in about two months – in June and July of 1926.

The result was well worth the effort. *The General* was critically hailed wherever it was seen. On its re-release in 1962, it found a new world-wide success. An international poll of film critics in 1967 saw it listed among the 'Twelve Best Comedy Films of All Time.'

The early- and mid-1930s brought four pictures set against a Civil War backdrop. In 1930, Walter Huston (though, perhaps because of the day's primitive sound equipment, he seemed to be 'speechifying' rather than simply speaking his dialogue) did an effective *Abraham Lincoln*, with fine direction by D W Griffith and excellent support from Kay Hammond as a tart Mary Todd Lincoln. Equally effective in *The Prisoner of Shark Island* (1936) was Warner Baxter's portrayal of Samuel Mudd, the physician who suffered imprisonment for treating the wounded Booth. The dimpled Shirley Temple spent 1935 in the service of the Confederacy, first as *The Littlest Rebel* and then as *The Little Colonel*. Singing and dancing in both, she successfully pleaded with President Lincoln to release her imprisoned father in the former. The latter was devoted to her post-war repair of a family split caused by the fighting.

And in 1939 came David O Selznick's monumental *Gone with the Wind*. So much has already been written about it and so well known is its story line and production history that any description of the picture at this date would be an exercise in repetition. For the purposes of this book, let it suffice to say that, as a war offering, *GWTW* is, as earlier mentioned, a behind-the-lines film, spending much of its first half on the efforts of upper-class Southerners to support the Confederate Cause while attempting to maintain their mannered lifestyle of old. It takes a first-hand look at the war itself only in the siege of

Left: An American Civil War battle scene from *Raintree County* (1958), a film based on the Pulitzer Prize novel.

Opposite top: David Niven (center left) and Charlton Heston in *55 Days at Peking* (1962).
Below: John Wayne and Richard Widmark in *The Alamo* (1960).
Bottom: Laurence Harvey in *The Alamo*.

Atlanta, concentrating then on the burning of the city. The sequence, in addition to the conflagration itself, is highlighted by two splendid scenes – Scarlett's flight when faced with assisting in an amputation surgery and her horror at the sight of wounded soldiers on stretchers for as far as the eye can see in the Atlanta railway station.

The film's latter half, when not dealing with Scarlett's passion for Ashley Wilkes and her marriage to Rhett Butler, provides a solid look at the post-war problems – the hunger, the invasion of carpetbaggers, the problems of freed and confused slaves, the stealthy emergence of the Klu Klux Klan and the tragedy of a graceful way of life now 'gone with the wind.'

The film still ranks as one of the most honored in Hollywood history. The long list of its Academy Award honors – and others – are to be found in the next chapter.

GWTW was followed by *Sante Fe Trail* (1940), an impressive western starring Errol Flynn as the cavalryman who captures John Brown (Raymond Massey), the abolitionist whose activities helped to bring on the war. Since then, the Civil War has received but scant screen attention – in Audie Murphy's sensitive portrayal of the Stephen Crane novel of cowardice recognized and heroism achieved, *The Red Badge of Courage* (1951); *Raintree County* (1958) starring Elizabeth Taylor, from the novel by Ross Lockridge Jr; and James Stewart's alternately tough and sentimental but always deeply moving performance in *Shenandoah* (1965). Possibly the most unusual film of the breed is *The Beguiled* (1971), starring Clint Eastwood as a wounded Union soldier who is harbored, fought over, and then murdered by a group of sexually starved women at a Southern finishing school for young ladies. It all sounds like sadistic and melodramatic claptrap (which it is), but turns out to be an effective and moody piece, principally because of the work done by Eastwood, Geraldine Page, and Elizabeth Hartman.

Above: Ashley Wilkes (Leslie Howard) is treated for a wound as Clark Gable, Vivien Leigh and Olivia DeHaviland look on in *GWTW*. Top: Vivien Leigh walks among the wounded in Atlanta in *Gone With the Wind* (1939).

Of the revolutions fought beyond American soil, moviegoers are best acquainted with the French Revolution (1789), the Russian Revolution of 1917 and the Spanish Civil War (1936-39). Receiving less attention have been the Philippine uprising at the turn of this century after the island nation had been ceded to the US, the Mexican Revolution of 1867 and Mexico's Madero Revolution of 1910. Set against the first is *The Real Glory* (1939) starring Gary Cooper; the second, *Juarez* (1939) with Paul Muni in the title role; and the third, *Viva Villa* (1934), an MGM biography of revolutionary bandit Francisco (Pancho) Villa (Wallace Beery) and a film that caused the company no end of trouble with the Mexican Government. The problem cropped up during one night off from location filming when actor Lee Tracy, playing an American newsman, stood on a Mexico City hotel balcony and, said to be a little worse for alcoholic wear, urinated on a military parade below. The Mexican Government immediately withdrew its cooperation in the production, and MGM just as hastily cancelled Tracy's contract. His scenes were reshot with Stuart Erwin. Tracy never fully lived down the scandal, though he returned to Hollywood in 1964 for a very effective appearance as the US President in *The Best Man*.

The French Revolution is best remembered from two productions, the first British and the second American – *The Scarlet Pimpernel* (1934) starring Leslie Howard and *A Tale of Two Cities* (1936) with Ronald Colman. Both are screen versions of novels – respectively, Baroness Orczy's thriller about the daring but outwardly foppish Englishman who rescues French aristocrats sentenced to the guillotine, and Charles Dickens' epic novel of Sidney Carton, the barrister who sacrifices his life to save a look-alike friend, who is the husband of the woman Carton loves,

from the guillotine. The production with Colman was the second, and best, of four screen tellings of *A Tale of Two Cities*. The first, with Maurice Costello in the Carton role, came from Vitagraph in 1911. The second, released by Fox in 1917, starred William Farnum. The final production to date was a modest 1956 effort that featured Dirk Bogarde at the head of a fine British cast. (The story was also filmed for television in the early 1980s). As for *The Scarlet Pimpernel*, it fathered two

Above: Wallace Beery (left) in *Viva Villa* (1934), with Joseph Schildkraut.
Left: Leslie Howard as *The Scarlet Pimpernel* (1935) discusses neckcloths with Raymond Massey.

British offerings – a stylish but nevertheless weak sequel, *The Return of the Scarlet Pimpernel* (1937) and Leslie Howard's entertaining modernization of the plot for World War II purposes, *Pimpernel Smith* (1941).

Also due mention here is MGM's *Marie Antoinette* (1938). Designed as a spectacle for Norma Shearer in the title role, the picture is an over-long, ponderous, snail-paced account of life in the French court that was to fall to the revolutionaries.

The Revolution led to the ascendancy of Napoleon Bonaparte and the Napoleonic Wars, which, in turn, led to a string of films, some of them entertaining and some of them memorably impressive. Ranking high among the former is *Captain Horatio Hornblower*

(1951; British title: *Captain Horatio Hornblower, RN*) starring Gregory Peck, while the latter are represented by 1935's *Becky Sharp*, an adaptation for Miriam Hopkins of William Makepeace Thackery's novel, *Vanity Fair*, and the first feature shot in the just-perfected three-color Technicolor process; *The Pride and the Passion* (1957), which, based on C S Forester's *The Gun*, has English officer Cary Grant assisting Frank Sinatra, Sophia Loren and Spanish troops in mounting a giant cannon in the hopes of repulsing an invading Napoleon; two top-notch versions of Leo Tolstoy's novel on the French invasion of Russia, *War and Peace* (1957 and 1967); and *Waterloo* (1970), with its superb action sequences depicting the 'little Corporal's' final battle. The great British naval hero, Lord Nelson, has been twice portrayed on the screen – by a somber Laurence Olivier in *That Hamilton Woman* (1942; British title: *The Lady Hamilton*) and a rambunctious Peter Finch in Britain's *Bequest to the Nation* (1973; US title: *The Nelson Affair*). Both are highlighted by excellent sequences of the battle of Trafalgar and Nelson's death of a wounded suffered in the fighting. The scenes of this great admiral's demise are overwhelming.

The Russian Revolution was put to use early on in Hollywood's sound history, in *Rasputin and the Empress* (1932; also released as *Rasputin the Mad Monk*), MGM's heavy-handed spectacle that assembled the Barrymore family – Ethel and brothers Lionel and John – for their first and only screen appearance together. Obviously enjoying himself thoroughly, Lionel had a scene-stealing field day as the charismatic monk who had an extraordinary influence on the Russian imperial family, while Ethel was cast as Empress Alexandra, the wife of Nicholas II (Ralph Morgan), whose naive mismanagement of government at last triggered the revolution of 1917. John Barrymore was cast as in a thinly-disguised portrait of Prince Youssoupoff.

Left: The Russian march out of Moscow in *War and Peace* (1956).
Opposite top: Peter Finch as Lord Nelson in *The Nelson Affair* (1973).
Below: Christopher Plummer as Wellington raises a stirrup cup before the battle in *Waterloo* (1970).

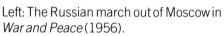

As did *Viva Villa* two years later, the film got MGM into hot water – but not because of any performer's misbehavior. This time, the script was the culprit. It portrayed Youssoupoff as Rasputin's murderer and contained a scene in which Princess Youssoupoff was raped. The real Prince and Princess, very much alive and annoyed by the whole thing, successfully sued MGM for libel. The court held that the Prince had been Rasputin's killer but that the rape had been dreamed up by the scenarist.

Aside from a few action scenes and the climactic moment when the royal family is removed from a railroad car and executed by revolutionaries, *Rasputin and the Empress* is played out in the Nicholas-Alexandra household. But not so the USSR's *Lenin v Octiabrye* (1937; English title: *Lenin in October*). Here, Boris Shchukin portrays Lenin during the revolution's fighting and

Right: Gregory Peck as *Captain Horatio Hornblower* (1951) threatens a French courier.

then during the subsequent year when he works with such figures as Stalin (I Golshtab) and Maxim Gorky (Nikolai Cherkassov). The film was made on Stalin's instructions to celebrate the uprising's twentieth anniversary. Shot in just three months, it served as a good and not-too-fictionalized propaganda item. In the wake of one success, the USSR tried for another and came up with the well directed and acted but historically inaccurate *Lenin v 1918* (1939; English title: *Lenin in 1918*).

Later years brought two fine re-creations of the upheaval – *Dr Zhivago* (1965) and *Reds* (1981). Adapted from the novel by Boris Pasternak and directed by David Lean, *Dr Zhivago*

chronicles the revolt as seen from both sides of the fence. A film that truly merits its publicity appelation – sweeping – it is photographically splendid, especially in its winter sequences with their vast expanses of snow and ice-mantled scenery, and provides more than ample opportunities for Omar Sharif, Julie Christie, Rod Steiger, Alec Guinness and Tom Courtenay to display their performing skills. Its visual magnificence and performances aside, however, *Dr Zhivago* has been accused of a deadly talkiness and of so reducing the complexities of the Pasternak novel to fit a 192-minute running time that many of its scenes make little or no sense.

Reds, a writing, directing and acting triumph for Warren Beatty, is based on the life of radical journalist John Reed, who chronicled the revolution. Much of the story concentrates on Reed's romance with fellow journalist Louise Bryant (beautifully portrayed by Diane Keaton), but gives an incisive account of the revolution's street fighting and the political and social upheavals that accompanied the uprising.

The Spanish Civil War received its earliest attention in Walter Wanger's *Blockade* (1938) and *Arise My Love* (1940), both of which have been mentioned previously. Its most ambitious treatment was on view in 1943, in Paramount's adaptation of the Ernest

Opposite: A desert attack from *Beau Geste* (1939).
Below: Anthony Quinn as Omar Mukhtar, the Bedouin hero who fought Mussolini, in *Lion of the Desert* (1979).

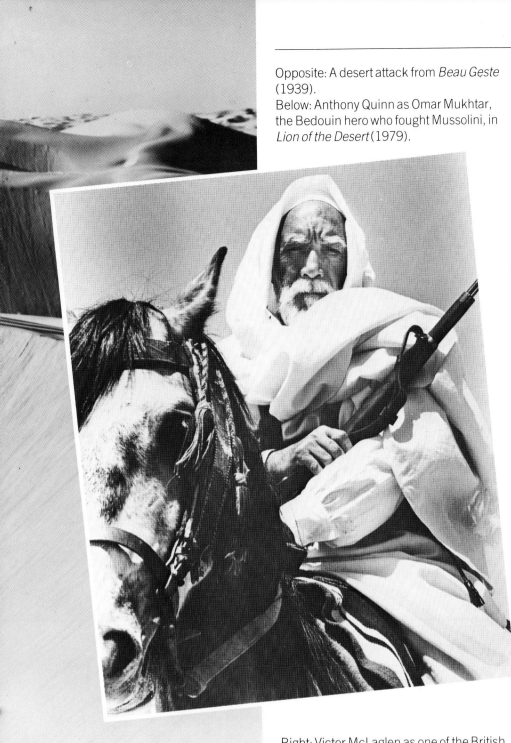

latter – *La Guerre Est Finie* (1966), a French-Swedish production whose English title is *The War Is Over* – Yves Montand portrays an aging professional revolutionary who, at the end of his quarter-century exile in Paris, re-examines his political ideals and returns to Spain, unaware that the national police are awaiting him. Though stars Montand, Ingrid Thulin and Genevieve Bujold were praised for their work, the film is considered a dullishly talky one and is chiefly remembered for its unique invention of flashforwards.

If ever a nation did moviemakers a favor, it was Great Britain when her explorers and colonizers took her to Arabia, Africa and India. Her military efforts to control these areas have provided the source of inspiration for dozens of films, from RKO's *The Lost Patrol* (1934) to director Richard Attenborough's acclaimed *Gandhi* (1982). Quite as well as any other examples, these two films demonstrate the disparity of themes attempted. *The Lost Patrol*, tautly directed by John Ford, concerns a handful of British troopers who, on losing their bearings in the Mesopotamian desert and taking refuge in an oasis, are systematically annihilated by unseen Arab riflemen; it stars Victor McLaglen, Wallace Ford and, in a memorable departure from his

Right: Victor McLaglen as one of the British troopers in the Mesopotamian desert in *The Lost Patrol* (1934).

Hemingway best-selling novel, *For Whom the Bell Tolls*. Telling the story of a group of peasant partisans who set out to blow up a bridge of strategic value to the enemy, the film stars Gary Cooper as the American mercenary, Robert Jordan, who lends them a needed hand. Ingrid Bergman is memorable (when was she not?) as the tragic Maria. Strong support comes from Katina Paxinou and Akim Tamiroff as peasants. For her work, Miss Paxinou received the year's Academy Award as best supporting actress, while Tamiroff's cowardly and oft-repeated line – 'I do not provoke' – become a US byword for several months.

The film, a critical and financial

success, was judged to be exciting and suspenseful, with the only sour note being the charge that it perhaps moved too slowly at times. In addition to the Paxinou award, *For Whom the Bell Tolls* received Academy nominations for best picture, best actor (Cooper), and best actress (Miss Bergman).

The subsequent years have seen two films concerning exiled veterans of the Spanish conflict. In the first – the beautifully made but, in great part, uninteresting comment on human and political morality, *Behold A Pale Horse* (1964) – Gregory Peck is cast as a guerrilla who goes into exile at the end of the war and then returns 20 years later to assassinate a brutal police chief. The

horror-film roles, Boris Karloff as a soldier whose religious fanaticism combines with the frightening presence of death to drive him mad. *Gandhi*, of course, tells the story of the pacifist leader, expertly played by Ben Kingsley, who worked so effectively for the liberation of his nation.

Africa has served as the setting for such diverse plots as *The Sun Never Sets* (1939), *Zulu* (1964) and *Khartoum* (1966), the first being a routinely done story of two brothers (Basil Rathbone and Douglas Fairbanks Jr) successfully thwarting a German munition maker's attempt to plunge the world into war, and the second a suspenseful and remarkably accurate account of the defense of a mission station in Natal by 120 British soldiers, against 4000 attacking Zulus in 1879. Featured here are fine performances by Stanley Baker and Michael Caine as two English soldiers. *Khartoum* describes the ten-month defense of that city in 1885-86 by General Charles 'Chinese' Gordon against an uprising by the Arabian leader, the Mahdi. Charlton Heston portrays Gordon, with the Mahdi being played by Laurence Olivier. Both men

do fine work in a film that, despite its excellent battle sequences and superb photography, has been generally dismissed as dullish.

At this point, it must be admitted that not Britain but another colonial power, France, with its Foreign Legion, has supplied moviegoers with their best African entertainments, including such films as *Under Two Flags*, Twentieth Century's 1936 adaptation (Universal did a silent version in 1921) of the Ouida novel that has a sultry cafe girl (Claudette Colbert) helping a dashing Legionnaire (Ronald Colman) in battle and losing her own life in the process; Laurel and Hardy's at-times-funny but generally sad reminder of better comic days now gone, *Flying Deuces* (1939) and, best of all, *Beau Geste* (1926, 1939, and 1966).

Of the three treatments given *Beau Geste*, those of 1926 and 1939 offer the superior film tellings of the Percival C Wren novel about the young English-

Below: Michael Caine aims a Martini-Henry in *Zulu* (1964).

Opposite: Mahatma Gandhi (Ben Kingsley) marches with Martin Sheen in *Gandhi* (1982). Opposite inset: Ava Gardner in *Bhowani Junction* (1955) with Bill Travers.

man who runs off to join the Foreign Legion after stealing a family diamond at the time it is to be sold by his beloved and financially hard-pressed aunt. He is followed and joined in uniform by his two loyal brothers. The inseparable threesome ultimately participate in the defense of a desert fortress against Arab attack, with the young Englishman dying and one of his brothers returning home to reveal his reason for the diamond theft – to protect the aunt from trying to sell a fake gem while at the same time enabling her to collect the insurance money for its theft.

Ronald Colman, Neil Hamilton and Ralph Forbes played the brothers in the silent 1926 version, with the same parts going to Gary Cooper, Ray Milland, and Robert Preston in 1939. The best role in any of the versions belongs to the martinet Legionnaire sergeant who, as his men die at the fort, props them up in the gun ports so that the Arabs will think the place is defended by a major force. Noah Beery (Sr) played the part in 1926. Brian Donlevy, with a handsome scar etched across one cheek and happily growling his most famous line – 'I will make you into sold-jers. I

promise you' – used the role to steal the 1939 edition from everyone except J Carrol Naish as a sniveling, traitorous soldier.

The 1966 remake has been called a slick retelling of the story, but simply does not live up to the tradition of good-fun melodrama established by its predecessors. The brothers were played by Guy Stockwell, Doug McClure, and Leslie Nielsen. Telly Savalas had a fine time as the sadistic sergeant.

The 1926 film was followed by a 1931 sequel, *Beau Ideal*, starring Lester Vail and Ralph Forbes. Here, one of the

Above: Tyrone Power explains the new cartridges to his Moslem soldiers in *King of the Khyber Rifles* (1954).

Top: Ralph Richardson receives a letter with a feather in it as June Duprez and C Aubrey Smith (left) look on in *Four Feathers* (1939).

brothers (Forbes) joins with a Legionnaire friend to thwart an uprising launched by a treacherous emir. It turned out to be pretty pallid stuff that was not at all helped by the primitive sound equipment of the day.

Italy's occupation of Libya has also provided audiences with screen fare, namely *Lion of the Desert* (1979; also known as *Omar Muktar – Lion of the Desert*), the battle-riddled story of a Bedouin leader who resisted the intruders with an unrelenting guerrilla campaign between 1912 and 1931. The picture, which is reported to have cost more than $30 million, is of epic proportions, not the least of which is

Anthony Quinn's vigorous portrayal of the Bedouin.

But back to the British. Director Zoltan Korda's excellent *Four Feathers* (1939) is principally set in Africa as it tells the story of the young Englishman (John Clements) who, thinking himself unfit for military life, resigns his regimental commission on the eve of a campaign to the Sudan and is branded a coward by his friends, receiving from each a white feather as a token of their contempt. He then travels to Africa and, in a series of private exploits, regains his self-respect and returns the feathers. Clements performs strongly as the young Englishman, only to have his work somewhat over-shadowed by Ralph Richardson's inspired portrayal of a comrade blinded in the Sudan fighting. The film, an adaptation of the A E W Mason novel, was widely praised not only for its performances and story line but for its fine use of

color. It is one of the first British color films.

Four Feathers was originally made in 1929 as an early Paramount talkie, with Richard Arlen doing well in the role later given to Clements. It appeared for a third time in 1955, under the title *Storm Over the Nile*. Here, though its battle scenes should have been given greater scope through the use of widescreen filming, it turned out to be feeble stuff. Laurence Harvey, Anthony Steele and Ian Carmichael starred.

And now we come to India, the source of many a film through the years – such fare, for instance, as *King of the Khyber Rifles* (1954), starring Tyrone Power in the often violent tale of a British regiment threatened by an Indian potentate in 1857 and saved by one of its officers, a half-caste. And, in *Bengal Brigade* (also 1954; British title: *Bengal Rifles*), there's noble officer Rock Hudson being cashiered out of the nineteenth century army on false evidence and going undercover to foil a nasty Indian plot and clear his name. On the more serious side, in *Bhowani Junction* (1955), sympathetic officer Stewart Granger watches India's fight for independence in the post-World War II era.

Of the various military films set against an Indian background, the two most fondly-remembered are, without doubt, *Lives of a Bengal Lancer* (1935) and *Gunga Din* (1939).

Lives of a Bengal Lancer, a highly entertaining mixture of comedy, drama, and adventure, casts Gary Cooper, Franchot Tone, and Richard Cromwell as three British officers who fall into the clutches of evil potentate Douglas Dumbrille. As he holds them prisoner and tortures them (with lighted bamboo sticks under the fingernails) for vital military information, their unit advances on his stronghold. They help to save the day for their comrades by breaking free and raising havoc within the fortress, a havoc that reaches its climax when Cooper, flaming torch in hand, dashes through a hail of bullets to an enemy ammunition building and blows the place sky high.

Cooper and Tone make an amusing pair as experienced officers who enjoy an off-handed friendship. Particularly memorable is the scene in which Cooper, toying with a fakir's flute in his quarters, attracts and 'charms' a deadly cobra. Passing by on his way to shave, Tone pauses to view the spectacle, nonchalantly remarks that the cobra

will strike when the music stops, and continues on his way. A desperate Cooper, running slowly out of breath, plays on. At the last moment, in the instant before Cooper can pipe no longer, Tone steps back into the room and kills the snake with a single revolver shot.

For sheer good fun, though, *Lives of a Bengal Lancer*, as good as it is, has always had to take a back seat to RKO's spectacular *Gunga Din*. Drawing its title – but precious little else – from Rudyard Kipling's poem about a British regiment's waterboy, the picture is an action delight throughout as it traces the adventures and misadventures of three inseparable sergeant friends who like nothing better than to fight with anyone in sight and make life miserable for stiff-backed fellow sergeant Robert Coote. Playing the threesome to the hilt are Cary Grant as the

Left: Gary Cooper at the head of his troop in *Lives of a Bengal Lancer* (1935).
Below: An attack scene from *Bengal Brigade* (1954).

gold-greedy Cutter, Douglas Fairbanks Jr as the about-to-leave-the-army-for-marriage Ballantine, and Victor McLaglen as McChesney, who impatiently endures Cutter's fancies of wealth and is determined to thwart Ballantine's wedding plans. Dancing about them throughout is a nimble and brown-faced Sam Jaffe as Gunga Din, the waterboy who yearns to be a regimental bugler.

and, as the sergeants stage a marvelous brawl with their captors, Gunga Din climbs to the dome and sounds a warning to the regiment with his beloved and ever-present bugle. The warning, which Jaffe repeats until – riddled with Thuggee bullets – he topples to his death, is all the regiment needs. It assembles itself in battle formation and brings the planned revolt crashing down with a cavalry charge. The film

ends with Cutter no wealthier than ever, with Ballantine deciding to remain in the service, and with McChesney quietly tearful as the poem 'Gunga Din,' composed on the spot by regimental visitor Kipling, is read in memory of the heroic waterboy. As for Gunga Din himself – now designated an honorary bugler with the regiment and buried with full military honors – he grins happily out at the audience as his

Expertly directed by George Stevens, the film builds to a breathtaking climax when Cutter, in his pursuit of riches, makes his way to a gold-domed mountain temple held by Eduardo Ciannelli and his Thuggees, a murderous religious sect. On entering and finding that Ciannelli is planning the conquest of India, Cutter is taken prisoner. McChesney and Ballantine learn of his whereabouts and, with Gunga Din, attempt his rescue, only to be themselves captured. The four are made to stand on a balcony beneath the gold dome and watch as their regiment unwittingly moves towards a Thuggee ambush. The prisoners break loose

Above: Warren Beatty and Diane Keaton in *Reds* (1981).
Right: Richard Gere and Debra Winger in *An Officer and a Gentleman* (1982).
Opposite top: Cary Grant is captured by Eduardo Ciannelli in *Gunga Din* (1939).
Opposite bottom: Grant and Fairbanks in *Gunga Din*.

spirit, to the soft swirl of bagpipes, offers a smart salute at final fade.

RKO, though it boasted the Astaire-Rogers dance team, was not a giant among Hollywood's major studios in 1939. *Gunga Din*, made for the then-staggering sum of $1,915,000, ranked as its most expensive investment to date. It was an investment that paid off handsomely. The picture attracted and thrilled audiences everywhere, earned widespread critical praise for its cheerful toughness and, on television today, continues to charm old-movie devotees.

Gunga Din, under the title *Soldiers Three*, was handed to Stewart Granger, David Niven, Robert Newton and Walter Pidgeon for a remake in 1951. Frank Sinatra, Dean Martin, and Sammy Davis Jr turned the whole idea into a western in 1961, calling it *Sergeants Three*. Neither version came anywhere near matching the original's quality. But, then, what could?

MEDALS WON
—The Most Decorated—

The finest examples of cinematic warfare have won honors over the years for their excellence and public impact. Considering that the films do not come from the larger of the industry's genres, the number of recognitions granted them is startling. Since early 1929, when the first Academy Awards banquet was held in Los Angeles, nearly 200 pictures with war themes or backgrounds have received tributes from the world's film evaluation groups. The recognitions themselves have ranged from those for a given year's best picture and best performances to those for best screenplay, best art decoration, and such technical achievements as best cinematography and best special effects.

And there have been periods – years, obviously, when the world was preoccupied with open conflict – in which war films have dominated the honors lists. For example, in 1943, the Academy Award for best picture went to *Casablanca*, with *Watch on the Rhine* and *For Whom the Bell Tolls* nominated for that same Oscar. Receiving nominations for various other Academy prizes were *So Proudly We Hail* for best supporting actress (Paulette Goddard), best original screenplay, and best black-and-white photography; *Destination Tokyo* and *Action in the North Atlantic* for best original screen stories; *North Star* for best original screenplay; and *Corvette K-225*, *Five Graves to Cairo*, *North Star*, *Sahara* and *Air Force* for best black-and-white cinematography. J Carroll Naish was nominated as best supporting actor for his work in *Sahara*.

1943 stands as a high-water mark so far as the recognitions given cinema warfare are concerned. Never before had so many war films appeared on the Academy's lists, and the number has never been equaled since. Nor did the honors stop with the Academy. Both *Casablanca* and *Watch on the Rhine* were named to the US National Board of Review's list of the 10 best English language films of the year. The National Board of Review placed Katina Paxinou of *For Whom the Bell Tolls* on its list of best actresses. The Golden Globe Awards singled out Paul Lukas as 1943's best actor for his work in *Watch on the Rhine*. He also won the Academy's Oscar for best actor.

While the passing years have seen approximately 200 war films receive honors, only a small percentage of the entrants can claim to have taken or been mentioned for the greatest share of the most coveted recognitions. In this chapter, we're going to pay homage to these 'most decorated' films as they pass in review. We'll do so by listing the honors accorded them by what are generally considered to be the world's five leading film evaluation groups.

In the order of their founding, the groups are: the US Academy of Motion Picture Arts and Sciences (1928), the US National Board of Review (1930), the New York Film Critics Circle (1935), the US Golden Globe Awards (1943), and the British Academy of Film and Television Arts, originally the British Film Academy (1948).

The honors and recipients, listed in chronological order, are:

1927/28

Seventh Heaven (USA)
US Academy Awards:
    Best Director (Frank Borzage)
    Best Actress (Janet Gaynor)
    Writing, Adaptation
US Academy Award Nomination: Best
  Picture

Wings (USA)
US Academy Awards:
    Best Picture
    Engineering Effects

1929/30

All Quiet on the Western Front (USA)
US Academy Awards:
    Best Picture
    Best Director (Lewis Milestone)
US Academy Award Nominations:
    Writing
    Cinematography
US National Board of Review:
  List of 10 Best Films

1938

La Grande Illusion/Grand Illusion (France)
US Academy Award Nomination: Best
  Picture
New York Film Critics: Best Foreign Film

1939

Gone With the Wind (USA)
US Academy Awards:
    Best Picture
    Best Director (Victor Fleming)
    Best Actress (Vivien Leigh)
    Best Supporting Actress (Hattie
      McDaniel)
    Screenplay
    Cinematography, Color
    Interior Decoration
    Film Editing
US Academy Award Nominations:
    Best Actor (Clark Gable)
    Best Supporting Actress (Olivia de
      Havilland)
US National Board of Review (1940):
  List of 10 Best American Films
  List of Best Performances (Leigh)
New York Film Critics: Best Actress (Leigh)

1940

Foreign Correspondent (USA)
US Academy Award Nominations:
    Best Picture
    Best Supporting Actor (Albert
        Basserman)
    Original Screenplay
    Cinematography, Black & White
US National Board of Review:
    List of 10 Best American Films

The Great Dictator (USA)
US Academy Award Nominations:
    Best Picture
    Best Actor (Charles Chaplin)
    Best Supporting Actor (Jack Oakie)
US National Board of Review:
    List of 10 Best American Films
    List of Best Performances (Chaplin)
New York Film Critics: Best Actor (Chaplin)

1941

Sergeant York (USA)
US Academy Awards:
    Best Actor (Gary Cooper)
    Film Editing
US Academy Award Nominations:
    Best Picture
    Best Director (Howard Hawks)
    Best Supporting Actor (Walter Brennan)
    Best Supporting Actress (Margaret
        Wycherly)
    Original Screenplay
    Cinematography, Black & White

1942

In Which We Serve (Great Britain)
US Academy Award Nominations (1943):
    Best Picture
    Original Screenplay
US National Board of Review:
    List of 10 Best English-Language Films
    List of Best Performances (Bernard
        Miles, John Mills)
New York Film Critics: Best Film

Mrs Miniver (USA)
US Academy Awards:
    Best Picture
    Best Director (William Wyler)
    Best Actress (Greer Garson)
    Best Support Actress (Teresa Wright)
    Screenplay
    Cinematography, Black & White
US Academy Award Nominations:
    Best Actor (Walter Pidgeon)
    Best Supporting Actor (Henry Travers)
    Best Supporting Actress (Dame May
        Whitty)
US National Board of Review:
    List of 10 Best English-Language Films
    List of Best Performances (Greer
        Garson, Teresa Wright)

Wake Island (USA)
US Academy Award Nominations:
    Best Picture
    Best Supporting Actor (William
        Bendix)
    Original Screenplay
US National Board of Review: List of 10 Best
    English-Language Films
New York Film Critics: Best Director (John
    Farrow)

1943

Casablanca (USA)
US Academy Awards:
    Best Picture
    Best Director (Michael Curtiz)
    Screenplay
US Academy Award Nominations:
    Best Actor (Humphrey Bogart)
    Best Supporting Actor (Claude Rains)
    Cinematography, Black & White
US National Board of Review:
    List of 10 Best English-Language Films
    List of Best Directors (Curtiz)

For Whom the Bell Tolls (USA)
US Academy Award: Best Supporting
    Actress (Katina Paxinou)
US Academy Award Nominations:
    Best Picture
    Best Actor (Gary Cooper)
    Best Actress (Ingrid Bergman)
    Best Supporting Actor (Akim Tamiroff)
    Cinematography, Color
US National Board of Review: List of Best
    Actresses (Paxinou)

1944

Lifeboat (USA)
US Academy Award Nominations:
    Best Director (Alfred Hitchcock)
    Original Story
    Cinematography, Black & White
US National Board of Review: List of 10 Best
    English Language Films
New York Film Critics: Best Actress
    (Tallulah Bankhead)

1946

The Best Years of Our Lives (USA)
US Academy Awards:
    Best Picture
    Best Director (William Wyler)
    Best Actor (Fredric March)
    Best Supporting Actor (Harold Russell)
    Screenplay
    Musical Score, Dramatic or Comedy
        Picture
    Special Award: To Harold Russell for
        the hope and courage he gave to his
        fellow veterans through his
        appearance in the film

US National Board of Review:
    Best Director (Wyler)
    List of 10 Best Films
New York Film Critics:
    Best Film
    Best Director (Wyler)
US Golden Globe:
    Best Motion Picture, Drama
    Best Non-Professional Actor
        (Russell)
British Academy (1947): Best Film

1947

Shoeshine (Italy)
US Academy Award: Special Award for
    Outstanding Film Made Under Adverse
    Conditions
National Board of Review: List of 10 Best
    Films

1948

The Search (USA)
US Academy Award: Motion Picture Story
US Academy Award Nominations:
    Best Director (Fred Zinnemann)
    Best Actor (Montgomery Clift)
    Screenplay
US National Board of Review: List of 10 Best
    Films
US Golden Globe:
    Best Screenplay
    Best Film Promoting International
        Understanding
    Special Award: Best Juvenile Actor
        (Ivan Yandl)
British Academy (1949): United Nations
    Award

1949

Battleground (USA)
US Academy Award: Cinematography,
    Black & White
US Academy Award Nominations:
    Best Picture
    Best Director (William A Wellman)
    Best Supporting Actor (James
        Whitmore)
US Golden Globe:
    Best Supporting Actor (Whitmore)
    Best Screenplay

The Bicycle Thief/Bicycle Thieves (Italy)
US Academy Award: Special Award as The
    Most Outstanding Foreign Film
US Academy Award Nomination:
    Screenplay
US National Board of Review:
    Best Film
    Best Director (Vittorio De Sica)
New York Film Critics: Best Foreign Film
US Golden Globe: Best Foreign Film
British Academy: Best Film

Twelve O'Clock High (USA)
US Academy Awards:
Best Supporting Actor (Dean Jagger)
Sound Recording
US Academy Award Nominations:
Best Picture
Best Actor (Gregory Peck)
US National Board of Review (1950):
List of 10 Best American Films
New York Film Critics (1950): Best Actor
(Peck)

1952

Les Jeux Interdits/Forbidden Games
(France)
US Academy Award: Best Foreign
Language Picture
US National Board of Review: List of Five
Best Foreign Films
New York Film Critics: Best Foreign Film
British Academy (1953): Best Film

1953

From Here to Eternity (USA)
US Academy Awards: Best Picture
Best Director (Fred Zinnemann)
Best Supporting Actor (Frank Sinatra)
Best Supporting Actress (Donna Reed)
Screenplay
Cinematography, Black & White
Sound Recording
Film Editing
US Academy Award Nominations:
Best Actor (Montgomery Clift)
Best Actor (Burt Lancaster)
Best Actress (Deborah Kerr)
US National Board of Review:
List of 10 Best American Films
New York Film Critics: Best Film
Best Director (Zinnemann)
Best Actor (Lancaster)
US Golden Globe:
Best Director (Zinnemann)
Best Supporting Actor (Sinatra)

1957

The Bridge on the River Kwai (Great Britain)
US Academy Awards: Best Picture
Best Director (David Lean)
Best Actor (Alec Guinness)
Screenplay Based on Material from
Another Medium
Cinematography/Musical Score
Film Editing
US Academy Award Nomination: Best
Supporting Actor (Sessue Hayakawa)
US National Board of Review:
Best American Film
Best Director (Lean)
Best Actor (Guinness)
Best Supporting Actor (Hayakawa)

New York Film Critics:
Best Film
Best Director (Lean)
Best Actor (Guinness)
US Golden Globe:
Best Film, Drama
Best Director (Lean)
Best Actor (Guinness)
British Academy:
Best Film
Best British Film
Best Actor (Guinness)
Screenplay

1959

The Bridge (West Germany)
US Academy Award Nomination: Best
Foreign Language Film
US National Board of Review (1961): Best
Foreign Film
US Golden Globe: List of Five Best Foreign
Films

1960

Ballad of a Soldier (USSR)
US Academy Award Nomination (1961):
Story and Screenplay Written Directly for
the Screen
British Academy (1961): Best Film

1961

The Guns of Navarone (USA)
US Academy Award: Special Effects
US Academy Award Nominations:
Best Picture
Best Director (J Lee Thompson)
Screenplay Based on Material from
Another Medium
US Golden Globe:
Best Film, Drama
Best Musical Score

Judgment at Nuremberg (USA)
US Academy Awards:
Best Actor (Maxmillian Schell)
Screenplay Based on Material from
Another Medium
US Academy Award Nominations:
Best Picture
Best Director (Stanley Kramer)
Best Actor (Spencer Tracy)
Best Supporting Actor (Montgomery
Clift)
Best Supporting Actress (Judy
Garland)
Cinematography, Black & White
US National Board of Review: List of 10 Best
American Films
New York Film Critics: Best Actor (Schell)
US Golden Globe:
Best Director (Kramer)
Best Actor (Schell)

1962

Lawrence of Arabia (Great Britain)
US Academy Awards:
Best Picture
Best Director (David Lean)
Cinematography, Color
Art Direction/Set Direction, Color
Sound/Musical Score
Film Editing
US Academy Award Nominations:
Best Actor (Peter O'Toole)
Best Supporting Actor (Omar Sharif)
Screenplay Based on Material from
Another Medium
US National Board of Review: List of 10 Best
English Language Films
US Golden Globe:
Best Film, Drama
Best Director (Lean)
Best Supporting Actor (Sharif)
Best Cinematography, Color
British Academy:
Best Film
Best British Film
Best British Actor (O'Toole)
Best Screenplay, British Film

The Longest Day (USA)
US Academy Awards:
Cinematography, Black & White
Special Effects
US Academy Award Nomination: Best Picture
US National Board of Review: Best English
Language Film
US Golden Globe: Cinematography, Black &
White

1964

**Dr Strangelove; or How I learned to Stop
Worrying and Love the Bomb** (Great Britain)
US Academy Award: Screenplay Based on
Material from Another Medium
US Academy Award Nominations:
Best Picture
Best Director (Stanley Kubrick)
Best Actor (Peter Sellers)
New York Film Critics: Best Director (Kubrick)
British Academy:
Best Film
Best British Film
United Nations Award
Art Direction, British Film, Black & White

1965

Dr Zhivago (USA)
US Academy Awards:
Screenplay Based on Material from
Another Medium
Cinematography, Color
Art Direction/Set Direction, Color
Costume Design
Musical Score, Substantially Original

US Academy Award Nominations:
  Best Picture
  Best Director (David Lean)
  Best Supporting Actor (Tom Courtenay)
US National Board of Review:
  Best Actress (Julie Christie)
  List of 10 Best English Language Films
US Golden Globe:
  Best Film
  Best Director (Lean)
  Best Actor, Drama (Omar Sharif)
  Best Screenplay
  Musical Score, Original

1969

Oh! What a Lovely War (Great Britain)
US Golden Globe: Best English Language
  Film
British Academy:
  United Nations Award
  Best Actor (Laurence Olivier)
  Cinematography
  Costume Design
  Sound
  Art Direction

1970

M★A★S★H (USA)
US Academy Award: Screenplay Based on
  Material from Another Medium
US Academy Award Nominations:
  Best Picture
  Best Director (Robert Altman)
  Best Supporting Actress (Sally
    Kellerman)
US Golden Globe: Best Film, Musical/
  Comedy
British Academy: United Nations Award

Patton (USA)
US Academy Awards:
  Best Picture
  Best Director (Franklin J Schaffner)
  Best Actor (George C Scott, declined)
  Story and Screenplay Based on
    Factual Material or Material Not
    Previously Published
  Art Direction/Set Direction
  Sound
  Film Editing
US Academy Award Nomination:
  Cinematography
US National Board of Review:
  Best English Language Film
  Best Actor (Scott)
US Golden Globe: Best Actor, Drama (Scott)

1978

Coming Home (USA)
US Academy Awards:
  Best Actor (Jon Voight)
  Original Screenplay
US Academy Award Nominations:
  Best Picture
  Best Director (Hal Ashby)
  Best Actress (Jane Fonda)
  Best Supporting Actor (Bruce Dern)
  Best Supporting Actress (Penelope
    Milford)
US National Board of Review:
  Best Actor (Voight)
  List of 10 Best English Language Films
New York Film Critics:
  Best Actor (Voight)
  Best Supporting Actor (Walken)
US Golden Globe:
  Best Actor, Drama (Voight)
  Best Actress, Drama (Fonda)

The Deer Hunter (USA)
US Academy Awards:
  Best Picture
  Best Director (Michael Cimino)
  Best Supporting Actor
    (Christopher Walken)
  Sound
  Film Editing
US Academy Award Nominations:
  Best Actor (Robert De Niro)
  Best Supporting Actress
    (Meryl Streep)
  Original Screenplay
  Cinematography
New York Film Critics: Best Film
US Golden Globe: Best Director (Cimino)
British Academy:
  Cinematography
  Film Editing

1979

Apocalypse Now (USA)
US Academy Awards:
  Cinematography
  Sound
US Academy Award Nominations:
  Best Picture
  Best Director (Francis Ford Coppola)
  Best Supporting Actor (Robert Duvall)
  Screenplay Adapted from Another
    Medium
US National Board of Review: List of 10 Best
  English Language Films
US Golden Globe:
  Best Director (Coppola)
  Best Supporting Actor (Duvall)
British Academy:
  Best Director (Coppola)
  Best Supporting Actor (Duvall)

As impressive as the above honors list is, it is an incomplete one. It does not – in fact, cannot – include a number of excellent films – namely, all those that were made either before film evaluation bodies came into being or during the first years of the US Academy of Motion Picture Arts and Sciences, when that organization was yet too provincial to acknowledge foreign products. And so this chapter – and this book – would not be complete without a salute to such notable and, in many intances, magnificent efforts as *The Birth of a Nation, Intolerance, War Brides, The Heart of Humanity, Shoulder Arms, The Big Parade, Arsenal, Battleship Potemkin, Les Croix de Bois,* and Abel Gance's *Napoleon.*

At present, undoubtedly because of the Vietnam debacle and the awful realization that the next conflict can well be our last, the public has turned away from realistic warfare and has sent it into eclipse. The battles, yes, are still there on view, but they have become mainly, as such fare as *Star Wars* and the James Bond thrillers make clear, the province of science fiction and espionage yarns. As for military life itself, as evidenced by *Stripes, Private Benjamin,* and *An Officer and a Gentleman,* it seems to be much in the hands of comedy and romance. How long the eclipse will last is anybody's guess. Since the popularity of any film type is a cyclical matter, we can expect to see, at some point in the future, a return to those air, sea, and land battles once so familiar to audiences everywhere. All other film genre have come and gone and come again. There is no reason to think that the same will not happen to filmed warfare.

But when? We hope soon. Ever since its birth, filmed warfare has appealed to audiences on several levels. Depending on the level, it has generated undiluted excitement, titillated (unhappily) our sense of violence, roused our patriotic spirit and strengthened our grasp of history. But, at its very deepest level, it has imbued us with keen sympathies and terrible understanding, as did *All Quiet on the Western Front.* It is because of what can be accomplished at this deepest level that the war film's rapid emergence from its present eclipse is to be hoped for. Only this kind of film, and none other, can, when realistically and sensitively presented, tell us the truth of what happens to humans and their world when that world is ripped asunder by the age-old business of war – the debasing, ennobling, exhilarating, exhausting and inhumane business that has ultimately come, over the centuries since the pointed stick, to threaten the destruction of us all.

FILMOGRAPHY

Above and Beyond 1952 (USA, MGM). D: Melvin Frank, Norman Panama. S: Robert Taylor, Eleanor Parker, James Whitmore.

Above Us the Waves 1955 (GB). D: Ralph Thomas. S: John Mills, John Gregson, James Robertson Justice.

Abraham Lincoln 1930 (USA, UA). D: D W Griffith. S: Walter Huston, Kay Hammond, Ian Keith.

Aces High 1976 (GB). D: Jack Gold. S: Malcolm McDowell, Christopher Plummer, John Gielgud.

Action in the North Atlantic 1943 (USA, War). D: Lloyd Bacon. S: Humphrey Bogart, Raymond Massey, Julie Bishop.

Advance to the Rear/British title: **Company of Cowards?** 1964 (USA, MGM). D: George Marshall. S: Glenn Ford, Melvyn Douglas, Stella Stevens.

Air Force 1943 (USA, Warner). D: Howard Hawks. S: John Garfield, Gig Young, Arthur Kennedy.

Air Raid Wardens 1943 (USA, MGM). D: Edward Sedgwick. S: Stan Laurel, Oliver Hardy, Edgar Kennedy.

Alamo, The 1960 (USA, UA-Wayne). D: John Wayne. S: John Wayne, Laurence Harvey, Richard Widmark.

Alexander Nevsky 1938 (USSR). D: Sergei Eisenstein. S: Nikolai Cherkassov, Nikolai Okhlapov.

Alexander the Great 1956 (USA, UA). D: Robert Rossen. S: Richard Burton, Danielle Darrieux, Fredric March.

All Quiet on the Western Front 1930 (USA, Univ). D: Lewis Milestone. S: Lew Ayres, Louis Wolheim, John Wray.

All the Young Men 1960 (USA, Col). D: Hal Bartlett. S: Alan Ladd, Sidney Poitier.

Ambush Bay 1966 (USA, UA). D: Ron Winston. S: Hugh O'Brian, Mickey Rooney.

Amere Victoire/English title: **Bitter Victory** 1957 (France). D: Nicholas Ray. S: Curt Jurgens, Richard Burton, Ruth Roman.

American Guerrilla in the Philippines, An/British title: **I Shall Return** 1950 (USA, 20th Cent). D: Fritz Lang. S: Tyrone Power, Micheline Presle, Tom Ewell.

Americanization of Emily, The 1964 (USA, MGM-Filmways). D: Arthur Hiller. S: James Garner, Julie Andrews, Melvyn Douglas.

Angels One Five 1952 (GB). D: George More O'Ferrall. S: Jack Hawkins, John Gregson, Michael Denison.

Anzio/British title: **The Battle for Anzio** 1968 (Italy). D: Edward Dmytryk. S: Robert Mitchum, Robert Ryan, Peter Falk.

Apocalypse Now 1979 (USA, UA). D: Francis Ford Coppola. S: Martin Sheen, Robert Duvall, Marlon Brando.

Appointment in London 1952 (GB). D: Philip Leacock. S: Dirk Bogarde, Ian Hunter.

Arsenal 1929 (USSR). D: Alexander Dovzhenko. S: S Svashenko, A Buchma.

Arise My Love 1940 (USA, Par). D: Mitchell Leisen. S: Ray Milland, Claudette Colbert, Walter Abel.

Armored Command 1961 (USA/Allied Artists). D: Byron Haskell. S: Howard Keel, Burt Reynolds, Tina Louise.

Assignment in Brittany 1943 (USA, MGM). D: Jack Conway. S: Jean-Pierre Aumont, Signe Hasso, Reginald Owen.

Attack 1956 (USA, UA). D: Robert Aldrich. S: Jack Palance, Eddie Albert, Lee Marvin.

Attack and Retreat 1964 (Italy/USSR). D: Giuseppe De Santis. S: Arthur Kennedy, Peter Falk, Tatiana Samilova.

Attack Squadron 1963 (Japan). D: Shue Matsubayashi. S: Toshiro Mifune.

Away All Boats 1956 (USA, Univ-Int). D: Joseph Pevney. S: Jeff Chandler, George Nader, Julie Adams.

Back to Bataan 1945 (USA, RKO). D: Edward Dmytryk. S: John Wayne, Anthony Quinn, Beulah Bondi.

Ballad of a Soldier 1959 (USSR). D: Grigori Chukrai. S: Vladimir Ivashev, Shanna Prokhorenko.

Barefoot Battalion 1954 (Greece). D: Gregg Tallas. S: Maria Costi, Nico Fermas.

Bataan 1943 (USA, MGM). D: Tay Garnett. S: Robert Taylor, Lloyd Nolan, Robert Walker.

Bataille Du Rail, La/English title: **The Battle of the Rails** 1945 (France). D: Rene Clement. S: Tony Laurent.

Battle Circus 1952 (USA, MGM). D: Richard Brooks. S: Humphrey Bogart, June Allyson, Keenan Wynn.

Battle Cry 1954 (USA, War). D: Raoul Walsh. S: Aldo Ray, Van Heflin, James Whitmore.

Battle Cry of Peace, The 1915 (USA, Vitagraph). D: J Stuart Blackton. S: Norma Talmadge, James Morrison, Charles Richman.

Battle Hymn 1957 (USA, Univ-Int). D: Douglas Sirk. S: Rock Hudson, Dan Duryea, Anna Kashfi.

Battle of Britain 1969 (GB). D: Guy Hamilton. S: Laurence Olivier, Michael Caine, Robert Shaw.

Battle of the Bulge 1965 (USA, War). D: Ken Annakin. S: Henry Fonda, Robert Shaw, Robert Ryan.

Battle of the River Plate 1956 (GB). D: Michael Powell. S: John Gregson, Peter Finch, Anthony Quayle.

Battleship Potemkin, The 1925 (USSR). D: Sergei Eisenstein. S: A Antonov, Grigori Alexandrov, Vladimir Barsky.

Beach Red 1967 (USA, UA). D: Cornel Wilde. S: Cornel Wilde, Rip Torn, Jean Wallace.

Beau Geste 1926 (USA, Par). D: Herbert Brenon. S: Ronald Colman, Neil Hamilton, Ralph Forbes, Noah Beery Sr.

Beau Geste 1939 (USA, Par). D: William Wellman. S: Gary Cooper, Ray Milland, Robert Preston, Brian Donlevy, Susan Hayward.

Beau Geste 1966 (USA, Univ). D: Douglas Heyes. S: Guy Stockwell, Telly Savalas, Doug McClure.

Beau Ideal 1931 (USA, RKO). D: Herbert Brenon. S: Ralph Forbes, Lester Vail, Loretta Young.

Becky Sharp 1935 (USA, RKO). D: Rouben Mamoulian. S: Miriam Hopkins, Cedric Hardwicke, Frances Dee.

Bedford Incident, The 1965 (USA, Col). D: James B Harris. S: Richard Widmark, Sidney Poitier, James MacArthur.

Before Winter Comes 1968 (GB). D: J Lee-Thompson. S: David Niven, Topal, Anna Karina.

The Beginning or the End 1947 (USA, MGM). D: Norman Taurog. S: Brian Donlevy, Tom Drake, Robert Walker, Beverly Tyler.

Beguiled, The 1971 (USA, Univ). D: Don Siegel. S: Clint Eastwood, Geraldine Page, Elizabeth Hartman.

Behold a Pale Horse 1964 (USA, Col). D: Fred Zinnemann. S: Gregory Peck, Omar Sharif, Anthony Quinn.

Bell for Adano, A 1945 (USA/20th Cent). D: Henry King. S: John Hodiak, William Bendix, Jean Tierney.

Bells Go Down, The 1943 (GB). D: Basil Deardon. S: James Mason, Tommy Trinder, Mervyn Johns.

Beloved Enemy 1936 (USA, Goldwyn). D: H C Potter. S: Brian Aherne, Merle Oberon, David Niven.

Bengal Brigade/British title: **Bengal Rifles** 1954. (USA, Univ-Int). D: Laslo Benedek. S: Rock Hudson, Dan O'Herlihy.

Bequest to the Nation/US title: **The Nelson Affair** 1973 (GB). D: James Cellan Jones. S: Peter Finch, Glenda Jackson, Michael Jayston.

Best of Enemies, The 1961 (USA/Italy). D: Guy Hamilton. S: David Niven, Alberto Sordi, Michael Wilding.

Best Years of Our Lives, The 1946 (USA, Goldwyn). D: William Wyler. S: Fredric March, Myrna Loy, Teresa Wright, Dana Andrews, Harold Russell.

Between Heaven and Hell 1956 (USA, 20th Cent). D: Richard Fleischer. S: Robert Wagner, Buddy Ebsen, Broderick Crawford.

Big Blockade, The 1941 (GB). D: Charles Frend. S: Leslie Banks, Michael Redgrave, John Mills, Will Hay.

Big Parade, The 1925 (USA, MGM). D: King Vidor. S: John Gilbert, Karl Dane, Renée Adorée, Hobart Bosworth.

Big Red One, The 1979 (USA). D: Samuel Fuller. S: Lee Marvin, Mark Hamill, Bobby DiCicco.

Birth of a Nation, The 1915/abbreviated sound version, with prologue, 1930 (USA, Epoch). D: D W Griffith. S: Henry B Walthall, Lillian Gish, Mae Marsh, Robert Harron.

Blockade 1938 (USA, Wanger). D: William Dieterle. S: Henry Fonda, Madeleine Carroll, Leo Carillo, John Halliday.

Blue Max, The 1966 (USA, 20th Cent). D: John Guillermin. S: George Peppard, James Mason, Jeremy Kemp, Ursula Andress.

Bombardier 1943 (USA, RKO). D: Richard Wallace. S: Pat O'Brien, Randolph Scott, Anne Shirley.

Bombers B-52/British title: **No Sleep till Dawn** 1957 (USA, War). D: Gordon Douglas. S: Karl Malden, Efrem Zimbalist Jr, Marsha Hunt.

Boot, Das/English title: **The Boat** 1981 (West Germany). D: Wolfgang Petersen. S: Jurgen Prochnow, Herbert Gronemeyer, Klaus Wennemann.

Boys in Company C, The 1978 (Hong Kong). D: Sidney J Furie. S: Stan Shaw, Andrew Stevens, Michael Lembeck.

Breaker Morant 1980 (Aus). D: Bruce Beresford. S: Bryan Brown, Edward Woodward.

Breakthrough 1950 (USA, War). D: Lewis Seiler. S: David Brian, John Agar, Frank Lovejoy.

Bridge, The 1959 (West Germany). D: Bernhard Wicki. S: Vokler Bohnet, Fritz Wepper, Michael Hinz.

Bridge at Remagen, The 1968 (USA, UA). D: John Guillermin. S: George Segal, Robert Vaughn, Ben Gazzara.

Bridge on the River Kwai, The 1957 (GB). D: David Lean. S: Alec Guinness, William Holden, Sessue Hayakawa, Jack Hawkins.

Bridge Too Far, A 1977 (GB/USA). D: Richard Attenborough. S: Dirk Bogarde, James Caan, Michael Caine, Sean Connery.

Bridges at Toko-Ri, The 1954 (USA, Par). D: Mark Robson. S: William Holden, Grace Kelly, Fredric March, Mickey Rooney.

Brown on Resolution/US title: **Born for Glory** 1935 (GB). D: Walter Forde. S: John Mills, Betty Balfour, Barry Mackay.

Buccaneer, The 1938 (USA, Par). D: Cecil B DeMille. S: Fredric March, Franciska Gaal, Akim Tamiroff.

Buccaneer, The 1958 (USA, Par). D: Anthony Quinn. S: Yul Brynner, Charles Boyer, Claire Bloom.

Buck Privates 1941 (USA, Univ). D: Arthur Lubin. S: Bud Abbott, Lou Costello, Lee Bowman, the Andrews Sisters.

Burmese Harp, The 1956 (Japan). D: Kon Ichikawa. S: Shoji Yasuri, Rentano Mikuni.

Caine Mutiny, The 1954 (USA, Col). D: Edward Dmytryk. S: Van Johnson, Humphrey Bogart, Fred MacMurray, Jose Ferrer.

Captain Carey USA/British title: **After Midnight** 1949 (USA, Par). D: Mitchell Leisen. S: Alan Ladd, Francis Lederer, Wanda Hendrix.

Captain Eddie 1945 (USA, 20th Cent). D: Lloyd Bacon. S: Fred MacMurray, Lynn Bari, Thomas Mitchell.

Captain Horatio Hornblower/British title: **Captain Horatio Hornblower, R.N.** 1951 (USA, War). D: Raoul Walsh. S: Gregory Peck, Virginia Mayo, James Robertson Justice.

Captains of the Clouds 1942 (USA, War). D: Michael Curtiz. S: James Cagney, Dennis Morgan, Alan Hale, Reginald Gardiner.

Captive Heart, The 1946 (GB). D: Basil Deardon. S: Michael Redgrave, Jack Warner, Basil Radford.

Casablanca 1942 (USA, War). D: Michael Curtiz. S: Humphrey Bogart, Ingrid Bergman, Claude Rains, Paul Heinreid, Conrad Veidt, Peter Lorre, Sidney Greenstreet.

Castle Keep 1969 (USA, Col). D: Sydney Pollack. S: Burt Lancaster, Peter Falk, Jean-Pierre Aumont.

Catch 22 1970 (USA, Par). D: Mike Nichols. S: Alan Arkin, Martin Balsam, Richard Benjamin.

Caught in the Draft 1941 (USA, Par). D: David Butler. S: Bob Hope, Dorothy Lamour, Lynne Overman, Eddie Bracken.

Chain Lightning 1950 (USA, War). D: Stuart Heisler. S: Humphrey Bogart, Eleanor Parker, Raymond Massey.

Charge of the Light Brigade, The 1936 (USA, War). D: Michael Curtiz. S: Errol Flynn, Olivia de Havilland, Patric Knowles, David Niven.

Charge of the Light Brigade, The 1968 (GB). D: Tony Richardson. S: Trevor Howard, John Gielgud, Vanessa Redgrave.

Che! 1969 (USA, 20th Cent). D: Richard Fleischer. S: Omar Sharif, Jack Palance, Cesare Danova.

China 1943 (USA, Par). D: John Farrow. S: Alan Ladd, Loretta Young, William Bendix, Philip Ahn.

Civilization 1916 (USA, Triangle). D: Thomas Ince. S: Enid Markey, J Barney Sherry, Howard Hickman.

Cockleshell Heroes 1955 (GB). D: Jose Ferrer. S: Jose Ferrer, Trevor Howard, Dora Bryan, Anthony Newley.

Colditz Story, The 1954 (GB). D: Guy Hamilton. S: John Mills, Eric Portman, Christopher Rhodes, Ian Carmichael.

Coming Home 1978 (USA, UA). D: Hal Ashby. S: Jane Fonda, Jon Voight, Bruce Dern.

Command Decision 1948 (USA, MGM). D: Sam Wood. S: Clark Gable, Walter Pidgeon, Van Johnson, Brian Donlevy.

Commandos Strike at Dawn, The 1942 (USA, Col). D: John Farrow. S: Paul Muni, Anna Lee, Cedric Hardwicke, Lillian Gish.

Conqueror, The 1955 (USA, Howard Hughes). D: Dick Powell. S: John Wayne, Susan Hayward, Pedro Armendariz.

Conquest 1937 (USA, MGM). D: Clarence Brown. S: Greta Garbo, Charles Boyer, Reginald Owen.

Convoy 1941 (GB). D: Pen Tennyson. S: Clive Brook, Edward Chapman, John Clements.

Corvette K-225/British title: **The Nelson Touch** 1943 (USA, Univ). D: Richard Rosson. S: Randolph Scott, Ella Raines, James Brown.

Cottage to Let/US title: **Bombsight Stolen** 1941 (GB). D: Anthony Asquith. S: John Mills, Leslie Banks, Alastair Sim.

Counterattack/British title: **One Against Seven** 1945 (USA, Col). D: Zoltan Korda. S: Paul Muni, Marguerite Chapman, Larry Parks.

Court-Martial of Billy Mitchell, The/British title: **One Man Mutiny** 1955 (USA, US Pictures). D: Otto Preminger. S: Gary Cooper, Rod Steiger, Ralph Bellamy, Charles Bickford.

Crash Dive 1943 (USA, 20th Cent). D: Archie Mayo. S: Tyrone Power, Dana Andrews, Anne Baxter.

Croix de Bois, Les 1932 (France). D: Raymond Bernard. S: Gabriel Gabrio, Charles Vanel, Pierre Blanchar.

Cross of Iron 1976 (GB/West Germany). D: Sam Peckinpah. S: James Coburn, Maxmillian Schell, James Mason.

Cross of Lorraine, The 1944 (USA, MGM). D: Tay Garnett. S: Gene Kelly, Jean-Pierre Aumont, Peter Lorre, Cedric Hardwicke.

Crossing of the Rhine, The 1960 (France/Italy/West Germany). D: Andre Cayatte. S: Charles Aznavour, Nicole Courcel.

Cruel Sea, The 1952 (GB). D: Charles Frend. S: Jack Hawkins, Donald Sinden, Stanley Baker.

Custer of the West 1968 (USA, Cinerama-Security). D: Robert Siodmak. S: Robert Shaw, Mary Ure, Robert Ryan.

Dam Busters, The 1954 (GB). D: Michael Anderson. S: Michael Redgrave, Richard Todd, Derek Farr, Basil Sydney.

Dangerous Moonlight/US title: **Suicide Squadron** 1941 (GB). D: Brian Desmond Hurst. S: Anton Walbrook, Sally Gray, Derrick de Marney.

Dawn Patrol, The 1930 (USA, War). D: Howard Hawks. S: Richard Barthelmess, Douglas Fairbanks Jr, Neil Hamilton.

Dawn Patrol 1938 (USA, War). D: Edmund Goulding. S: Errol Flynn, David Niven, Basil Rathbone, Donald Crisp.

Day Will Dawn, The 1942 (GB). D: Harold French. S: Ralph Richardson, Deborah Kerr, Hugh Williams.

Days of Glory 1944 (USA, RKO). D: Jacques Tourneur. S: Gregory Peck, Tamara Toumanova, Alan Reed.

D-Day the Sixth of June 1956 (USA, 20th Cent). D: Henry Koster. S: Robert Taylor, Richard Todd, Dana Wynter.

Decision Before Dawn 1951 (USA, 20th Cent). D: Anatole Litvak. S: Richard Basehart, Oskar Werner, Gary Merrill, Hildegarde Neff.

Deep Six, The 1958 (USA, Jaquar). D: Rudolph Mate. S: Alan Ladd, William Bendix, Efrem Zimbalist Jr.

Deer Hunter, The 1978 (USA, Univ). D: Michael Cimino. S: Robert De Niro, John Cazale, Christopher Walken, John Savage.

Desert Fox, The/British title: **Rommel, Desert Fox** 1951 (USA, 20th Cent). D: Henry Hathaway. S: James Mason, Jessica Tandy, Cedric Hardwicke.

Desert Rats, The 1953 (USA, 20th Cent). D: Robert Wise. S: James Mason, Richard Burton, Robert Newton.

Desperate Journey 1942 (USA, War). D: Raoul Walsh. S: Errol Flynn, Ronald Reagan, Arthur Kennedy.

Destination Gobi 1953 (USA, 20th Cent). D: Robert Wise. S: Richard Widmark, Don Taylor, Casey Adams.

Destination Tokyo 1943 (USA, War). D: Delmar Daves. S: Cary Grant, John Garfield, Alan Hale.

Destroyer 1943 (USA, Col). D: William A. Seiter. S: Edward G Robinson, Glenn Ford, Edgar Buchanan, Marguerite Chapman.

Devil Dogs of the Air 1935 (USA, War). D: Lloyd Bacon. S: James Cagney, Pat O'Brien, Margaret Lindsay, Frank McHugh.

Devil's Brigade, The 1968 (USA, UA-Wolper). D: Andrew V McLagen. S: William Holden, Cliff Robertson, Vince Edwards.

Dirty Dozen, The 1967 (USA/Spain). D: Robert Aldrich. S: Lee Marvin, Robert Ryan, Ernest Borgnine, George Kennedy, Jim Brown.

Dive Bomber 1941 (USA, War). D: Michael Curtiz. S: Errol Flynn, Fred MacMurray, Alexis Smith, Ralph Bellamy.

Dr Strangelove — or How I Learned to Stop Worrying and Love the Bomb 1963 (GB). D: Stanley Kubrick. S: Peter Sellers, George C Scott, Sterling Hayden, Slim Pickens.

Dr Zhivago 1965 (USA, MGM). D: David Lean. S: Omar Sharif, Julie Christie, Rod Steiger, Alec Guinness.

Don't Go Near the Water 1957 (USA, MGM). D: Charles Walters. S: Glenn Ford, Fred Clark, Gia Scala, Anne Francis.

Doughboys 1930 (USA, MGM). D: Edward Sedgwick. S: Buster Keaton, Sally Eilers, Cliff Edwards.

Drum Beat 1954 (USA, Jaguar). D: Delmer Daves. S: Alan Ladd, Audrey Dalton, Robert Keith.

Dunkirk 1958 (GB). D: Leslie Norman. S: John Mills, Richard Attenborough, Bernard Lee.

Eagle and the Hawk, The 1933 (USA, Par). D: Stuart Walker. S: Cary Grant, Fredric March, Jack Oakie, Carole Lombard.

Eagle Has Landed, The 1976 (GB). D: John Sturges. S: Michael Caine, Robert Duvall, Donald Sutherland, Jenny Agutter.

Eagle Squadron 1942 (USA, Univ). D: Arthur Lubin. S: Robert Stack, Diana Barrymore, John Loder.

Edge of Darkness 1943 (USA, War). D: Lewis Milestone. S: Errol Flynn, Ann Sheridan, Walter Huston.

Enemy Below, The 1957 (USA, 20th Cent). D: Dick Powell. S: Robert Mitchum, Curt Jurgens, Theodore Bikel.

Enemy General, The 1960 (USA, Col). D: George Sherman. S: Van Johnson, Jean-Pierre Aumont, Dany Carrel.

Ensign Pulver 1964 (USA, War). D: Joshua Logan. S: Robert Walker, Walter Matthau, Burl Ives.

Eroica/English title: **Heroism** 1957 (Poland). D: Andrzej Munk. S: Barbara Polomska, L Niemszyk, Roman Klosowski.

Escape/reissued as **When the Door Opened** 1940 (USA, MGM). D: Mervyn LeRoy. S: Robert Taylor, Norma Shearer, Conrad Veidt.

Escape to Glory/also released as **Submarine Zone** 1940 (USA, Col). D: John Brahm. S: Pat O'Brien, Constance Bennett, John Halliday.

Eternal Sea, The 1955 (USA, Rep). D: John H Auer. S: Sterling Hayden, Alexis Smith, Dean Jagger.

Eve of St Mark, The 1944 (USA, 20th Cent). D: John M Stahl. S: Anne Baxter, William Eythe, Michael O'Shea.

Fail Safe 1964 (USA, Col). D: Sidney Lumet. S: Henry Fonda, Walter Matthau, Frank Overton, Dan O'Herlihy.

Fall of Berlin, The 1949 (USSR). D: M Chiaureli. S: B Andreyev, M Gelovani.

Farewell to Arms, A 1932 (USA, Par). D: Frank Borzage. S: Gary Cooper, Helen Hayes, Adolph Menjou.

Farewell to Arms, A 1957 (USA, 20th Cent). D: Charles Vidor. S: Rock Hudson, Jennifer Jones, Vittorio de Sica.

Father Goose 1964 (USA, Univ-Inter). D: Ralph Nelson. S: Cary Grant, Leslie Caron, Trevor Howard.

55 Days at Peking 1962 (USA/Spain). D: Nicholas Ray, Andrew Marton. S: Charlton Heston, Ava Gardner, David Niven.

Fighter Squadron 1948 (USA, War). D: Raoul Walsh. S: Edmond O'Brien, Robert Stack, Tom D'Andrea.

Fighting Seabees, The 1944 (USA, Rep). D: Edward Ludwig. S: John Wayne, Dennis O'Keefe, Susan Hayward.

Fighting 69th, The 1940 (USA, War). D: William Keighley. S: James Cagney, Pat O'Brien, George Brent, Jeffrey Lynn.

Fire Over England 1936 (GB). D: William K Howard. S: Laurence Olivier, Flora Robson, Vivien Leigh.

First of the Few, The/US title: **Spitfire** 1942 (GB). D: Leslie Howard. S: Leslie Howard, David Niven, Rosamund John.

First to Fight 1967 (USA, War). D: Christian Nyby. S: Chad Everett, Gene Hackman, Dean Jagger.

Five Fingers 1952 (USA, 20th Cent). D: Joseph L Mankiewicz. S: James Mason, Michael Rennie, Danielle Darrieux.

Five Graves to Cairo 1943 (USA, Par). D: Billy Wilder. S: Franchot Tone, Erich Von Stroheim, Anne Baxter.

Fixed Bayonets 1951 (USA, 20th Cent). D: Samuel Fuller. S: Richard Basehart, Gene Evans, Michael O'Shea.

Flight Command 1940 (USA, MGM). D: Frank Borzage. S: Robert Taylor, Walter Pidgeon, Ruth Hussey.

Flying Deuces, The 1939 (USA, Morros). D: Edward Sutherland. S: Stan Laurel, Oliver Hardy, Jean Parker.

Flying Fortress 1942 (GB). D: Walter Forde. S: Richard Greene, Carla Lahmann, Donald Stewart.

Flying Leathernecks 1951 (USA, RKO). D: Nicholas Ray. S: John Wayne, Robert Ryan, Janis Carter.

Flying Tigers 1942 (USA, Rep). D: David Miller. S: John Wayne, Anna Lee, John Carroll.

For Whom the Bell Tolls 1943 (USA, Par). D: Sam Wood. S: Gary Cooper, Ingrid Bergman, Akim Tamiroff, Katina Paxinou.

Force of Arms 1951 (USA, War). D: Michael Curtiz. S: William Holden, Nancy Olson, Frank Lovejoy.

Force Ten from Navarone 1978 (GB). D: Guy Hamilton. S: Robert Shaw, Edward Fox, Harrison Ford.

Foreign Correspondent 1940 (USA, Wanger). D: Alfred Hitchcock. S: Joel McCrea, Laraine Day, Herbert Marshall, George Sanders, Albert Basserman.

Foreman Went to France, The/US title: **Somewhere in France** 1941 (GB). D: Charles Frend. S: Tommy Trinder, Constance Cummings, Clifford Evans.

Forty-Ninth Parallel, The/US title: **The Invaders** 1941 (GB). D: Michael Powell. S: Eric Portman, Raymond Massey, Laurence Olivier, Leslie Howard, Anton Walbrook.

Four Feathers, The 1929 (USA, Par). D: Lothar Mendes, Merian C Cooper, Ernest Schoedsack. S: Richard Arlen, Clive Brook, Fay Wray.

Four Feathers, The 1939 (GB). D: Zoltan Korda. S: John Clements, Ralph Richardson, June Duprez.

Four Horsemen of the Apocalypse, The 1921 (USA, Metro). D: Rex Ingram. S: Rudolph Valentino, Alice Terry, Alan Hale.

Four Horsemen of the Apocalypse, The 1961 (USA, MGM). D: Vincente Minnelli. S: Glenn Ford, Charles Boyer, Ingrid Thulin.

Four in a Jeep 1951 (Switzerland). D: Leopold Lindtberg. S: Ralph Meeker, Viveca Lindfors, Michael Medwin.

Four Sons 1940 (USA, 20th Cent). D: Archie Mayo. S: Don Ameche, Eugenie Leontovich, Alan Curtis, Mary Beth Hughes.

Frogmen, The 1951 (USA, 20th Cent). D: Lloyd Bacon. S: Richard Widmark, Dana Andrews, Gary Merrill.

From Here to Eternity 1953 (USA, Col). D: Fred Zinnemann. S: Burt Lancaster, Deborah Kerr, Frank Sinatra, Donna Reed, Montgomery Clift, Ernest Borgnine.

Gallant Hours, The 1960 (USA, UA). D: Robert Montgomery. S: James Cagney, Dennis Weaver, Richard Jaeckel.

Gathering of Eagles, A 1962 (USA, Univ-Inter). D: Delbert Mann. S: Rock Hudson, Rod Taylor, Mary Peach.

General, The 1926 (USA, Keaton). D: Buster Keaton, Clyde Bruckman. S: Buster Keaton, Marion Mack, Glen Cavander.

Generale della Rovere, Il/English title: **General della Rovere** 1959 (France/Italy). D: Roberto Rossellini. S: Vittorio de Sica, Hannes Messemer, Sandra Milo.

Germania, Anno Zero/English title: **Germany Year Zero**/also released as **Exit Street** and **Allemagne, Annee Zero** 1947 (Italy/France). D: Roberto Rossellini. S: Franz Gruger and non-professional actors.

Glory Brigade, The 1953 (USA, 20th Cent). D: Robert D Webb. S: Victor Mature, Lee Marvin, Richard Egan, Alexander Scourby.

Go for Broke 1951 (USA, MGM). D: Robert Pirosh. S: Van Johnson, Lane Nakano, George Miki.

Go Tell the Spartans 1978 (USA, Spartan). D: Ted Post. S: Burt Lancaster, Craig Wasson, Marc Singer.

God Is My Co-Pilot 1945 (USA, War). D: Robert Florey. S: Dennis Morgan, Dane Clark, Andrea King, Raymond Massey.

Gone with the Wind 1939 (USA, MGM). D: Victor Fleming, Sam Wood, George Cukor. S: Clark Gable, Vivien Leigh, Leslie Howard, Olivia de Havilland, Thomas Mitchell.

Gordon's War 1973 (USA, 20th Cent). D: Ossie Davis. S: Paul Winfield, David Downing, Carl Lee.

Grande Illusion, La/English title: **Grand Illusion** 1937 (France). D: Jean Renoir. S: Pierre Fresnay, Erich Von Stroheim, Jean Gabin, Marcel Dalio.

Grande Vadrouille, La/English title: **Don't Look Now — We're Being Shot At** 1966 (France). D: Gerard Oury. S: Terry-Thomas, Bourvil, Louis de Funes.

Great Dictator, The 1940 (USA, Chaplin). D: Charles Chaplin. S: Charles Chaplin, Paulette Goddard, Jack Oakie.

Great Escape, The 1963 (USA, UA). D: John Sturges. S: Steve McQueen, James Garner, Richard Attenborough, Charles Bronson.

Great Guns 1941 (USA, 20th Cent). D: Monty Banks. S: Stan Laurel, Oliver Hardy, Sheila Ryan, Dick Nelson.

Great Waldo Pepper, The 1975 (USA, Univ). D: George Roy Hill. S: Robert Redford, Bo Svenson, Susan Sarandon.

Green Berets, The 1968 (USA, War). D: John Wayne, Ray Kellogg. S: John Wayne, David Janssen, Jim Hutton, Aldo Ray.

Guadalcanal Diary 1943 (USA, 20th Cent). D: Lewis Seiler. S: Preston Foster, Lloyd Nolan, William Bendix, Richard Jaeckel.

Guerre Est Finie, La/English title: **The War Is Over** 1966 (France/Sweden). D: Alain Resnais. S: Yves Montand, Ingrid Thulin, Genevieve Bujold.

Gung Ho! 1943 (USA, Univ). D: Ray Enright. S: Randolph Scott, Alan Curtis, Noah Beery Jr, J Carroll Naish, Robert Mitchum, Grace MacDonald.

Gunga Din 1939 (USA, RKO). D: George Stevens. S: Cary Grant, Victor MaLaglen, Douglas Fairbanks Jr, Joan Fontaine, Sam Jaffe.

Guns of Navarone, The 1961 (GB). D: J Lee-Thompson. S: Gregory Peck, David Niven, Anthony Quinn, Stanley Baker.

Guy Named Joe, A 1944 (USA, MGM). D: Victor Fleming. S: Spencer Tracy, Irene Dunne, Van Johnson, Ward Bond.

Halls of Montezuma 1951 (USA, 20th Cent). D: Lewis Milestone. S: Richard Widmark, Jack Palance, Robert Wagner.

Hannibal Brooks 1968 (GB). D: Michael Winner. S: Oliver Reed, Michael J Pollard, Karen Baal.

Hasty Heart, The 1949 (GB). D: Vincent Sherman. S: Richard Todd, Patricia Neal, Ronald Reagan.

Heart of Humanity, The 1919 (USA, Univ-Jewel). D: Allen Holuber. S: Dorothy Phillips, William Stowell, Erich Von Stroheim.

Hearts of Humanity 1918 (USA, Zukor). D: D W Griffith. S: Lillian Gish, Robert Harron, Erich Von Stroheim.

Heaven Knows, Mr Allison 1957 (USA, 20th Cent). D: John Huston. S: Robert Mitchum, Deborah Kerr.

Hell Divers 1931 (USA, MGM). D: George Hill. S: Clark Gable, Wallace Beery, Conrad Nagel.

Hell in the Pacific 1969 (USA, Cinerama). D: John Boorman. S: Lee Marvin, Toshiro Mifune.

Hell Is for Heroes 1962 (USA, Par). D: Don Siegel. S: Steve McQueen, Bobby Darin, Fess Parker, James Coburn.

Hell to Eternity 1960 (USA, Allied Artists). D: Phil Karlsen. S: David Janssen, Jeffrey Hunter, Vic Damone.

Hell's Angels 1930 (USA, Hughes). D: Howard Hughes. S: Ben Lyon, Jean Harlow, James Hall.

Here Comes the Navy/originally titled **Hey, Sailor** 1934 (USA, War). D: Lloyd Bacon. S: James Cagney, Pat O'Brien, Gloria Stuart.

Heroes 1977 (USA, Univ). D: Jeremy Paul Kagan. S: Henry Winkler, Sally Field, Harrison Ford.

Heroes of Telemark, The 1965 (GB). D: Anthony Mann. S: Kirk Douglas, Richard Harris, Ulla Jacobsson.

High Flight 1958 (GB). D: John Gilling. S: Ray Milland, Bernard Lee, Kenneth Haigh.

Hill in Korea, A 1956 (GB). D: Julian Amyes. S: George Baker, Stanley Baker, Michael Medwin, Harry Andrews.

Hitler 1961 (USA, Three Crown). D: Stuart Heisler. S: Richard Basehart, Martin Kosleck, Maria Emo.

Hitler – The Last Ten Days 1973 (GB/Italy). D: Ennio de Concini. S: Alec Guinness, Simon Ward, Adolfo Celli.

Hitler's Children 1943 (USA, RKO). D: Edward Dmytryk. S: Bonita Granville, Tim Holt, Otto Kruger.

Home of the Brave 1949 (USA, Kramer). D: Mark Robson. S: James Edwards, Lloyd Bridges, Frank Lovejoy, Jeff Corey.

Horizontal Lieutenant, The 1962 (USA, MGM). D: Richard Thorpe. S: Jim Hutton, Paula Prentiss, Miyoshi Umeki.

Hostages 1943 (USA, Par). D: Frank Tuttle. S: Luise Rainer, Paul Lukas, William Bendix.

Hotel Sahara 1951 (GB). D: Ken Annakin. S: Peter Ustinov, Yvonne de Carlo, Roland Culver, David Tomlinson.

How I Won the War 1967 (GB). D: Richard Lester. S: John Lennon, Michael Crawford, Roy Kinnear.

Howards of Virginia, The 1940 (USA, Col). D: Frank Lloyd. S: Cary Grant, Martha Scott, Richard Carlson.

I Wanted Wings 1941 (USA, Par). D: Mitchell Leisen. S: Ray Milland, William Holden, Brian Donlevy, Veronica Lake.

I Was a Male War Bride 1949 (USA, 20th Cent). D: Howard Hawks. S: Cary Grant, Ann Sheridan, Randy Stuart.

I Was Monty's Double/US title: **Hell, Heaven and Hoboken** 1958 (GB). D: John Guillermin. S: John Mills, Cecil Parker.

Immortal Sergeant, The 1943 (USA, 20th Cent). D: John Stahl. S: Henry Fonda, Maureen O'Hara, Thomas Mitchell.

In Harm's Way 1965 (USA, Par). D: Otto Preminger. S: John Wayne, Kirk Douglas, Patricia Neal, Tom Tryon.

In Love and War 1958 (USA, 20th Cent). D: Philip Dunne. S: Jeffrey Hunter, Robert Wagner, Bradford Dillman.

In Which We Serve 1942 (GB). D: Noel Coward, David Lean. S: Noel Coward, Bernard Miles, John Mills, Celia Johnson.

International Squadron 1941 (USA, War). D: Lothar Mendes. S: Ronald Reagan, Julie Bishop, James Stephenson.

Intolerance 1916 (USA, Wark). D: D W Griffith. S: Lillian Gish, Mae Marsh, Howard Gaye, Margery Wilson, Constance Talmadge.

Introduction to the Enemy 1974 (USA). D: Jane Fonda, Tom Hayden, Haskell Wexler.

Invasion Quartet 1961 (GB). D: Jay Lewis. S: Bill Travers, Spike Milligan, Grégoire Aslan.

Iron Duke, The 1935 (GB). D: Victor Saville. S: George Arliss, Emlyn Williams, Gladys Cooper.

Is Paris Burning? 1965 (France/USA). D: Rene Clement. S: Gert Frobe, Leslie Caron, Charles Boyer, Orson Welles.

It Happened Here 1963 (GB). D: Kevin Brownlow, Andrew Mollo. S: Sebastian Shaw, Pauline Murray.

Jackboot Mutiny 1955 (Germany). D: G W Pabst. S: Bernhard Wicki, Carl Ludwig Diehl.

Jeux Interdits, Les/English titles: **Forbidden Games, The Secret Game** 1952 (France). D: Rene Clement. S: Brigitte Fossey, Georges Poujouly, Amedee.

Joan of Paris 1942 (USA, 20th Cent). D: Robert Stevenson. S: Michele Morgan, Paul Henried, Thomas Mitchell.

John Paul Jones 1959 (USA, War). D: John Farrow. S: Robert Stack, Charles Coburn, Bette Davis.

Johnny Got His Gun 1971 (USA, World Entertainment). D: Dalton Trumbo. S: Timothy Bottoms, Jason Robards Jr, Diane Varsi.

Journey Together 1944 (GB). D: John Boulting. S: Richard Attenborough, David Tomlinson.

Journey's End 1930 (GB). D: James Whale. S: Colin Clive, David Manners, Ian MacLaren.

Judgment at Nuremberg 1961 (USA, UA). D: Stanley Kramer. S: Spencer Tracy, Maxmillian Schell, Burt Lancaster, Richard Widmark.

Jump into Hell 1955 (USA, War). D: David Butler. S: Jacques Sernas, Arnold Moss, Kurt Kasznar.

Kanal/English title: **They Loved Life** 1956 (Poland). D: Andrzef Wajda. S: Tadeusz Janczar, Teresa Izewska.

Keep 'Em Flying 1941 (USA, Univ). D: Arthur Lubin. S: Bud Abbott, Lou Costello, Martha Raye, Carol Bruce.

Keep Your Powder Dry 1945 (USA, MGM). D: Edward Buzzell. S: Lana Turner, Laraine Day, Susan Peters.

Kelly's Heroes 1970 (USA/Yugoslavia). D: Brian G Hutton. S: Clint Eastwood, Donald Sutherland, Don Rickles.

Key, The 1958 (GB). D: Carol Reed. S: William Holden, Trevor Howard, Sophia Loren.

Khartoum 1966 (GB). D: Basil Dearden. S: Charlton Heston, Laurence Olivier, Ralph Richardson.

Killing Fields, The 1984 (USA, Goldcrest-International Film Investors). D: Roland Joffe. S: Sam Waterston, Haing S Ngor, Craig T Nelson.

King of the Khyber Rifles 1954 (USA, 20th Cent). D: Henry King. S: Tyrone Power, Michael Rennie, Terry Moore.

King Rat 1965 (USA, Col). D: Bryan Forbes. S: George Segal, John Mills, Tom Courtenay.

Ladies Courageous 1944 (USA, Univ). D: Edward H Griffith. S: Loretta Young, Geraldine Fitzgerald, Diana Barrymore.

Lafayette 1961 (France/Italy). D: Jean Dreville. S: Michel Le Royer, Jack Hawkins, Orson Welles.

Lafayette Escadrille 1957 (USA, War). D: William A Wellman. S: Tab Hunter, David Janssen, Clint Eastwood.

Last Blitzkrieg, The 1959 (USA, Col). D: Arthur Dreifuss. S: Van Johnson, Dick York, Kerwin Mathews.

Lawrence of Arabia 1962 (GB). D: David Lean. S: Peter O'Toole, Alec Guinness, Claude Rains, Omar Sharif, Arthur Kennedy.

Lenin v Octiabrye/English title: **Lenin in October** 1937 (USSR). D: Mikhail Romm. S: Boris Shchukin, Nikolai Oklopkov.

Lenin v 1918/English title: **Lenin in 1918** 1939 (USSR). D: Mikhail Romm. S: Boris Schhukin, Nikolai Cherkassov.

Life and Death of Colonel Blimp, The 1943 (GB). D: Michael Powell. S: Roger Livesey, Deborah Kerr, Anton Walbrook.

Lifeboat 1944 (USA, 20th Cent). D: Alfred Hitchcock. S: Tallulah Bankhead, John Hodiak, Walter Slezak.

Light Up the Sky 1960 (GB). D: Lewis Gilbert. S: Ian Carmichael, Tommy Steele, Benny Hill.

Lilac Time 1928 (USA, First National). D: George Fitzmaurice. S: Colleen Moore, Gary Cooper.

Lion Has Wings, The 1939 (GB). D: Michael Powell. S: Ralph Richardson, Merle Oberon, June Duprez.

Lion of the Desert/also known as **Omar Muktar – Lion of the Desert** 1979 (GB). D: Moustapha Akkad. S: Anthony Quinn, Oliver Reed.

Little Colonel, The 1935 (USA, 20th Cent). D: David Butler. S: Shirley Temple, Lionel Barrymore, Evelyn Venable.

Littlest Rebel, The 1935 (USA, 20th Cent). D: David Butler. S: Shirley Temple, John Boles, Karen Morley.

Lives of a Bengal Lancer 1935 (USA, Par). D: Henry Hathaway. S: Gary Cooper, Franchot Tone, Richard Cromwell, Douglas Dumbrille.

Long and the Short and the Tall, The/US title: **Jungle Fighters** 1960 (GB). D: Leslie Norman. S: Laurence Harvey, Richard Todd.

Long Day's Dying, The 1968 (GB). D: Peter Collinson. S: David Hemmings, Tom Bell, Alan Dobie.

Long Gray Line, The 1955 (USA, Col). D: John Ford. S: Tyrone Power, Maureen O'Hara, Donald Crisp.

Long Voyage Home, The 1940 (USA, Wanger). D: John Ford. S: John Wayne, Thomas Mitchell, Ian Hunter.

Longest Day, The 1972 (USA, 20th Cent). D: Andrew Marton, Ken Annakin, Bernhard Wicki. S: Robert Mitchum, John Wayne, Henry Fonda, Robert Ryan, Robert Wagner.

Lost Command 1966 (USA, Col). D: Mark Robson. S: Anthony Quinn, George Segal, Alain Delon.

Lost Patrol, The 1934 (USA, RKO). D: John Ford. S: Victor McLagen, Wallace Ford, Boris Karloff.

Lost Squadron, The 1932 (USA, RKO). D: George Archainbaud. S: Richard Dix, Joel McCrea, Erich Von Stroheim.

Love, Soldiers and Women 1953 (France/Italy). D: Marcel Pagliero, Jean Delannoy, Christian-Jaque. S: Claudette Colbert, Michele Morgan, Martine Carol.

MacArthur/also known as **MacArthur the Rebel General** 1977 (USA, Univ). D: Joseph Sargent. S: Gregory Peck, Ed Flanders, Dan O'Herlihy.

McConnell Story, The/British title: **Tiger in the Sky** 1955 (USA, War). D: Gordon Douglas. S: Alan Ladd, June Allyson, James Whitmore.

McKenzie Break, The 1970 (GB). D: Lamont Johnson. S: Brian Keith, Ian Hendry, Helmut Griem.

Magnificent Doll, The 1946 (USA, Univ). D: Frank Borzage. S: Ginger Rogers, David Niven, Burgess Meredith.

Man of Conquest 1939 (USA, Rep). D: George Nicholls Jr. S: Richard Dix, Joan Fontaine, Edward Ellis, Gail Patrick.

Man Who Never Was, The 1955 (GB). D: Ronald Neame. S: Clifton Webb, Robert Flemying, Gloria Grahame.

March or Die 1977 (GB). D: Dick Richards. S: Gene Hackman, Terence Hill, Catherine Deneuve.

Marie Antoinette 1938 (USA, MGM). D: W S Van Dyke. S: Norma Shearer, Tyrone Power, John Barrymore.

Marines Let's Go 1961 (USA, 20th Cent). D: Raoul Walsh. S: Tom Tryon, David Hedison.

Marseillaise, La 1937 (France). D: Jean Renoir. S: Pierre Renoir, Lise Delemare.

M★A★S★H 1970 (USA, 20th Cent). D: Robert Altman. S: Donald Sutherland, Elliott Gould, Sally Kellerman, Tom Skerritt.

Mata Hari 1932 (USA, MGM). D: George Fitzmaurice. S: Greta Garbo, Ramon Novarro, C Henry Gordon.

Me and the Colonel 1958 (USA, Col). D: Peter Glenville. S: Danny Kaye, Curt Jurgens, Nicole Maurey.

Men, The/later released as **Battle Stripes** 1950 (USA, Kramer). D: Fred Zinnemann. S: Marlon Brando, Teresa Wright, Everett Sloane, Jack Webb.

Men in War 1957 (USA, Security). D: Anthony Mann. S: Robert Ryan, Robert Keith, Aldo Ray.

Men of the Fighting Lady 1954 (USA, MGM). D: Andrew Marton. S: Van Johnson, Louis Calhern, Walter Pidgeon.

Merrill's Marauders 1962 (USA, War). D: Samuel Fuller. S: Jeff Chandler, Andrew Duggan, Ty Hardin.

Message to Garcia, A 1936 (USA, 20th Cent). D: George Marshall. S: Barbara Stanwyck, Wallace Beery, John Boles.

Midway 1976 (USA, Univ). D: Jack Smight. S: Charlton Heston, Henry Fonda, Robert Mitchum, Glenn Ford, Toshiro Mifune.

Millions Like Us 1943 (GB). D: Frank Launder, Sidney Gilliat. S: Patricia Roc, Gordon Jackson, Eric Portman.

Miniver Story, The 1950 (GB). D: H C Potter. S: Greer Garson, Walter Pidgeon.

Missing in Action 1984 (USA, Cannon Group). D: Joseph Zito. S: Chuck Norris, M Emmet Walsh, Lenore Kasdorf.

Mister Roberts 1955 (USA, War). D: John Ford, Mervyn LeRoy. S: Henry Fonda, Jack Lemmon, James Cagney, William Powell.

Mr Winkle Goes to War/British title: **Arms and the Woman** 1944 (USA, Col). D: Alfred E Green. S: Edward G Robinson, Ruth Warrick.

Mrs Miniver 1942 (USA, MGM). D: William Wyler. S: Greer Garson, Walter Pidgeon, Teresa Wright, Dame May Whitty.

Moon Is Down, The 1943 (USA, 20th Cent). D: Irving Pichel. S: Henry Travers, Lee J Cobb, Cedric Hardwicke.

Mortal Storm, The 1940 (USA, MGM). D: Frank Borzage. S: Margaret Sullavan, Robert Young, James Stewart.

Murphy's War 1971 (GB). D: Peter Yates. S: Peter O'Toole, Sian Phillips, Philippe Noiret.

Mussolini: Ultimo Atto/English titles: **The Last Four Days, Last Days of Mussolini** 1974 (Italy). S: Rod Steiger.

Mystery Submarine/US title: **Decoy** 1962 (GB). D: C M Pennington-Richards. S: Edward Judd, James Robertson Justice.

Naked and the Dead, The 1958 (USA, RKO). D: Raoul Walsh. S: Aldo Ray, Cliff Robertson, Raymond Massey.

Napoleon/also known as **Napoleon vu par Abel Gance** 1927 (France). Later versions titled **Napoleon-Bonaparte** (1955) and **Bonaparte et la Revolution** (1971). D: Abel Gance. S: Albert Dieudonné, Antonin Artaud.

Never So Few 1959 (USA, MGM). D: John Sturges. S: Frank Sinatra, Peter Lawford, Gina Lollobrigida.

Next of Kin, The 1942 (GB). D: Thorold Dickinson. S: Mevyn Johns, Nova Pilbeam.

Night of the Generals, The 1967 (GB). D: Anatole Litvak. S: Peter O'Toole, Omar Sharif, Tom Courtenay.

Night People 1954 (USA, 20th Cent). D: Nunnally Johnson. S: Gregory Peck, Broderick Crawford, Buddy Ebsen.

Night Train to Munich/US titles: **Gestapo, Night Train** 1940 (GB). D: Carol Reed. S: Rex Harrison, Margaret Lockwood.

1941 1979 (USA, Univ). D: Steven Spielberg. S: John Belushi, Dan Aykroyd, Ned Beatty, Treat Williams.

Nobi/English title: **Fires on the Plain** 1959 (Japan). D: Kon Ichikawa. S: Eijji Funakoshi, Osamu Takizawa, Mickey Curtis.

None But the Brave 1965 (USA, War). D: Frank Sinatra. S: Frank Sinatra, Clint Walker, Tommy Sands.

None Shall Escape 1945 (USA, Col). D: Andre de Toth. S: Alexander Knox, Marsha Hunt, Henry Travers.

North Star/later released as **Armored Attack** 1943 (USA, Goldwyn). D: Lewis Milestone. S: Anne Baxter, Farley Granger, Dana Andrews.

Northern Pursuit 1943 (USA, War). D: Raoul Walsh. S: Errol Flynn, Helmut Dantine, Julie Bishop.

Northwest Passage 1940 (USA, MGM). D: King Vidor. S: Spencer Tracy, Robert Young, Walter Brennan, Ruth Hussey.

Nun and the Sergeant, The 1962 (USA, US). D: Franklin Adreon. S: Robert Webber, Anna Sten, Leon Gordon.

OSS 1946 (USA, Par). D: Irving Pichel. S: Alan Ladd, Geraldine Fitzgerald, Patric Knowles.

Objective Burma 1944 (USA, War). D: Raoul Walsh. S: Errol Flynn, William Prince, James Brown.

Odette 1950 (GB). D: Herbert Wilcox. S: Anna Neagle, Trevor Howard, Peter Ustinov.

Oh What a Lovely War 1969 (GB). D: Richard Attenborough. S: Ralph Richardson, Meriel Forbes, John Gielgud, Laurence Olivier.

On the Beach 1959 (USA, US). D: Stanley Kramer. S: Gregory Peck, Ava Gardner, Anthony Perkins, Fred Astaire.

On the Double 1961 (USA, Par). D: Melville Shavelson. S: Danny Kaye, Dana Wynter, Wilfred Hyde-White.

One Minute to Zero 1952 (USA, RKO). D: Tay Garnett. S: Robert Mitchum, Ann Blyth, William Talman.

One of Our Aircraft Is Missing 1941 (GB). D: Michael Powell, Emeric Pressburger. S: Godfrey Tearle, Eric Portman, Hugh Williams.

One That Got Away, The 1957 (GB). D: Roy Baker. S: Hardy Kruger, Michael Goodliffe, Alec McCowan.

Operation Amsterdam 1958 (GB). D: Michael McCarthy. S: Peter Finch, Eva Bartok, Tony Britton.

Operation Crossbow/also released as **The Great Spy Mission** 1965 (GB). D: Michael Anderson. S: George Peppard, John Mills, Tom Courtenay.

Operation Daybreak 1975 (USA, War). D: Lewis Gilbert. S: Timothy Bottoms, Martin Shaw, Nicola Pagett.

Operation Mad Ball 1957 (USA, Col). D: Richard Quine. S: Jack Lemmon, Ernie Kovaks, Mickey Rooney.

Operation Pacific 1950 (USA, War). D: George Waggner. S: John Wayne, Patricia Neal, Ward Bond.

Operation Petticoat 1959 (USA, Univ). D: Blake Edwards. S: Cary Grant, Tony Curtis, Dina Merrill.

Operation Secret 1952 (USA, War). D: Lewis Seiler. S: Cornel Wilde, Steve Cochran.

Operation Thunderbolt/also released as **Entebbe: Operation Thunderbolt** 1977 (Israel). D: Menahem Golan. S: Klaus Kinski, Assaf Dayan.

Orders to Kill 1958 (GB). D: Anthony Asquith. S: Paul Massie, Irene Worth, James Robertson Justice.

Overlord 1975 (GB). D: Stuart Cooper. S: Brian Stirner, Nicholas Ball.

Paisa/also released as **Paisan** 1946 (Italy). D: Roberto Rossellini. S: William Tubbs, Gar Moore, Maria Michi.

Paris Underground 1945 (USA, UA). D: Gregory Ratoff. S: Constance Bennett, Gracie Fields.

Passage to Marseilles 1944 (USA, War). D: Michael Curtiz. S: Humphrey Bogart, Peter Lorre, Sydney Greenstreet, Victor Francen.

Password Is Courage, The 1962 (GB). D: Andrew L Stone. S: Dirk Bogarde, Maria Perschy.

Paths of Glory 1957 (USA, UA). D: Stanley Kubrick. S: Kirk Douglas, Adolphe Menjou, Ralph Meeker, George Macready.

Patton/British title: **Patton — Lust for Glory** 1970 (USA, 20th Cent). D: Franklin Schaffner. S: George C Scott, Karl Malden, Stephen Young.

Perfect Strangers/US title: **Vacation from Marriage** 1945 (GB). D: Alexander Korda. S: Robert Donat, Deborah Kerr, Ann Todd.

Pied Piper, The 1942 (USA, 20th Cent). D: Irving Pichel. S: Monty Woolley, Otto Preminger, Anne Baxter, Roddy McDowell.

Pilot Number Five 1943 (USA, MGM). D: George Sidney. S: Franchot Tone, Gene Kelly, Van Johnson, Marsha Hunt.

Pimpernel Smith/US titles: **Mister V; The Fighting Pimpernel** 1941 (GB). D: Leslie Howard. S: Leslie Howard, Francis L Sullivan, Mary Morris.

Play Dirty 1969 (GB). D: Andre de Toth. S: Michael Caine, Nigel Davenport, Nigel Green.

Plough and the Stars, The 1936 (USA, RKO). D: John Ford. S: Barbara Stanwyck, Preston Foster, Barry Fitzgerald.

Pork Chop Hill 1959 (USA, UA). D: Lewis Milestone. S: Gregory Peck, George Shibata, Harry Guardino.

President's Lady, The 1953 (USA, 20th Cent). D: Henry Levin. S: Charlton Heston, Susan Hayward, John McIntire.

Pride and the Passion, The 1957 (USA, UA). D: Stanley Kramer. S: Cary Grant, Frank Sinatra, Sophia Loren.

Pride of the Marines/British title: **Forever in Love** 1945 (USA, War). D: Delmer Daves. S: John Garfield, Eleanor Parker, Dane Clark.

Prisoner of War 1954 (USA, MGM). D: Andrew Marton. S: Ronald Reagan, Dewey Martin, Steve Forrest.

Private Angelo 1949 (GB). D: Peter Ustinov. S: Peter Ustinov, Godfrey Tearle.

Proud and Profane, The 1956 (USA, Par). D: George Seaton. S: William Holden, Deborah Kerr.

PT 109 1963 (USA, War). D: Leslie H Martinson. S: Cliff Robertson, James Gregory, Ty Hardin.

Purple Heart, The 1944 (USA, 20th Cent). D: Lewis Milestone. S: Dana Andrews, Richard Conte, Farley Granger, Sam Levene.

Purple Plain, The 1954 (GB). D: Robert Parrish. S: Gregory Peck, Maurice Denham, Win Min Than.

Q Planes/US title: **Clouds over Europe** 1939 (GB). D: Tim Whelan. S: Laurence Olivier, Ralph Richardson, Valerie Hobson.

Rack, The 1956 (USA, MGM). D: Arnold Laven. S: Paul Newman, Walter Pidgeon, Lee Marvin, Edmond O'Brien.

Raid on Rommel 1971 (USA, Univ). D: Henry Hathaway. S: Richard Burton, Clinton Greyn, John Colicos.

Raintree County 1958 (USA, MGM). D: Edward Dmytryk. S: Elizabeth Taylor, Montgomery Clift, Eva Marie Saint.

Rasputin and the Empress/also released as **Rasputin the Mad Monk** 1932 (USA, MGM). D: Richard Baleslawski. S: Ethel, Lionel, and John Barrymore, Ralph Morgan.

Reach for Glory 1962 (GB). D: Philip Leacock. S: Harry Andrews, Kay Walsh.

Reach for the Sky 1956 (GB). D: Lewis Gilbert. S: Kenneth More, Muriel Pavlow, Alexander Knox.

Red Badge of Courage, The 1951 (USA, MGM). D: John Huston. S: Audie Murphy, Bill Mauldin, Douglas Dick.

Red Beret, The/US title: **Paratrooper** 1953 (GB). D: Terence Young. S: Alan Ladd, Susan Stephen, Leo Genn.

Reds 1981 (USA, Par). D: Warren Beatty. S: Warren Beatty, Diane Keaton, Jack Nicholson.

Retreat, Hell! 1952 (USA, War). D: Joseph H. Lewis. S: Frank Lovejoy, Richard Carlson, Anita Louise.

Reunion in France/British title: **Mademoiselle France** 1943 (USA, MGM). D: Jules Dassin. S: John Wayne, Joan Crawford, Philip Dorn.

Road Back, The 1937 (USA, Univ). D: James Whale. S: Richard Cromwell, Slim Summerville, John King.

Road to Glory, The 1936 (USA, 20th Cent). D: Howard Hawks. S: Warner Baxter, Fredric March, Lionel Barrymore, June Lang.

Roma, Citta Aperta/English titles: **Open City; Rome, Open City** 1945 (Italy). D: Roberto Rossellini. S: Anna Magnani, Aldo Fabrizzi.

Run Silent, Run Deep 1958 (USA, UA). D: Robert Wise. S: Clark Gable, Burt Lancaster, Jack Warden.

Russians Are Coming, The Russians Are Coming, The 1966 (USA, UA). D: Norman Jewison. S: Carl Reiner, Eva Maria Saint, Alan Arkin, Brian Keith.

Sahara 1943 (USA, Col). D: Zoltan Korda. S: Humphrey Bogart, Lloyd Bridges, Bruce Bennett, J Carroll Naish.

Sailors Three 1940 (GB). D: Walter Forde. S: Tommy Trinder, Michael Wilding, Claude Hulbert.

Salute John Citizen 1942 (GB). D: Maurice Elvey. S: Stanley Holloway, Edward Rigby.

Salute to the Marines 1943 (USA, MGM). D: S Sylan Simon. S: Wallace Beery, Fay Bainter.

Sand Pebbles, The 1966 (USA, 20th Cent). D: Robert Wise. S: Steve McQueen, Richard Crenna, Richard Attenborough.

Sands of Iwo Jima 1949 (USA, Rep). D: Allan Dwan. S: John Wayne, John Agar, Forrest Tucker.

Sante Fe Trail 1940 (USA, War). D: Michael Curtiz. S: Errol Flynn, Olivia de Havilland, Raymond Massey.

Sayonara 1957 (USA, Goetz/Pennebaker). D: Joshua Logan. S: Marlon Brando, Red Buttons, Miyoshi Umeki, James Garner.

Scarlet Pimpernel, The 1934 (GB). D: Leslie Howard. S: Leslie Howard, Raymond Massey, Merle Oberon.

Sea Chase, The 1955 (USA, War). D: John Farrow. S: John Wayne, Lana Turner, David Farrarr.

Sea of Sand 1958 (GB). D: Guy Green. S: Richard Attenborough, John Gregson.

Search, The 1948 (USA/Switzerland). D: Fred Zinnemann. S: Montgomery Clift, Aline MacMahon, Wendell Corey, Ivan Jandl.

Secret Invasion, The 1964 (USA, UA). D: Roger Corman. S: Stewart Granger, Raf Vallone, Mickey Rooney, Henry Silva.

Secret Mission 1942 (GB). D: Harold French. S: Hugh Williams, James Mason, Carla Lehmann.

Secret of Santa Vittoria, The 1969 (USA, UA). D: Stanley Kramer. S: Anthony Quinn, Anna Magnani, Virna Lisi, Hardy Kruger.

Secret War of Harry Frigg, The 1967 (USA, Univ). D: Jack Smight. S: Paul Newman, Sylva Koscina, John Williams, Andrew Duggan, Tom Bosley.

See Here, Private Hargrove 1944 (USA, MGM). D: Wesley Ruggles. S: Robert Walker, Donna Reed, Robert Benchley.

Sergeant York 1941 (USA, War). D: Howard Hawks. S: Gary Cooper, Walter Brennan, Joan Leslie, Margaret Wycherly.

Sergeants Three 1961 (USA, UA). D: John Sturges. S: Frank Sinatra, Dean Martin, Sammy Davis Jr.

Seventh Cross, The 1944 (USA, MGM). D: Fred Zinnemann. S: Spencer Tracy, Signe Hasso, Hume Cronyn.

Seventh Heaven 1927 (USA, Fox). D: Frank Borzage. S: Janet Gaynor, Charles Farrell, David Butler.

Seventh Heaven 1937 (USA, 20th Cent). D: Henry King. S: James Stewart, Simone Simon, Jean Hersholt.

Ships with Wings 1941 (GB). D: Sergei Nolbandov. S: John Clements, Leslie Banks, Ann Todd.

Shenandoah 1965 (USA, Univ). D: Andrew V McLaglen. S: James Stewart, Rosemary Forsyth, Doug McClure.

Shoeshine 1946 (Italy). D: Vittorio de Sica. S: Franco Interlenghi, Rinaldo Smordoni.

Shop on Main Street, The/also released as **The Shop on the High Street** 1965 (Czechoslovakia). D: Jan Kadar, Einar Klos. S: Ida Kaminska, Jozef Kroner, Hana Slivkova.

Shoulder Arms 1918 (USA, Chaplin/First National). D: Charles Chaplin. S: Charles Chaplin, Edna Purviance, Sydney Chaplin.

Silent Enemy, The 1958 (GB). D: William Fairchild. S: Laurence Harvey, John Clements, Dawn Addams.

Since You Went Away 1944 (USA, Selznick). D: John Cromwell. S: Claudette Colbert, Joseph Cotten, Jennifer Jones, Shirley Temple.

Sink the Bismarck 1960 (GB). D: Lewis Gilbert. S: Kenneth More, Dana Wynter, Laurence Naismith, Karel Stepanek.

633 Squadron 1964 (GB). D: Walter Grauman. S: Cliff Robertson, Harry Andrews, George Chakiris.

So Ends Our Night 1941 (USA, UA). D: John Cromwell. S: Fredric March, Margaret Sullavan, Glenn Ford.

So Proudly We Hail 1943 (USA, Par). D: Mark Sandrich. S: Claudette Colbert, Paulette Goddard, Veronica Lake, Sonny Tufts.

Soldiers Three 1951 (USA, MGM). D: Tay Garnett. S: Stewart Granger, David Niven, Robert Newton, Walter Pidgeon.

Song of Russia 1944 (USA, MGM). D: Gregory Ratoff. S: Robert Taylor, John Hodiak, Susan Peters.

Sons O' Guns 1936 (USA, War). D: Lloyd Bacon. S: Joe E Brown, Joan Blondell, Eric Blore.

Sound Barrier, The/US title: **Breaking the Sound Barrier** 1952 (GB). D: David Lean. S: Ralph Richardson, Ann Todd, Nigel Patrick.

Spartacus 1960 (USA, Univ-Int). D: Stanley Kubrick. S: Kirk Douglas, Laurence Olivier, Charles Laughton.

Squadron Leader X 1942 (GB). D: Lance Comfort. S: Eric Portman, Ann Dvorak, Barry Jones.

Stalag 17 1953 (USA, Par). D: Billy Wilder. S: William Holden, Robert Strauss, Don Taylor, Harvey Lembeck, Otto Preminger.

Stand by for Action/British title: **Cargo of Innocents** 1943 (USA, MGM). D: Robert Z Leonard. S: Robert Taylor, Brian Donlevy, Charles Laughton.

Steel Bayonet, The 1957 (GB). D: Michael Carreras. S: Leo Genn, Michael Medwin, Kieron Moore.

Steel Helmet, The 1951 (USA, 20th Cent). D: Samuel Fuller. S: Gene Evans, James Edwards, Robert Hutton.

Storm over the Nile 1965 (GB). D: Terence Young. S: Laurence Harvey, Anthony Steel, Ian Carmichael.

Story of Dr Wassell, The 1964 (USA, Para). D: Cecil B DeMille. S: Gary Cooper, Laraine Day, Dennis O'Keefe.

Story of GI Joe, The/also released as **War Correspondent** 1945 (USA, UA). S: Burgess Meredith, Robert Mitchum, Wally Cassell.

Strategic Air Command 1955 (USA, Par). D: Anthony Mann. S: James Stewart, June Allyson, Barry Sullivan.

Submarine Command 1951 (USA, Par). D: John Farrow. S: William Holden, Nancy Olsen, Don Taylor.

Submarine D-1 1937 (USA, War). D: Lloyd Bacon. S: Pat O'Brien, Wayne Morris, Doris Weston.

Submarine X-1 1967 (GB). D: William Graham. S: James Caan, Norman Bowler.

Sullivans, The/later released as **The Fighting Sullivans** 1944 (USA, 20th Cent). D: Lloyd Bacon. S: Thomas Mitchell, Selena Royle, Anne Baxter, Edward Ryan.

Take the High Ground 1953 (USA, MGM). D: Richard Brooks. S: Richard Widmark, Karl Malden, Elaine Stewart.

Target Zero 1955 (USA, War). D: Harmon Jones. S: Richard Conte, Charles Bronson, Chuck Connors.

Task Force 1949 (USA, War). D: Delmer Daves. S: Gary Cooper, Jane Wyatt, Walter Brennan.

Teahouse of the August Moon, The 1956 (USA, MGM). D: Daniel Mann. S: Marlon Brando, Glenn Ford, Eddie Albert, Paul Ford.

Tell It to the Marines 1926 (USA, MGM). D: George Hill. S: Lon Chaney, Eleanor Boardman, Warner Oland.

Teresa 1951 (USA, MGM). D: Fred Zinnemann. S: Pier Angeli, John Ericson, Patricia Collinge.

That Hamilton Woman/British title: **Lady Hamilton** 1942 (USA, London Films). D: Alexander Korda. S: Laurence Olivier, Vivien Leigh, Gladys Cooper, Alan Mowbray, Henry Wilcoxon.

They Died with Their Boots On 1941 (USA, War). D: Raoul Walsh. S: Errol Flynn, Olivia de Havilland, Arthur Kennedy, Anthony Quinn.

They Were Expendable 1945 (USA, MGM). D: John Ford. S: Robert Montgomery, John Wayne, Donna Reed, Ward Bond.

They Were Not Divided 1951 (GB). D: Terence Young. S: Edward Underdown, Helen Cherry, Ralph Clanton.

They Who Dare 1953 (GB). D: Lewis Milestone. S: Dirk Bogarde, Akim Tamiroff, Denholm Elliott.

Thin Red Line, The 1964 (USA, Security/ACE). D: Andrew Marton. S: Keir Dullea, Jack Warden, Kieron Moore.

This Above All 1942 (USA, 20th Cent). D: Anatole Litvak. S: Tyrone Power, Joan Fontaine, Thomas Mitchell.

Three Came Home 1950 (USA, 20th Cent). D: Jean Negulesco. S: Claudette Colbert, Sessue Hayakawa, Patric Knowles.

Three Comrades 1938 (USA, MGM). D: Frank Borzage. S: Robert Taylor, Margaret Sullavan, Franchot Tone, Robert Young.

300 Spartans, The 1962 (USA, 20th Cent). D: Rudolph Mate. S: Richard Egan, Ralph Richardson, Diane Baker, David Farrar.

Three Stripes in the Sun/British title: **The Gentle Sergeant** 1955 (USA, Col). D: Richard Murphy. S: Aldo Ray, Dick York, Phil Carey.

Thunderbirds 1942 (USA, 20th Cent). D: William A Welmman. S: Preston Foster, Gene Tierney, John Sutton.

Thunderbirds 1952 (USA, Rep). D: John H Auer. S: John Derek, Mona Freeman, John Barrymore Jr.

Till the End of Time 1946 (USA, RKO). D: Edward Dmytryk. S: Guy Madison, Dorothy McGuire, Robert Mitchum.

Time to Love and a Time to Die, A 1958 (USA, Univ). D: Douglas Sirk. S: John Gavin, Lilo Pulver, Keenan Wynn.

To Hell and Back 1955 (USA, Univ-Int). D: Jesse Hibbs. S: Audie Murphy, Marshall Thompson, Charles Drake.

To the Shores of Tripoli 1942 (USA, 20th Cent). D: Bruce Humberstone. S: John Payne, Randolph Scott, Maureen O'Hara.

To the Victor 1948 (USA, War). D: Delmer Daves. S: Dennis Morgan, Viveca Lindfors, Bruce Bennett.

Tobruk 1967 (USA, Univ). D: Arthur Hiller. S: Rock Hudson, George Peppard, Guy Stockwell.

Tomorrow We Live/US title: **At Dawn We Die** 1942 (GB). D: George King. S: John Clements, Hugh Sinclair, Greta Gynt.

Too Late the Hero 1969 (USA, Associates & Aldrich/Palomar). D: Robert Aldrich. S: Michael Caine, Cliff Robertson, Henry Fonda.

Tora! Tora! Tora! 1970 (USA, 20th Cent). D: Richard Fleischer, Ray Kellogg, Toshio Masuda, Kinji Fukasaku. S: Joseph Cotten, Martin Balsam, Jason Robards, James Whitmore.

Torpedo Run 1958 (USA, MGM). D: Joseph Pevney. S: Glenn Ford, Ernest Borgnine, Diane Brewster.

Triumph of the Will 1936 (Germany). D: Leni Riefenstahl. Documentary.

True Glory, The 1945 (USAGB). D: Carol Reed, Garson Kanin. Documentary.

Twelve O'Clock High 1949 (USA, 20th Cent). D: Henry King. S: Gregory Peck, Gary Merrill, Millard Mitchell.

Uncommon Valor 1983 (USA, Par). D: Ted Kotcheff. S: Gene Hackman, Fred Ward, Robert Stack.

Under Fire 1983 (USA, Lion's Gate). D: Roger Spottiswoode. S: Gene Hackman, Nick Nolte, Richard Masur.

Under Ten Flags 1960 (USA, Par). D: Duilio Coletti, Silvio Narizzano. S: Van Heflin, Charles Laughton, John Ericson.

Under Two Flags 1936 (USA, 20th Cent). D: Frank Lloyd. S: Claudette Colbert, Ronald Colman, Victor McLaglen.

Underground 1941 (USA, War). D: Vincent Sherman. S: Jeffrey Lynn, Philip Dorn, Karen Verne.

Underground 1970 (USA, UA). D: Arthur H Nader. S: Robert Goulet, Daniele Gaubert, Lawrence Dobkin.

Up from the Beach 1965 (USA, 20th Cent). D: Robert Parrish. S: Cliff Robertson, Françoise Rosay, Red Buttons.

Up Periscope 1959 (USA, War). D: Gordon Douglas. S: James Garner, Edmond O'Brien.

Valiant, The 1961 (GB/Italy). D: Roy Baker. S: John Mills, Robert Shaw, Ettore Manni.

Victors, The 1963 (USA, Col). D: Carl Foreman. S: George Peppard, Eli Wallach, Vince Edwards, Melina Mercouri.

Victory 1981 (USA, Lorimar). D: John Huston. S: Michael Caine, Sylvester Stallone, Pelé.

Victory Through Air Power 1943 (USA, Disney). D: H C Potter (live action sequences). Animated/live action documentary.

Vikings, The 1958 (USA, UA). D: Richard Fleischer. S: Kirk Douglas, Tony Curtis, Janet Leigh, Ernest Borgnine.

Von Richthofen and Brown 1971 (USA, UA). D: Roger Corman. S: John Phillip Law, Don Stroud.

Von Ryan's Express 1965 (USA, 20th Cent). D: Mark Robson. S: Frank Sinatra, Trevor Howard, Sergei Fantoni.

Wackiest Ship in the Army, The 1960 (USA, Col). D: Ralph Murphy. S: Jack Lemmon, John Lund, Ricky Nelson.

Wake Island 1942 (USA, Par). D: John Farrow. S: Brian Donlevy, MacDonald Carey, William Bendix, Robert Preston.

Wake Me When It's Over 1960 (USA, 20th Cent). D: Mervyn LeRoy. S: Ernie Kovacs, Jack Warden, Dick Shawn.

Walk in the Sun, A 1946 (USA, Milestone). D: Lewis Milestone. S: Dana Andrews, Richard Conte, John Ireland, Sterling Holloway.

War and Peace 1956 (USA/Italy). D: King Vidor, Mario Soldati. S: Henry Fonda, Audrey Hepburn, Mel Ferrer, Herbert Lom.

War and Peace 1967 (USSR). D: Sergei Bondarchuk. S: Lyudmilla Savelyeva, Sergei Bondarchuk.

War Brides 1916 (USA, Selznick). D: Herbert Brenon. S: Alla Nazimova, Charles Hutchinson, Charles Bryant.

WarGames 1983 (USA, Goldberg). D: John Badham. S: Dabney Coleman, Matthew Broderick, John Wood.

War Hunt 1962 (USA, TD Enterprises). D: Denis Sanders. S: John Saxon, Robert Redford.

War Lover, The 1962 (GB). D: Philip Leacock. S: Steve McQueen, Robert Wagner, Shirley Anne Field.

Warrens of Virginia, The 1915 (USA, Lasky Feature Play Co). D: Cecil B DeMille. S: Blanche Sweet, James Neill, House Peters.

Watch on the Rhine 1943 (USA, War). D: Herman Shumlin. S: Paul Lukas, Bette Davis, George Coulouris, Lucile Watson.

Waterloo 1970 (Italy/USSR). D: Sergei Bondarchuk. S: Rod Steiger, Orson Welles, Christopher Plummer.

Way Ahead, The/US title: **Immortal Battalion** 1944 (GB). D: Carol Reed. S: David Niven, Stanley Holloway, William Hartnell.

We Dive at Dawn 1943 (GB). D: Anthony Asquith. S: John Mills, Eric Portman.

Went the Day Well?/US title: **Forty-Eight Hours** 1942 (GB). D: Alberto Cavalcanti. S: Leslie Banks, Elizabeth Allen.

Westfront 1918/also released as **Shame of a Nation, Four from the Infantry, Comrades of 1918** 1930 (Germany). D: G W Pabst. S: Fritz Kampers, Gustav Diessl, Claus Clausen.

West Point of the Air 1935 (USA, MGM). D: Richard Rosson. S: Robert Young, Wallace Beery, Maureen O'Sullivan.

What Did You Do in the War, Daddy? 1966 (USA, UA). D: Blake Edwards. S: James Coburn, Sergei Fantoni, Dick Shawn.

What Price Glory? 1926 (USA, Fox). D: Raoul Walsh. S: Victor McLagen, Edmond Lowe, Dolores Del Rio, Leslie Fenton.

What Price Glory? 1952 (USA, 20th Cent). D: John Ford. S: James Cagney, Dan Dailey, Corinne Calvet.

Where Eagles Dare 1969 (GB). D: Brian G Hutton. S: Richard Burton, Clint Eastwood, Mary Ure.

Whisky Galore/US title: **Tight Little Island** 1948 (GB). D: Alexander Mackendrick. S: Joan Greenwood, Basil Radford, Gordon Jackson.

White Angel, The 1936 (USA, War). D: William Dieterle. S: Kay Francis, Ian Hunter, Donald Woods, Donald Crisp.

White Cliffs of Dover, The 1944 (USA, MGM). D: Clarence Brown. S: Irene Dunne, Alan Marshall, Frank Morgan.

Why We Fight 1942-45 (USA, US War Office). D: Frank Capra, Anatole Litvak, Anthony Veiller. Series of seven documentaries.

Wife Takes a Flyer, The/British title: **A Yank in Dutch** 1942 (USA, Col). D: Richard Wallace. S: Constance Bennett, Franchot Tone, Allyn Joslyn.

Wild Blue Yonder, The 1952 (USA, Rep). D: Allan Dwan. S: Wendell Corey, Vera Hruba Ralston, Forrest Tucker.

Wing and a Prayer 1944 (USA, 20th Cent). D: Henry Hathaway. S: Don Ameche, Dana Andrews, Richard Jaeckel, Cedric Hardwicke.

Winged Victory 1944 (USA, 20th Cent). D: George Cukor. S: Lon McAllister, Edmond O'Brien, Jeanne Crain.

Wings 1927, silent; 1928, sound (USA, Par). D: William A Wellman. S: Charles Buddy Rogers, Richard Arlen, Clara Bow, Gary Cooper.

Wings for the Eagle 1942 (USA, War). D: Lloyd Bacon. S: Dennis Morgan, Ann Sheridan, Jack Carson.

Wings of the Navy 1939 (USA, War). D: Lloyd Bacon. S: George Brent, John Payne, Olivia de Havilland.

Yank in the RAF, A 1942 (USA, 20th Cent). D: Henry King. S: Tyrone Power, Betty Grable, John Sutton.

Yank in Vietnam, A 1964 (USA). D: Marshall Thompson. S: Marshall Thompson, Enrique Magalona.

Yellow Jack 1938 (USA, MGM). D: George B Seitz. S: Robert Montgomery, Lewis Stone, Virginia Bruce, Buddy Ebsen.

Yesterday's Enemy 1959 (GB). D: Val Guest. S: Stanley Baker, Guy Rolfe, Leo McKern.

Young Eagles 1930 (USA, Par). D: William A Wellman. S: Charles Buddy Rogers, Paul Lukas, Jean Arthur.

Young Lions, The 1958 (USA, 20th Cent). D: Edward Dmytryk. S: Marlon Brando, Montgomery Clift, Dean Martin, Hope Lange.

You're in the Navy Now 1951 (USA, 20th Cent). D: Henry Hathaway. S: Gary Cooper, Millard Mitchell, Jane Greer.

Zulu 1964 (GB). D: Cy Enfield. S: Stanley Baker, Michael Caine, Jack Hawkins.

Acknowledgments
The author and publisher would like to thank the following people who have helped in the preparation of this book: Alan Gooch, who designed it; Thomas G Aylesworth, who edited it; Sheila A Byrd, who did the photo research; Cynthia Klein, who prepared the index.

INDEX

Abbott, Bud *43*
Above and Beyond 86-7, *88*
Abraham Lincoln 162
Adorée, Renée *21, 21*
Air Force 48
Air Raid Wardens 43, *43*
Alamo, The 159, *163*
Alexander Hamilton 146
Alexander Nevsky 148
Alexander the Great 148, *149*
All Quiet on the Western Front 8, *14-15*, 26, 2708, *28*, 31, 82, 113, 176
All the Young Men 108, *109*
Allyson, June 106, *107*
Ameche, Don 49
America's Answer 20
Americanization of Emily, The 93, 95-6
Andrews, Dana 49, 69, 72, *80*, 80
Andrews, Julie 96
antiwar films 13, 16, 19, 23, 34-5, 113, 117, 120, 154
Anzio 88, 89
Apocalypse Now 2-3, 7, *109*, *118*, *119*, 120-21, 179
Arise My Love 40, 168
Arkin, Alan 97, *97*, *130*, 130
Arlen, Richard 23, 172
Arliss, George 146, 148
Arsenal 26, 2607
Attenborough, Richard 82, 169-70
aviation 23, 31-2, 34, 48, 59, 81, 87, 88-9, 120-21, 135, 136
Ayres, Lew *8*, 28, 31

Back to Bataan 52, 53
Baker, Stanley 109, 170
Ballad of a Soldier 178
Bari, Lynn *136*, 136
Barry, Gene *115*
Barrymore (Ethel, John, Lionel) 166
Basehart, Richard 102, 140
Bataan 47, 48
Battle Circus 104, 106, *107*
Battle Cry 78, *78*
Battle Cry of Peace 16, 17
Battle Hymn 142, 144, *145*
Battle of Britain 11, 88
Battle of San Pietro, The 65
Battle of the Beaches 65
Battle of the Bulge 92, 95
Battle of the River Plate 88
Battleground 24, 80-1, 177
Beatty, Warren *10*, 168, *175*
Beau Geste 24, *168*, 170-71
Becky Sharp 166
Bedford Incident, The 129
Beery, Wallace 126, *165*
Beguiled, The 164
Behind the Rising Sun 51, 51
Behold a Pale Horse 169
Bell for Adano, A 68
Bellamy, Ralph *42*, 146
Beloved Enemy 155
Bendix, William 68
Bengal Brigade 172, *172*
Bergman, Ingrid 169

Berlin, Irving *45*
Best Years of Our Lives, The, 68, 69, 72-3, 138, 177
Bhowani Junction 171, 172
Bicycle Thief, The 177
Big Blockade, The 64
Big Parade, The 21, 22
Big Red One, The 11, 86, 87, 104
biographical films 86, 134-51, 154
Birth of a Nation, The 7, 9-10, 12, 16, 17, 159, *160*
Blackton, J Stuart 8, 20, 159
Blockade 39, *39*, 168
Blue Max, The 1, *34*, 34
Boer War 154
Bogarde, Dirk 140, 165
Bogart, Humphrey 55, 56, 57, 59, *63*, 106, *107*
Bombadier 51
Bombers B52 128
Bonaparte, Napoleon 148-59, 151, 165
Boone, Richard *139*
Das Boot 99
Borgnine, Ernest 76
Bottoms, Timothy *34*
Bow, Clara 23
Boxer Rebellion 154-55
Boyer, Charles *150*
Boys in Company C, The 116, 119-20
Brando, Marlon 46, 82, *92*, 95, 120, 149, *150*
Brass Target, The 134, *137*
Breaker Morant 154, *155*
Brennan, Walter 74, 146
Brent, George 126
Bridge, The 82, 178
Bridge Too Far, A 75, 92
Bridge at Remagen, The 92, 94
Bridge on the River Kwai, The 12, 78, 79, 79-80, 178
Bridges, Lloyd 72
Bridges at Toko-Ri, The 111, 113, *113*
Brigade 154
British Empire 169-70
Bronson, Charles 86, 109
Brown on Resolution 32
Buccaneer, The 158
Buck Privates 43, *43*, 93
Burton, Richard 74, 82, *92*, 148, *149*
Brynner, Yul 158

Cagney, James 29, 34, 44, 59, *60*, 126, 140
Caine, Michael *170*, 170
Caine Mutiny, The 73, *74*
Calvet, Corinne *22*
Capra, Frank 65
Captain Eddie 135-36
Captain Horatio Hornblower 165
Captains of the Clouds 59, *60*
Carroll, Madeleine 155, *156*
Casablanca 55, 56-7, 177
Cast a Giant Shadow 52
Castle Keep 66-7, 8405
Catch 22 97, *97*
Caught in the Draft 93
Chaney, Lon 17
Chaplin, Charlie 9, *18*, 19, *41*, 41-2, 161

Charge of the Light Brigade, The 154
Che! 144
China 51
China Gate 51, 104, *115*, 115, 116-17
Christie, Julie *32*
Cimino, Michael 120
Civil War 158, 159-64
Civilization 16, *17*
Clark, Dane 139
Clark, Fred 95, *96*
Clements, John 172
Clift, Montgomery 77, *82*
Coburn, James 99
Cold War 128-31
Colditz Story, The 82-3
Colman, Ronald 165, 171
combat films 73-84, 104, 111-13, 119-20, 137-38
Coming Home 117-19, *129*, 179
Command Decision 80, 81
Commandos Strike at Dawn, The 58
Connery, Sean 75
Conqueror, The 148
Conquest 149, *150*
Conte, Richard 80, *108*, 109
Convoy 63-4, *64*
Cooper, Gary 6, *24*, 24, *30*, 32, 50, 74, 98, 144-46, *146*, 155, *156*, 165, 169, 171, 172, *173*
Coppola, Francis Ford 120, 122
Costello, Lou *43*
Court-Martial of Billy Mitchell, The 24, *24*, *146*, 146
Coward, Noël 61-3, *62*
Croix de Bois, Les 22-3
Cross of Lorraine, The 58
Curtis, Tony 154, *155*
Custer, George *146*, 146
Custer of the West 148, *146*

Dam Busters, The 88-9, *91*
Dane, Karl 21-22
Dangerous Moonlight 61, *63*
Dawn Patrol, The 24, *25*, 26
De Carlo, Yvonne 94
De Niro, Robert *104*, 120
Deer Hunter, The 103, 120, *121*, 179
De Haviland, Olivia *164*
DeMille, Cecil B 50, 145, 159, 160
Desert Fox, The 55, 81, *139*, 139
Desert Rats, The 81, 81
Desiree 149, *150*
Destination Tokyo 48
Devil's Brigade, The 78, 84
Devil Dogs of the Air 126
Dietrich, Marlene 155
Dieudonne, Albert 149, *151*
Dirty Dozen, The 83-4, 86
Disney, Walt 65
Dive Bomber 42, *43*
Dr Strangelove . . . *129*, 130-31, 178
Doctor Zhivago 32, 34, 168, 178-79
Donat, Robert 73
Donlevy, Brian 171
Don't Go Near the Water 95, 96

Doughboys 31
Douglas, Kirk *31*, 34, 154, *155*
Douglas, Melvyn 96
Duvall, Robert *120*, 121-22

Eagle's Eye 18
Eastwood, Clint *74*, 164
Ebsen, Buddy *128*
editing techniques 20, 74, 87-8, 104, 169
Edwards, James *72*, *103*
Enemy Below, The 81, *82*
Ermey, Lee 120
espionage 64, 89, 91
Eternal Sea, The 142, 142, 144
Evans, Gene 102-03, *103*
Exodux 155, *157*

*FTA*Free the Army* 117
Face of War, A 117
Fail Safe 130, 131
Fairbanks, Douglas Jr 26, 174, *176*
Fairbanks, Douglas Sr 19
Fall of Berlin, The 92-3
Fall of a Nation, The 16-17
Farewell to Arms, A 24, *30*, 32
Father Goose 98, 99
55 Days at Peking 155, *164*
Fighting Lady, The 65
Fighting 69th, The 29, 32, 34, 59
Finch, Peter *167*
Fire over England 154
First of the Few 134
Five Graves to Cairo 55
Fixed Bayonets 102, *103*, 104
Flanders, Ed 142
Flying Tigers 52
Flynn, Errol 26, *27*, *42*, 146, *148*, 164
Fonda, Henry *349*, 55, *93*, *130*, *160*
Fonda, Jane 117, 119, *129*
For Whom the Bell Tolls 169, 177
Ford, Glenn *92*, 95
Ford, Harrison *116*
Ford, John 23, 40, 148, 159, 169
Foreign Correspondent 40, 177
Fort Apache 159, *160*
Forty-Ninth Parallel, The 61, 61
Four Feathers 172, 172
Four Horsemen of the Apocalypse, The 20, 120, 122
Four in a Jeep 72
French Foreign Legion 170-71
French Revolution 165
Frobe, Gert 92
From Here to Eternity 76-8, 76-77, 126, 178
Fuller, Samuel 102-04, 115
futuristic films 130-31

Gable, Clark *80*, 81, 126, *164*
Gallant Hours, The 140
Gance, Abel 149-51
Gandhi 169, 170, *171*
Garbo, Greta *150*, 149

Gardner, Ava *171*
Garfield, John 137, *138*, 138-39
Garner, James 82, *93*, 97
Garson, Greer 59
Gathering of Eagles, A 128
Gazzara, Ben *94*
General, The 161, 161-62
General della Rovere 72
General Died at Dawn, The 113, 155, *156*
Genghis Khan 148
Gere, Richard *175*
Germany Year Zero 68-9
Gilbert, John *21*, 21-2
Gish, Lillian 9, *17*, *160*
Glory Brigade, The 107
Go Tell the Spartans 117, 120, 123
God Is My Co-Pilot 136-37
Gone With the Wind 159, 162-63, *164*, 176
Gordon's War 116, 117
Gould, Elliot *10*, *105*, *112*, 113
Grande Illusion, La 39, 39, 176
Grant, Cary 48, *98*, 98, *99*, 166, *173*, *176*
Great Dictator, The 19, 40, *41*, 41-3, *93*, 177
Great Escape, The 82, 82
Great Guns 43
Great Santini, The 120, 121-22
Great Waldo Pepper, The 35, 35
Green Berets, The 13, *53*, 55, 116-17
Griffith, D W 8-9, *16*, 16, 17-18, 20, 24, 159, 162
Griffith, Raymond 28
Guadacanal Diary 48-9
Guerre Est Finie, La 169
Guiness, Alec *12*, *79*, 79, 92
Gung Ho! 40, 47, 51-2
Gunga Din 173-75, *176*
Guns of Navarone, The 82, *83*, 178

Hackman, Gene *122*
Halsey, William 140
Halls of Montezuma 113
Hammond, Kay 162
Hardy, Stan *43*, 43
Harrison, Rex 61
Harvey, Laurence 159, *163*
Hawkins, Jack 79
Hawks, Howard 20, 22, 26, 32, 48
Hayakawa, Sessue 79
Hayden, Sterling 142
Hayes, Helen *30*, 32
Hayfoot, Strawfoot 161
Heart of Humanity 19, 20
Heart of Maryland, The 161
Heart of the World 17-18
Heaven Knows, Mr Allison 76, 78
Held by the Enemy 161
Hell Divers 126
Hell's Angels 31, 113
Here Comes the Navy 126
Heroes 116, 117
Heston, Charlton *158*, *164*, 170
High Flight 128-29

Hill in Korea, A 109
historical films 89-92, 115, 154
Hitchcock, Alfred 40, 59
Hitler 140
Hitler – The Last Ten Days 92
Hitler's Children 58
Hitler's Madman 45
Hodiak, John 59, 68, *80*
Hoffman, Dustin *135*
Holden, William 79, *79*, 82, 85, 111, *113*
Home of the Brave 72
Homolka, Oscar *110*
Hope, Bob 43
Hotel Sahara 92, 94
How I Won the War 96
Howard, Leslie 61, *61*, 134, *164*, *165*, 165
Howard, Trevor *84*, 154
Hudson, Rock *127*, 144, *145*, 172
Huston, Walter 159, 162

I Wanted Wings 43
I Was a Male War Bride 98
Ice Station Zebra 127, 129-30
Immortal Sergeant, The 55
In Harm's Way 74-5
In Which We Serve 61-3, *62*, 177
Ince, Thomas 16
Indian wars (American) 159; (continental) 172
Intolerance 16, 16, 154
Introduction to the Enemy 117
The Iron Duke 148
Is Paris Burning? 92

Jackson, Gordon 94
Jaeckel, Richard 49
Jaffe, Sam 174
John Paul Jones 146
Johnny Got His Gun 34, 35
Johnson, Celia 62
Johnson, Van *73*, *80*
Journey's End 32
Juarez 165
Judgement at Nuremberg 178
Jump Into Hell 115, 115
Jurgens, Curt 81, 95

Karloff, Boris 170
Kaye, Danny 95
Keaton, Buster 31, *161*, 161-62
Keaton, Diane 168, *175*
Kelly, Grace 111
Kennedy, George *86*, 134
Kennedy, John F 140
Kerr, Deborah 73, *76*, 7708
Khartoum 170
Killing Fields, The 100-01, 121, 125, *125*
King of the Khyber Rifles *172*, 173
King Rat 85
Kingsley, Ben *170*, 171
Korean War 102-08, 109-114, *142-43*
Kovacs, Ernie 95
Kubrick, Stanley *130*
Ladd, Alan *51*, 51, 159
Lancaster, Burt 76, 76, 84, *117*, 120
The Last Four Days 142
Laurel, Stan *43*, 43

Lawrence of Arabia 34, 148, *149*, 178
Lean, David 35, 63, 78, 168
Leigh, Vivian *164*
Lemmon, Jack *93*, 95, *98*, 98
Lenin in October 167-68
Lest We Forget 17
The Life and Death of Colonel Blimp 64
Lifeboat 59, *62*, 177
Lincoln, Abraham 161, 162
Lindfors, Viveca 68
Lion of the Desert 169, 172
Little American, The 8, 12, 17
Little Big Man 134, *135*
Little Colonel, The 162
Lives of a Bengal Lancer 24, 172-73, *173*
Long Gray Line, The 146, 148
Long Voyage Home, The 40, 40, 52
Longest Day, The 10, *12* 54-5, *91*, 178
Loo, Richard *50*, *103*
The Lost Patrol 47, 169, 169-70
Lovejoy, Frank *72*, *106*
Lowe, Edmund 32

*M*A*S*H* *10*, 104-06, *105*, 111, *112*, 113-14, 179
MacArthur, Douglas 53-4, 142
MacArthur 140, *141*, 142
McConnell Story, The 142
McKenzie Break, The 82, *84*
McLaglen, Victor *22*, 23, *160*, 169, 174
MacMurray, Fred *42*, 135, 136, *136*
McQueen, Steve *82*, 82, 155
Magnificent Doll, The 159
Malden, Karl *106*, 142
Man of Conquest 146, 158
Man Who Never Was, The 89, 91
March, Fredric 69, 72, 111, 158
Marie Antoinette 165
Marines Let's Go 111
Martin, Dean 82
Marvin, Lee 86, *87*, 110
Massey, Raymond 59, *63*, 165
Mason James 55, 81, *139*, 139
Me and the Colonel 95
Men in War 110, *111*
Men of the Fighting Lady 110, *111*
Meredith, Burgess 24, 56, *159*
Merrils' Marauders 102, 104
Mexican wars 158-59, 165
Midway 87-8
Milestone, Lewis 27, 80, 113
Milland, Ray 171
Mission in Action 122
Mitchell, Thomas *40*, 50
Mitchum, Robert 24, 56, 76, 78, 81, *82*, 92, 106, *107*
Montgomery, Robert 140
Montand, Yves 169
More, Kenneth 88, 139

More the Merrier, The 94
Morgan, Dennis *68*, 136
Mortal Storm, The 40, 40
Muni, Paul 165
Murphy, Audie 139, 164
Murphy, George *48*
musical scores 61, 151, 159
Mussolini, Benito 142

Naked and the Dead, The 78
Naish, J Carroll 51, 171
Napoleon 140, 149-51, *151*
Navy Way, The 43
Nazimova, Alla 16, *17*
Neal, Tom 51
Nelson, Horatio 165
Nelson Affair, The 167
Nelson Touch, The 51
Nelson, Ricky 98
Newman, Paul 97, 98, *110*, 110, 155
Next of Kin 64
Night and Fog 64, 65
Night People, The 128, 129
Night Train to Munich 39-40, 61
1941 97, 98-9
Niven, David 26, 64, *159*, 164
Northwest Passage 158, *159*

Oakie, Jack 42
O'Brien, Pat *29*, 126
O'Brien, George *160*
O'Connell, Arthur *98*
O'Donnell, Cathy 73
An Officer and a Gentleman 175, 179
Oh, What a Lovely War 31, 34, 179
Olivier, Lawrence *38*, 88, 154, 170
On the Beach 128, 131
One Minute to Zero 104, 106, *107*
One of Our Aircraft is Missing 62, 63
Open City 69
Operation Mad Ball 95
Operation Pacific 74, 75
Operation Petticoat 98, 98
Operation Thunderbolt 156, *157*
O'Toole, Peter 148, *149*
Our Russian Front 113

Q Planes 38, 39
Quinn, Anthony *83*, *169*, 171

PT 109 113, *140*, 140
Pabst, G W *26*, 31
Paisan 69
Parker, Eleanor 139
Password is Courage, The 140, 140
Paths of Glory 22, *31*, 34
Patton, George S 134
Patton 7, *132*-33, *136*, *137*, 140-42, 179
Paxinou, Katina 169
peacetime films 126
Peck, Gregory 58, 81, *83*, *112*, 113, *128*, 129, *141*, 142, 166, *167*, 169
Peppard, George *34*
Perkins, Anthony *128*

Phillips, Dorothy 19
photographic techniques 9-10, 12, 69, 111-13, 120, 149-51, 159, 161
Pickford, Mary 8, 17, *19*
Pidgeon, Walter 59, *80*, *110*, 110, *111*
Pied Piper, The, 46, *46*
Pleasance, Donald 82
Plough and the Stars, The 155
Poitier, Sidney *109*, 109
Pork Chop Hill 111, *112*, 113
Porter, Edwin 6
Portman, Eric *61*
post-war films 20, 68-73, 99, 108-09, 117-19, 123, 125
Powell, William *93*
Power, Tyrone 59, 146, 172, *173*
Prelude to War 65
Preminger, Otto 46, *46*
President's Lady, The 158, *159*
Preston, Robert 171
Pride and the Passion, The 166
Pride of the Marines 137-39
Prisoner of Shark Island, The 162
Prisoner of War 110, *110*
prisoners of war 79, 83-4, 110, 140
propaganda films 12, 17, 18, 20, 21, 40, 44, 49, 64, 65, 93, 117, 168
Purple Heart, The 12, 49, *50*, 113

Rack, The 110, 110
Rains, Claude 56
Raintree County 162, 164
Rasputin and the Empress 166-67
Rathbone, Basil 26, *27*
Reach for the Sky 139
Reagan, Ronald *45*, 59, *110*, 110
Real Glory, The 165
Red Badge of Courage, the 164
Red Dawn 131, 131
Redford, Robert *35*, 75, 111
Redgrave, Michael 89
Reds 10, 168, *175*
Reed, Donna 76
Reiner, Carl *130*
Retreat, Hell 104, *106*
Revolutionary War 159
Richardson, Ralph *172*, 172
Rickenbacker, Edward 135, 136
Road Back, The 32
Road to Glory, The 22
Robertson, Cliff *140*, 140
Rogers, Charles (Buddy) *23*, 23
Rogers, Ginger *159*
Rommel, Erwin 55, 81, 139
Rooney, Mickey 111, *113*
Roosevelt, Theodore 8, 16
Rossellini, Roberto 68-9, 72
Rough Rider, The 8
Russell, Harold 69, 72-3, 138
Russians are Coming! 130, *130*
Russian Revolution 26, 166-68

Ryan, Robert *51*, *111*

Sahara 55
Sand Pebbles, The 155
Sands of Iwo Jima 36-7, *53*, 54, 74
Sante Fe Trail 164
Saunders, John Monk 24
Savalas, Telly 86
Scarlet Pimpernel, The 59, *165*, 165
Schell, Maximillian 46
Scott, George C 59, 130, 134, *137*, 140
Scott, Randolph *51*, 51-2
Sea Chase, the 54
Search, The 72, 177
Secret of Santa Vittoria, The 95, 96
Secret War of Harry Frigg, The 97, 98
Segal, George 85
Sellers, Peter *129*, 130
Selznick, David 162
Selznick, Lewis 16
Sergeant York 6, 24, 34, 145-46, *146*, 177
Seventh Heaven 32, 176
Sharif, Omar *32*, *144*, 148
Shanghai Express 155, *156*
Shaw, Robert 146, *148*
Shawn, Dick 99
Shearer, Norma 165
Sheen, Martin *118*, 120, *131*, *171*
Shenandoah 164
Shoeshine 177
Shoulder Arms 9, *18*, 19
Sinatra, Frank 76, *77*, 83
Sink the Bismarck 88
Skerrit, Tom 13
So Proudly We Hail 47-8
sound effects, 82, 151, 159. *See also* musical scores
Spanish American War 8
Spanish Civil War 39-40, 168-69
Spartacus 154, 154
special effects 87, 89, 106, 154
Spielberg, Steven 98
Spitfire 134-35
Stack, Robert 146
Stage Door Canteen 43
Stalag 17, *85*, 95
Stallings, Laurence 21
Stepanek, Karl 88
Stewart, James *40*, *126*, 126, 164
The Steel Helmet 86, 102-03, *103*, 104
Steiger, Rod 142, 146, 149
Stevens, George 174
Stone, Lewis 161
Story of Dr Wassell, The 50
Story of GI Joe, The 24, 55-6
Strategic Air Command 126, 128
Streep, Meryl 120
stunts: actors/activities 24, 34, 161
submarine warfare 48, 50-1, 61
Sullavan, Margaret 32, *40*
Sullivans, The 50
Sun Never Sets, The 170
Sutherland, Donald *10*, *105*, *112*, 113, 117

Tale of Two Cities, A 165
Take the High Ground 106, 106-07
Tamiroff, Akim 155, *156*, 169
Target Zero 108, 109
Task Force 24, 74
Tawny Pipit 94
Taylor, Robert 32, *48*, *88*
Teahouse of the August Moon, The 92, 95
Tell It to the Marines 126
Temple, Shirley 162
Terry-Thomas 98
They Died With Their Boots On 146, *148*
They Were Expendable 53-4
They Who Dare 113
Things to Come 38, 39
Thirty Seconds over Tokyo 49-50, *50*
This is the Army 44, *45*
Thompson, Marshall *115*, 116, 139
Three Comrades 32
300 Spartans, The 154
Tierney, Gene 68
Tight Little Island 94
Till The End of Time 73
To Hell and Back 138, 139
To the Shores of Tripoli 51
To the Victor 72
Todd, Richard 89, *91*
Tone, Franchot 32, 55, 172
Tora! Tora! Tora! 71, 86-7
Tracy, Lee 165
Tracy, Spencer, 50, *50*, *159*
Triumph of the Will 39, 64, *65*
Twelve O'Clock High 81, 178

Uncle Tom's Cabin 159
Uncommon Valor 122, 123
Under Two Flags 170
Ustinov, Peter *92*, 94

Valentino, Rudolph 20
Vidor, King 20, 22
Victors, The 83
Victory 83, 99
Vietnam War 115-122
Vikings, The 154, *155*
Viva Villa 165, 165
Voight, Jon 119, *129*
Von Richthofen 35
Von Richthofen and Brown 35
Von Ryan's Express 83, *84*
Von Stroheim, Erich 17, 19, 39, 55

Wackiest Ship in the Amry, The 98, 98
Wake Island 47, 177
Wake Me When It's Over 96
Walk in the Sun, A 80, 80, 113
Walken, Christopher 120
Walker, Robert 47
Wanger, Walter 39, 40
war: national attitudes to 8-9, 12, 16-17, 34, 38-9, 42-3, 116, 120, 123, 179
war films: awards 42, 57, 73, 80, 139, 141, 162, 169, 176, 179; battle scenes 22, 23, 81, 87-8, 89, 91-2, 115 (*See also* combat films); comedy in 13, 41-2, 43,

84, 113-14, 117; as comedy 93-9, 130, 161-62, 170; as documentary 19-20, 39, 61-2, 64-5, 87, 117; European 6, 59, 63-5; as genre 12-13, 21, 23, 51 (*See also* antiwar films; futuristic films; peacetime; propaganda; post-war films); and government cooperation/sponsorship 20, 24, 26, 57-8; as musicals 43-4, 126, 159; parodies/satire 18, 41; racism in 12, 18, 74; realism in 22, 69, 74, 115 (*See also* historical films); themes 16, 23, 24, 27, 38-9, 44-6, 59, 68, 73-4, 79-80, 83, 111, 113, 115, 126, 128, 129 (*See also* specific wars; biography; historical films); violence in 83, 88. *See also* editing techniques; photography
War and Peace 166, 166
War Brides 16, 17
War Games 131, 131
War Hunt 110-11
Warrens of Virginia, The 160-61
Waterloo 4-5, 149, *152-53*, 166
Waterson, Sam *121*, 125
Way Ahead, the 64
Wayne, John *13*, *40*, 40, 52-5, *52*, 75, 91, 116, 148, 158, *160*, 163
Webb, Clifton 91
Wellman, William 20, 23-4, 34
Westfront 1918 26, 31
What Did You Do in the War, Daddy? 98, 99
What Price Glory? 22, *22*, 23
Where Eagles Dare 74, 74
White Angel, The 154
Whitmore, James 81, *88*
Widmark, Richard *106*, 107, 129, *163*
Wilder, Billy 55
Winfield, Paul *116*, 117
Winkler, Henry *116*, 117
Wing and a Prayer 48, 49
Wings 23, 23-4, 176
Wings of the Navy 126
Wings Over the Pacific 50
Woolley, Monty 46, *46*
World War I 17, 22, 27, 31, 161; battles 23
World War II 40-65, 134; European theater 55-7, 61, 81-2, 86; Pacific theater 47-55, 74-9, 86; and home front/refugees 58, 64; film types 43. *See also* post-war
Wycherley, Margaret 146
Wyler, William 73
Wynn, Keenan 106

Yank in Vietnam, A 115, 116
Yankee Doodle Dandy 44
Yellow Jack 8
Yoshimura, Kimisaburo 65
Young, Robert 126

Young Winston 154
Young Lions, The 45, 6, 81-2

Zanuck, Daryl 91
Zinneman, Fred 76
Zulu 170, 170

Photo Credits
All photos from The Bison Picture Library, with the following exceptions:
Museum of Modern Art: 8, 16, 17, 20, 25, 26, 38 (below), 39 (below), 44, 45 (right), 51 (top right), 62 (top), 64 (below), 80 (top), 148 (below), 160 (top), 163 (top), 164 (top), 167 (below), 168.
National Film Archives: 184 (top), 135.
Phototeque: 13-14 (below), 100-101, 175 (top).
The Silver Screen Archives: 149 (top).